Teaching Shakespeare

Teaching Shakespeare
Passing it On

G. B. Shand

⟨W⟩WILEY-BLACKWELL

A John Wiley & Sons, Ltd., Publication

This edition first published 2009
© 2009 Blackwell Publishing Ltd

Blackwell Publishing was acquired by John Wiley & Sons in February 2007. Blackwell's publishing program has been merged with Wiley's global Scientific, Technical, and Medical business to form Wiley-Blackwell.

Registered Office
John Wiley & Sons Ltd, The Atrium, Southern Gate, Chichester, West Sussex, PO19 8SQ, United Kingdom

Editorial Offices
350 Main Street, Malden, MA 02148-5020, USA
9600 Garsington Road, Oxford, OX4 2DQ, UK
The Atrium, Southern Gate, Chichester, West Sussex, PO19 8SQ, UK

For details of our global editorial offices, for customer services, and for information about how to apply for permission to reuse the copyright material in this book please see our website at www.wiley.com/wiley-blackwell.

The right of G. B. Shand to be identified as the author of the editorial material in this work has been asserted in accordance with the Copyright, Designs and Patents Act 1988.

Library of Congress Cataloging-in-Publication Data

Teaching Shakespeare : passing it on / [edited by] G.B. Shand.
    p. cm.
    Includes bibliographical references and index.
    ISBN 978–1–4051–4045–4 (acid-free paper)—ISBN 978–1–4051–4046–1 (pbk. : acid-free paper) 1. Shakespeare, William, 1564–1616—Study and teaching. 2. Shakespeare, William, 1564–1616—Appreciation. I. Shand, G. B.

    PR2987.T365 2008
    822.3 3—dc22

                                                                    2008000138

A catalogue record for this book is available from the British Library.

Set in 10.5/13pt Minion by Graphicraft Limited, Hong Kong
Printed and bound in Singapore by Markono Print Media Pte Ltd

1   2009

Contents

Notes on Contributors

David Bevington's books include *From "Mankind" to Marlowe* (1962), *Tudor Drama and Politics* (1968), *Action is Eloquence* (1984), and *This Wide and Universal Theatre: Shakespeare in Performance Then and Now* (2007). In addition to editing and reediting *The Complete Works of Shakespeare* throughout his career, he has produced *Medieval Drama* (1975), and free-standing editions of *Henry IV* (1987), *Antony and Cleopatra* (1990), and *Troilus and Cressida* (1998). He was awarded the Quantrell Award for Teaching Excellence, University of Chicago, in 1979, and Guggenheim Fellowships in 1964–5 and 1981–2.

Anthony B. Dawson has been teaching Shakespeare and related subjects at the University of British Columbia for many years and was awarded a Killam Teaching Prize in 2004. He has written extensively on performance history and theory, on early modern theatre and culture, and on editing and textual theory. His books include *Hamlet* (for the *Shakespeare in Performance* series, 1995), *The Culture of Playgoing in Shakespeare's England* (2001, with Paul Yachnin), and an edition of *Troilus and Cressida* (2003). He is currently collaborating with Gretchen Minton on an edition of *Timon of Athens*.

Frances E. Dolan is Professor of English at the University of California, Davis. Her teaching is indebted to her own teachers, Suzanne Gossett, David Bevington, Janel Mueller, Mary Beth Rose, and Richard Strier, and to inspiring colleagues, Susan Morgan and Margaret Ferguson. She is the editor of *The Taming of the Shrew: Texts and Contexts* (1996), and of five plays for the new Pelican Shakespeare. She has served as President of the

Shakespeare Association of America. Her most recent publication is *Marriage and Violence: The Early Modern Legacy* (2008).

Richard Dutton has been Humanities Distinguished Professor of English at Ohio State University since 2003. Before that he taught for 29 years at Lancaster University, UK. He has published widely on early modern drama, especially on issues of censorship and authorship. His publications include *Mastering the Revels: the Regulation and Censorship of English Renaissance Drama* (1991), *Licensing, Censorship and Authorship in Early Modern England: Buggeswords* (2000), and the Revels Plays edition of Jonson's *Epicene* (2003). He is editing *Volpone* for the *Cambridge Ben Jonson*, and has a monograph on the Gunpowder Plot context of that play in press.

Miriam Gilbert has taught since 1969 at the University of Iowa, where she has received the University's Philip G. Hubbard Award for Outstanding Education (2002) and the John C. Gerber Award for Excellence in Teaching (Department of English, 1998). She has directed six National Endowment for the Humanities summer seminars for school teachers and two for college teachers, all focusing on the issue of performance and interpretation. Her publications include performance histories of *Love's Labour's Lost* and *The Merchant of Venice*, a major drama anthology, and articles on teaching Shakespeare.

Barbara Hodgdon, Professor of English at the University of Michigan, is the author of *The Shakespeare Trade: Performances and Appropriations*, *The End Crowns All: Closure and Contradiction in Shakespeare's History*, and numerous essays on Shakespearean performances. She is coeditor of *A Blackwell Companion to Shakespeare and Performance* and editor of the Arden3 *Taming of the Shrew*. While at Drake University, she twice received the President's Award for Outstanding Undergraduate Teaching.

Jean E. Howard is George Delacorte Professor in the Humanities at Columbia University. Her publications include *Shakespeare's Art of Orchestration: Stage Technique and Audience Response* (1984), *The Stage and Social Struggle in Early Modern England* (1994), *Engendering a Nation: A Feminist Account of Shakespeare's Early Histories* (1997), and *Theater of a City: The Places of London Comedy 1598–1642* (2006). An editor of The Norton Shakespeare (2nd edition 2007), she was the recipient at Syracuse University of the first William Wasserstrom Prize for Excellence in Graduate Teaching and at Columbia University of the 2006 Faculty Mentoring Award.

Alexander Leggatt is Professor Emeritus of English at University College, University of Toronto. His publications include *Shakespeare's Comedy of Love* (1974) and *Shakespeare's Tragedies: Violation and Identity* (2005). He is the editor of *The Cambridge Companion to Shakespearean Comedy* (2002) and coeditor, with Karen Bamford, of *Approaches to Teaching English Renaissance Drama* (2002). In 1995 he was given an Outstanding Teaching Award by the Faculty of Arts and Science, University of Toronto, and in 2005 he was elected a Fellow of the Royal Society of Canada.

Ania Loomba is Catherine Bryson professor of English at the University of Pennsylvania. She researches and teaches early modern studies, histories of race and colonialism, feminist theory, and contemporary postcolonial issues, often exploring the intersections between these fields. Her publications include *Gender, Race, Renaissance Drama* (1989) *Colonialism/ Postcolonialism* (1998), *Shakespeare, Race, and Colonialism* (2002) and (with Jonathan Burton) *Race in Early Modern England: A Documentary Companion* (2007).

Russ McDonald is the recipient of multiple teaching awards, first at the University of Rochester and later at the University of North Carolina at Greensboro. In 2003 he was named Professor of the Year for North Carolina by the CASE/Carnegie Foundation. The author of *The Bedford Companion to Shakespeare*, a book adopted in undergraduate and graduate classes throughout North America, he teaches now at Goldsmiths College, University of London.

Kate McLuskie, Director of the Shakespeare Institute in Stratford upon Avon, has written numerous articles on the plays of Shakespeare and his contemporaries, and is author of *Feminist Readings of Renaissance Dramatists* and *Dekker and Heywood: Professional Dramatists*. She has edited Webster's *The Duchess of Malfi*, and coedited collections of *Plays on Women* and essays on *Shakespeare and the Modern Theatre*. She has taught at the Universities of Kent and Southampton (where she was also deputy-vice chancellor responsible for education and widening access), and as a visiting professor in the Universities of the West Indies, Colorado, and Massachusetts.

Carol Chillington Rutter, Professor of English at the University of Warwick, received a student-nominated Warwick Award for Teaching Excellence in 2007. She directs the CAPITAL Centre, a government-funded Centre of Excellence in Teaching and Learning that establishes a partnership between Warwick and the Royal Shakespeare Company. Widely published, her most recent book is *Shakespeare and Child's Play: Performing Lost Boys on Stage and Screen* (2007).

G. B. Skip Shand, Senior Scholar at York University's Glendon College, writes on teaching early modern drama, and on text and performance. He edited both prose and poetry for Oxford's *Complete Middleton*. As text coach, he has assisted on professional productions in Canada and at Shakespeare's Globe Theatre. His mentors in graduate school were the quietly gifted Guy Hamel, and Clifford Leech, whose personal generosity and formidable scholarship made him the definitive graduate supervisor.

Ramona Wray is Lecturer in English at Queen's University, Belfast and a recipient of the 2005–6 QUB Teaching Award. She is the author of *Women Writers of the Seventeenth Century* (2004) and the coeditor, most recently, of *Screening Shakespeare in the Twenty-First Century* (2006) and *Reconceiving the Renaissance: A Critical Reader* (2005).

Acknowledgments

Many thanks to Emma Bennett, who first imagined this project, and who has guided it from beginning to end; to Barbara Hodgdon, M. J. Kidnie, Sandy Leggatt, and Carol Rutter, who were part of the formative thinking from day one; to Jean Howard, for much wise counsel at a crucial stage; to all the many supportive colleagues, near and far, who helped with suggestions about contributors and topics; to the contributors themselves, who have been enthusiastic, diligent, kindly, and endlessly patient, as required; to Hannah Morrell and Louise Butler, for easing our progress through the Press; to Jenny Roberts, for diplomatic and exacting vigilance in making our words presentable; and to Patricia Martin Shand, for saintly tolerance and forbearance on the home front.

This book is for our mentors and for our students, with equal gratitude to all.

Introduction: Passing it On

Skip Shand

Lear is crying out "Oh sides, you are too tough!" The anguished speaker is small, grey-bearded, black-gowned, with intense kindly eyes. He perches at his lectern. His voice, light yet gravelly and resonant, takes intimate possession of Lear's words and emotions, or they of him. As he reads, a roomful of third-year undergraduates at a small Canadian prairie college sits transfixed, even awed. Bob Hallstead is teaching Shakespeare, and I am hearing intimations of a vocation. To this day, despite the subsequent interventions of a dozen or more great Lears on stage and film, when I read the play I hear Hallstead. When I speak its words, as Barbara Hodgdon will put it in her essay, I am no doubt ventriloquizing him – as well as whichever professorial forerunner he himself was echoing.

Hallstead labored in relative obscurity at United College in Winnipeg, then a church-affiliated institution that rationalized the constraints of a small budget and an overloaded faculty by seeking to privilege teaching above all other academic arts. United College could afford little time for scholarship. Hallstead had one short research trip in his entire career, spent it in heaven at the Folger Library, where he wrote what I believe was his only scholarly article, a *Shakespeare Quarterly* argument for idolatrous love as the heartbeat of *Othello* (Hallstead 1968).

He lived, in the classroom, for the stories within the stories, the stories in the gaps and silences, the narrative and emotional subtext. And he took us through the texts scene by scene, moment by moment, in a progressive question-and-answer unpacking process he called Socratic. He would have loved David Bevington's closely read contribution to this volume.

Hallstead's interrogation proceeded up one aisle and down the next, so that you always knew when your turn with the words was imminent. As Dr Johnson said of the death sentence: "Depend upon it, sir, when a man knows he is to be hanged in a fortnight, it concentrates his mind wonderfully." Knowing that Hallstead's next question would be yours had the same salutary effect.

He mentored by befriending – a hard kind of mentoring to practice in a large university, no doubt, and harder still to teach except by example. Nonetheless it can be superbly effective: it invites the novice into the inner circle, accepts her or him as potential equal, shares the joy of the subject and the humanity of the professor. Hallstead openly treated teaching Shakespeare as a privilege, as a calling to be cherished and to be passed on. Around the world, classrooms are peopled by women and men just like him – teachers who are reminded constantly of the many-faceted wonder that is the Shakespeare opus, and of their great good fortune to be spending a career sharing the plays with generations of new students. As Tony Dawson says, we would almost do it for nothing. Almost. This book is directed to all those many teachers of Shakespeare, and perhaps especially to those now preparing to carry on.

Running through all the essays in this volume is a thread of engaged pleasure – pleasure taken in the subject itself, in pedagogical process, in the students with whom that process is shared. Among them, the contributors have chalked up something close to five hundred years of experience in the Shakespeare classroom, and several shelves of teaching awards, but their idealism about the project continues undiminished; their engagement with student, text, and context seems unflagging. They are different personalities, of course; they differ in the manner of their teaching, in its emphasis, in their ways of talking about it. Some lecture, some prefer the seminar or tutorial, some treat the classroom as a kind of idealized rehearsal hall. Some are devoted to the text as aesthetic, linguistic, poetic object; others explore it as revelatory of interpretive or theatrical possibility; some focus on its links to historical and contemporary social issues such as gender, race, and religion; some explore the ways in which it is reshaped, illuminated, deployed, in film and television versions and adaptations. And of course, most of them actually juggle all these concerns and strategies as they accompany students on the journey through the plays. Ania Loomba's chapter on Shakespeare and race ends with her students creating their own adaptations. Ramona Wray, focusing on gender and difference, offers multiple readings of Shakespearean film. At the foundation of their teaching activities, all the contributors are consumed with transferring critical and reading skills from themselves to their students, with empowering the "clientele," with making themselves, in Russ McDonald's happy formulation, obsolete. But the wonderful difference between pedagogical obsolescence and that of last year's automobile or cell phone, is that we get to do it all over again, semester after semester, term after term. With a little thoughtfulness and a lot of luck, we even get to do it better. The Shakespeare vocation is organic and ongoing, more like sourdough starter than like a dead computer – the absolutely essential catalytic ingredient in every new student's fresh encounter with the plays and the playwright.

Reading these teachers one after another, my strongest recurrent wishes are to be a fly on the wall in their classrooms (which, happily, their essays frequently permit), and to have the impossible opportunity to start over myself, to return to the outset of this career – if I had known then what I have been lucky enough to learn since! In a sense, the contributors were invited to mentor their readership, and to be as candid, as reflective, even as anecdotal, as they saw fit, to highlight something of the personal side of the endeavor. Noted practitioners were asked to speak to their experience of teaching Shakespeare: what they do, why they do it, why they do it their way, why it's worth doing at all. The results are frequently courageous. I sought distinguished scholars, well known for their books and editions, their essays and conference papers, but not so well known – except by hearsay, and sometimes among their immediate colleagues – for their undergraduate and graduate teaching. It's a curious fact that although teaching and supervision occupy the greater part of any Shakespearean's day-to-day life in the profession, and reach many more people over the course of a career than does the whole of one's scholarly output (David Bevington's ubiquitous Shakespeare editions probably make him the exception here), they are the area of most people's practice that we tend to know least about. This collection offers a look in.

Although attention to a variety of approaches was built in to the range of scholars invited, classroom reputation always trumped any particular critical angle on the discipline, and so the coverage is inevitably partial. The essays fall loosely into several broad and quite permeable categories: text; text and performance, including film and adaptation; text and contexts – history, gender, race, nation, systems of education; and mentoring the teachers of the future. Most essays, though appearing in one category in the Table of Contents, nonetheless have much to say about or to other categories. Kate McLuskie's chapter, for example, was originally imagined as part of a section on graduate education, but it speaks more broadly to many issues in Shakespeare teaching, in particular the potential friction between academic rigor and the now not so new orthodoxy of performative reading and experiential teaching. So her thoughtfully overarching exploration appears here as a kind of crossroads, picking up and assessing concerns implied in the sections on text and on performance, but moving forward also into the ensuing essays on Shakespeare and contexts cultural and educational.

Many universities are beginning – my own certainly is – to be systematic and attentive when it comes to the professional mentoring of graduate students and junior faculty, but it is still frequently the case that such activity on the part of senior scholars goes largely unacknowledged – and most often uncompensated. And it is also the case, as we are all aware, that some unfortunate students proceed unassisted and unaccompanied through their graduate experience, their survival and even success something of a miracle for which the university deserves no credit. With luck, however, even the most isolated graduate student has been fortunate enough to witness excellent teaching in action. I'd argue (with Russ McDonald, I believe) that good teaching is in itself a form of positive mentoring, and one hope is that these essays, in their wisdom about teaching and their committed demonstrations of strategies and emphases, might even stand as attitudinal and actual models, and so invite readers to renewed idealism about the possibilities of the vocation. Logically, then, Jean Howard's careful reflection on the desired supportive professional relationship between senior faculty and graduate students opens the collection. Her sense of graduate study as a kind of apprenticeship in the scholarly craft, and of herself as bearing solemn professional responsibility for overseeing that apprenticeship, defines a context for the subsequent essays, which might be seen as mentoring by example, if not always by direct intent. At the other end of the collection, Carol Rutter's essay, virtually a Shakespeare teacher's credo, embraces so many of the pleasures and privileges shared by teachers of Shakespeare, and in such a forward-looking fashion, that it cries out to conclude the volume. As Howard is eloquent about the nuts and bolts of the mentoring process, so Rutter is eloquent about how well guided she was as teacher, as scholar, as theatrical witness. She pays lively tribute to her academic predecessors, to her students, and to the educational and institutional culture that currently links her academic department to the RSC, and enables her to live her professional life in a classroom that is theatre, a theatre that is classroom. Her commitment, shared by all contributors to the volume, is to pass it on. "I was well taught," she says. "I was left an inheritance that I must leave as a legacy."

Between these bookends, Russ McDonald lays out vivid thumbnail rules for fostering close appreciation of the text's artistry, along with a celebration of the lecture, and a call to the professoriat to embrace and exemplify its own authority. McDonald's stress is on *imitatio*: the student is tacitly invited to emulate, and then to refine and transform, the example of the teacher. To teach otherwise, he argues, is "to deny the value of our own education." Fittingly, David Bevington mines his vast editorial experience to model the textual teacher at work, taking us through the same meticulous exercise in close reading that informs the best editorial commentaries and that launches the most attentive explorations in the rehearsal room. Like the editor and the actor, he says, "The teacher in the classroom . . . is passing along the same pleasure and the same intimate relationship with the playwright's words in action." And then Sandy Leggatt, seeming almost to respond to Russ McDonald's take on authority, presents an exploratory and rehearsal-like teaching strategy, based on posing questions about text and action and interpretive possibility, questions open to so many answers that in the end, as he suggests, they have no answer at all. The instructor is to be ready for the unexpected, indeed to invite it. Leggatt's approach honors and engages the student's best curiosity, seeking always to send that student away hungry for more, to be like one of Carol Rutter's students who reports that Rutter often ends a seminar with a great question. "We then spend the rest of the day thinking about it."

Bevington and Leggatt anticipate the series of essays describing the pleasures of performative teaching. Increasingly, these essays speak with and to one another. Tony Dawson's engagingly personal treatment of "script" dovetails with the linguistic emphasis of the more purely textual essays, as he addresses a current need to recuperate literary/textual work and merge it with theatrical reading. His undergraduates, creating their own adapted performances, are invited to learn about multiple texts and textual instability, for instance, and to cope practically with them. (Richard Dutton laments that the majority of his American students have their first encounter with these issues only in graduate school.) Dawson stresses the mutual learning that goes on in his best classes: a student performance throws emphasis on a particular gesture at a particular moment in the play; together class and instructor are led to assemble a pattern of related gesture invited by the playtext, building finally to an exemplified reading style that recapitulates those image-hunting strategies we once considered purely literary. Fran Dolan's students are likewise alerted to meaningful patterns of gesture, prop use in this case, invited by the playtext, and Barbara Hodgdon describes a comparable formalist reading process when she and her students "follow the noose," seeking out and assessing imagistic visual patterns in Shakespearean film. The best performative teaching often does not lie far from the literary training of most of its practitioners.

We teach constantly in unacknowledged traditions, and we are busy scavengers when it comes to the techniques of others. Crediting Miriam Gilbert as the source of one of her opening classroom gambits, Barbara Hodgdon speaks of the oral tradition in teaching. Indeed, it would be hard to quantify the positive impact, through personal contact, that Gilbert has had on the teaching of all who know her.[1] Her contribution to this collection, actorly as always, begins with the value of student questions and first responses, and goes on to speak directly to the basic student interest in character and motive. Gilbert honors that interest, using it, as Fran Dolan also suggests in her chapter, to lay down an organic pathway toward more sophisticated critical skills, such as more precise descriptive categories and vocabulary. Gilbert's chapter, bolstered by her encyclopedic knowledge of Shakespearean performances, offers a recuperation of the place of character in our studies: she says, in essence, to those who would dismiss character study as an interpretive pursuit, "Tell it to the actor."

Barbara Hodgdon's essay on the uses of film is, as it happens, exemplary of McDonald's "planned obsolescence" in action: beginning self-mockingly with her own first tentative classroom experiences, she moves on to embrace the support available to the teacher from the world of film and adaptation, but by the end the filmic adaptations of her students have completely taken over the essay. In the process, Hodgdon starts this collection's response to one of our most persistent questions about teaching Shakespeare, and indeed about the usefulness of teaching the humanities: what earthly contribution can we possibly be making to a world torn apart by difference, hatred, fear? Russ McDonald has earlier observed that while the humanities are anything but worthless, they are nonetheless useless in any public sense. Shakespeare's texts, he asserts, are "a source of limitless pleasure" to be shared through teaching – but they will not cure illness nor drive arrogant political leaders from office. In the end of Hodgdon's chapter, as her students speak to these issues, they are clearly seeking a more politically engaged form of outreach from their encounter with Shakespeare, creating new and responsive work that does at least have the barricades in sight.

Kate McLuskie revisits and redirects the issues of performative and academic/scholarly reading, opening them out into a rich assessment of the contours of Shakespeare teaching at all levels in the wake of England's Bardbiz controversy and Rex Gibson's *Teaching Shakespeare* (1998). Drawing on Samuel Beckett's *Waiting for Godot*, she uses the hapless Lucky's conflicted roles as dancer and thinker to stand in for the gulf that has opened up between the performative readers – now demonstrably in official institutional ascendancy – and those whose critical and classroom emphases might be called intellectual, a gulf she characterizes as "the comic misalignment between the experience of the physical arts and the discursive meanings that we demand of them." She points to the "contest over pedagogic practice that polarizes reading the plays and performing them," that contest between the exciting world of plays experienced on one's feet and the supposedly dull dull world of plays thoughtfully studied in (or on) one's seat. There is, as she implies, a potential trivializing of the subject in the new pedagogical world of playing with plays, where characters can be "hot seated," their complex and profound questions about ethical and behavioral choices "easily answered by engaged and enthusiastic eight year olds."

Carrying on into the rich question of the uses of Shakespeare are the several essays that advocate confronting a troubled world and teaching toward awareness and enlightened change. Writing from Northern Ireland about teaching gender, Ramona Wray points to the potentially transformative benefit of a pedagogy that moves from definitions to redefinitions of basic social and critical assumptions, awakening students to "a fresh sense of their agency [and] a consciousness about their own positions in a society that has historically traded upon fixed roles and that has often elected to judge on the basis of predetermined affiliations." One of the initial aims of the meticulously cumulative undergraduate English/Shakespeare program at Queen's University Belfast is, in Wray's words, unteaching the student, "disabusing him or her of assumptions culled from high school" – "unpicking bad habits," as one of Kate McLuskie's sources puts it. Fran Dolan, too, speaks of "challenging, perhaps even confiscating, some of their assumptions" about the truths of history. And Ania Loomba addresses the racial, religious, and national dimensions of the issue even more insistently, pointing to all the traditionally racialized appropriations of Shakespeare worldwide, and stating flatly, "We must necessarily either challenge these histories, or rehearse them. There is no middle ground." These are essays with a heartening sense of transformative purpose, and implicit valuing of the Shakespeare project.

Loomba's essay weaves together three narrative strands. She takes the reader through a delicate analysis of the complex hidden intersections, historical and current, among Shakespeare, race, and colonialism, and through the immense challenge of sensitizing students, particularly in the United States, to the insidious depth and force of these tacit conjunctions. As with McLuskie in England, Loomba is intensely aware of the project of the dominant culture in America, seeking to remake Shakespeare in its own voice and to universalize that voice, to claim it as the voice of the nation. She grounds her argument in an engagingly candid rehearsal of her own personal journey from "unracialized" and privileged beginnings in India, through her abrupt discovery of Black Sisterhood as a doctoral student in England, and now to her still-growing understanding of the complicated heterogeneity underpinning early modern and contemporary issues of race and nation. And she ends by taking us into her classrooms at the University of Pennsylvania, where the daily task of fostering heightened awareness goes on.

The best teaching of many of these contributors centers on asking or entertaining great questions. Fran Dolan comments that "The untutored or unedited question has the most in common with the best criticism because eye-opening essays begin when a critic asks a great question or takes a fresh look or notices something strange." Her piece on locating Shakespeare in an early modern context and encouraging students to produce historical knowledge speaks to the pleasure and revelation that so often spring from fresh student observations and responses. Embracing the unanticipated moments of improvisation and discovery celebrated by Sandy Leggatt and Tony Dawson, she defines a dull class as "one in which no student was able to throw me off my charted course." This is not the inchoate diffidence of the unfortunate instructor experienced by Russ McDonald in his student days, but the openness and flexibility of a rigorous authority who is also requiring her students to immerse themselves in early modern pamphlets and homilies in their entirety, and insisting yet again on close engagement with Shakespearean text. Dolan is not prescriptive about historical learning. She is implicitly in accord with Leggatt when he observes that while history is rightly to be acknowledged, "there are times when it should be thanked and sent on its way." And Dolan herself sends on their way those performance-based voices (happily not represented in this collection) who would argue that there is no time for closely historicized reading. As she says, "Nobody ever ruined anything by looking at it more carefully. Critique *is* pleasure."

The Shakespeare experience in the northern hemisphere has frequently been transatlantic. Russ McDonald and Carol Rutter are Americans ensconced in English universities, McDonald fairly recently, Rutter for many years. Miriam Gilbert divides her teaching time among Iowa City, Stratford-upon-Avon, and the Bread Loaf program in Oxford. And after what must have seemed a whole lifetime at Lancaster University, Richard Dutton has now set up Shakespeare shop at Ohio State, from which vantage point he looks back on the recent history of the national system he left behind. As does Ania Loomba in her account of the Indian experience, Dutton tunes in to the impact of class and privilege on higher education and the English study of Shakespeare, and situates himself autobiographically in the story. In the process, and in concert with Kate McLuskie and Carol Rutter, he provides North American readers with a vivid picture of academic life in England for the student and teacher of Shakespeare. In the end, he assesses his move to North America in terms of professorial autonomy. At Ohio State, he says, "I was, for the first time ever, absolute master of my own classroom. I set my own syllabus, chose my own plays, the order in which to study them, and the perspective from which they would be studied; I chose and set my own forms of assessment – all freedoms which US professors take for granted, but which are still rarities in England." Taken as a whole, the contributors to this collection seem to bear out this distinction, in that while no one from North America discusses the university or governmental systems (whether of constraint or opportunity) within which their Shakespeare teaching happens, all the British contributors – and Ania Loomba, whose voice is the most international of all – are concerned to place their teaching in its institutional contexts, from the individual department up to the impact of governmental policy and public attitude.

I'm drawn repeatedly to an observation made by Anne Michaels in her beautiful novel, *Fugitive Pieces*, that "The best teacher lodges an intent not in the mind but in the heart" (1996: 121). Leaving aside the debatable binary of mind and heart, the idea of "lodging an intent" is arresting: to lodge something is both to fix it firmly and to give it a dwelling place; intent is inner thoughtfulness and purpose moving forward, issuing in action. The best teacher does indeed lodge an intent in the minds *and* hearts of her or his students. From Jean Howard's specific embrace of the high calling of mentor, through the 12 subsequent essays exemplifying something of the range of long and fulfilling pedagogical experience, this collection (yet another manifestation of the many books called *Teaching Shakespeare*) seeks to communicate some of the pleasures and satisfactions of life in the Shakespearean classroom. Lodging Shakespearean intents in our students and our successors, reshaping and passing on the legacy we've received, is the hope we all share.

Note

1   My own first encounter was in a 1976 conversation arranged by Malcolm Scully of *The Chronicle of Higher Education*, a conversation which led to her sharing exercises and practical strategies on which I have never stopped relying in the years since.

References and Further Reading

Gibson, Rex (1998). *Teaching Shakespeare: A Handbook for Teachers*. Cambridge, UK: Cambridge University Press.
Hallstead, R. N. (1968). "Idolatrous Love: A New Approach to Othello." *Shakespeare Quarterly* 19: 107–24.
Michaels, Anne (1996). *Fugitive Pieces*. Toronto: McClelland & Stewart.

Part I

Mentoring

1

Teaching Shakespeare, Mentoring Shakespeareans

Jean E. Howard

In an average week during a typical semester, I will spend at least 10 hours in activities related to the mentoring of students, mostly graduate students who hope to make a career teaching Renaissance literature in a college or university. This is one of the most pleasurable, delicate, and complex activities of the many that comprise my life as a Shakespearean. So what is it that we do when we mentor those who will go on to become our professional colleagues and successors? Is it a teachable skill, a highly individual art, or simply a duty? What do we mean by mentoring, anyway? I welcomed Skip Shand's request to think about these issues in print because I realize that though by my own lights I have been an active mentor of graduate students for nearly 30 years, I have not ever formally put to myself the questions I just posed. This essay is therefore an attempt to reflect, in a nonprescriptive way, on my own practice and to invite others to similar reflections. As with so many aspects of academic life, there is much that is deeply intuitive and individual about many of the activities – teaching and research, as well as advising and mentoring – that fill our days. And yet there is sometimes something to be gained from thinking more systematically about aspects of our daily practice. It is in that spirit, then, that I put forward these reflections on mentoring.

Of course, the Shakespearean's first move is typically to think about what Shakespeare's plays offer by way of ruminations on a given topic. Unfortunately, those plays are not a sufficient guide to academic mentoring, any more than to fly fishing. In a few, something resembling a mentoring relationship is portrayed, but usually in a way that shows how misguided, comic, or irrelevant the mentor can be; or how intractable the mentee. Young women in Shakespeare's plays, for example, are often given the benefit of their elders' wisdom, and usually to bad effect. One can think of the nurse, counseling Juliet to marry the County Paris and forget Romeo since the second match "excels your first; or if it did not, / Your first is dead, or 'twere as good he were / As living hence and you no use of him" (*Romeo and Juliet*, 3.5.223–5).[1] Judging only by expediency, the nurse fails to understand what Juliet really values and so makes herself irrelevant and Juliet hopelessly isolated. Polonius and Laertes, giving advice to Ophelia, do no better, treating her as incapable of independent judgment, turning her into an object into which they pour their maxims and positioning her as a counter in their plots to unravel Hamlet's mystery. A dutiful daughter who heeds the advice she receives, Ophelia eventually goes mad.

In the history plays, older men sometimes give young men the kind of counsel we now associate with mentoring. In *Henry VI, I* and *II* the Duke of Gloucester, assigned the position of Lord Protector to the young Henry VI, tries to teach his charge how to govern wisely. But the Duke's authority is undermined by his wife's treasonous activities, and the young King is in thrall to his French spouse and swayed, by her and a court faction opposed to the Lord Protector's power, to remove Gloucester from office. In this case, good counsel is not enough to rescue a weak man from his own folly and the bad advice of others. The Duke of Gloucester is murdered in his bed, and Henry VI goes on to have a disastrous reign. These examples should all be a warning to those who feel that giving counsel is an easy, automatically efficacious endeavor. The literature on mentoring is full of warnings about mentors who are tone-deaf, inattentive, or smothering, and of mentees who feel, alternatively, neglected or bullied by those positioned to mentor them.

Perhaps the most complex relationship analogous to mentoring that we find in the histories involves Prince Hal, Falstaff, and King Henry. The King is also a father who periodically and without much success tries to teach his son, Hal, how to be a prince and future king. With considerable acuity, the plays devoted to the reign of Henry IV probe the complexities of succession and the psychological barriers that prevent a son from accepting the advice of a father whom he will follow upon the throne. The paradoxical cry, "The King is dead; long live the King," pinpoints the ideology of replication that lies at the heart of the succession process and goes some way to explaining the reasons one so destined might fall out of love with future greatness even while pursuing it. Is replicating the father all that life has to offer?

Shakespeare, however, allows the recoil from the role of successor to be played out in another arena with another father, Falstaff, who counter-mentors the Prince in the arts of time-wasting and dissipation and seems to chart a course for Hal quite different from that of dutiful successor. As has often been pointed out, however, this particular form of "bad counsel" has some unpredictable results: teaching Hal the common touch and how to "drink with any tinker in his own language" (*I Henry IV*, 2.5.16–17), an art he finds useful at Agincourt as well as in Eastcheap. That Hal ends up as a remarkably successful king, if not always a likable person, seems in the end to owe as much to the lessons in pragmatism he learned directly from his father (i.e., to "busy giddy minds / With foreign quarrels" (*2 Henry IV*, 4.3.341–2) as to those in wit, rhetorical skill, and sheer opportunism he garnered from Falstaff. Mentoring here seems in some sense to pay off, but the collateral costs are huge. Henry IV is harried until the moment of death by his sense that his son is an irresponsible maverick rather than a fit successor. To prove his worthiness, Hal has publicly to humiliate and repudiate the man, Falstaff, who encouraged his wildness and hoped to benefit from it. Both of the older men appear driven by their own needs as much as, if not more than, the needs of the young Prince, and this particular triangle offers a miniature case study of the very complex motives, many of them not selfless, that can plague attempts to prepare young people for the professional roles they will soon assume.

These few examples drawn from the plays are not, of course, truly close approximations of the kind of situation university professors and their students face, but they nonetheless highlight some of the pitfalls that bedevil academic mentoring, and I will return to some of them below. They include the urge to replicate oneself through one's students; the temptation to stifle independence and creativity by prescribing too closely what a student must do; and the danger of mistaking mentoring for fathering or mothering and so falling prey to all the psychological traps and hazards that inform parent-child relationships. If distance is a problem, never letting students into the professional game and into our carefully protected reservoirs of knowledge and time, closeness may pose an even greater problem, fostering an inability to distinguish between guidance and cloning.

It is easy to spot pitfalls in mentoring relationships, harder to define a positive model of what might work and be useful. For me it's helpful to narrow the focus, first, and to look at the very particular situation of graduate students. What is it that makes mentoring such a crucial aspect of their graduate experience? While we all advise undergraduates about their course work, their majors, and often their life decisions, except in special cases we are not preparing them to enter the profession of which we are members. And they pass through our hands very quickly, often encountered in one or two courses. Untenured faculty also require special kinds of professional advice and mentoring as they come fully to occupy their roles as teacher/scholars and pass through the tenure process, but they are colleagues, not students, with their graduate training behind them. Graduate students, however, are both in close relationship with faculty for a long time, typically five to eight years, and also face an unusually steep learning curve in terms of mastering the professional skills they will need for success as a scholar/teacher at the university level. Above all, of course, they need to reaffirm their decision to acquire a PhD. Not every entering master's student is sure of his or her vocation, and they often need help in figuring out if they have really chosen the right path. If they have, then the array of skills for them to acquire is sometimes dauntingly large. They need to learn how to use specialized tools and skills to do original research; how to write a seminar paper, a conference paper, a dissertation chapter, a grant proposal, a book review, and a job letter; how to study for and pass qualifying exams; how to design a course syllabus and manage a classroom; how to define a dissertation topic they can live with and enjoy for three to four years or longer; how to break that topic into manageable segments; how to assess and write about other scholars' work; how to approach scholars at other schools to read their work or be on their conference panels; how to search for a job; and how to maintain balance between the unceasing demands of teaching and research and other parts of their lives.

All of these are difficult jobs requiring new skills and mental and emotional resources. In the pursuit of them it is easy for students to feel overwhelmed, insecure, and lonely. While most love the literature they have chosen to study, they are in a competitive environment where the love of their subject matter is not enough. They must also pass over many professional hurdles and learn how to channel their passion for literature into a research project that they will pursue, often largely by themselves, for many years. It is an astonishing fact that even in the most successful graduate programs, only 60 percent of entering students complete the PhD. A full quarter of those completing the MPhil never make it to the PhD (Damrosch 1995: 144, 146), confirming my own sense that as one researcher has put it, the biggest challenge of graduate mentoring involves "helping students make a successful transition from the familiar and highly structured world of coursework, with its short-term goals and predictable closure, to the unfamiliar, loosely structured, and relatively open-ended world of thesis or dissertation research" (King n. d.: 7). This open-ended world is the one in which they will live as professional teachers/scholars but for which we do not always adequately prepare them.

Mentoring is integral to the successful negotiation of this long process of training and supporting young scholars to become full members of the professoriate or, very occasionally, to find a better path for themselves outside the academy. Almost no one learns all the requisite professional tasks and skills without a lot of help from experienced faculty members. At Columbia students get quite a bit of institutional help learning how to become good teachers. There is, for example, a mandatory seminar in the second year that prepares them to teach their own section of University Writing in the third year in the program. Besides the content of the writing course, students learn about syllabus and assignment design, classroom management, assigning grades, responding to papers, and handling controversial and sensitive topics that arise in the classroom. There are many different ways to handle the training of graduate students as classroom teachers, but departments need to have developed one. Individual faculty can help by visiting their graduate students' classrooms, when asked, to give feedback on their effectiveness as teachers; and, when they are assigned teaching assistants for lecture classes, they can spend time with those graduate students on how to grade papers, handle classroom discussion, and even do lectures. Typically, I give my TAs a chance to give one lecture per term. Sometimes I help them figure out how they will focus the lecture and how they will open up their presentations to invite student participation. We also talk about how to handle certain recurring situations: the question that is met with deafening silence, the undergrad who won't stop talking, the "back row phenomenon" by which some students opt out of active participation in the class.

My personal goal is to help grad students emerge from this period of intensive training in research and in teaching with their intellectual independence and critical spirit intact, but with their professional naivety dispelled. That is, I want them well-schooled in the ways of the profession, and I want them to feel empowered by that knowledge to try for the jobs best suited to their ambitions, the fellowships most likely to further their research, and the professional contacts most likely to make them smarter.

But I also hope that becoming professional, which it is my job to help effect, does not entail a diminution of the passions that drove them to graduate school in the first place or the independence of mind that will make their work, in the last analysis, consequential. I like students who are always a little wild, the ones never entirely tamed to the merely professional, but who inhabit that space with their own special grace and integrity.

In helping students make it through graduate school intact and well-prepared for the profession they are entering, a little distance on my part is important. Overinvestment makes everything harder: it makes it harder to stand back and be genuinely critical of imperfect work, harder to avoid inappropriately shaping an emerging project, harder to send students off to get advice from someone besides myself. This is a particular challenge when dealing with those students for whom one often feels the greatest empathy: those not to the manor born, those from working-class backgrounds whose parents perhaps did not go to college, or those from ethnic or racial groups traditionally underrepresented in American higher education. Academically gifted, they nonetheless have to work harder than some other students to feel at home and empowered in PhD programs, partly because they may not see themselves reflected in the demographics of the senior faculty. It is imperative to be responsive to the particular situation of such students, yet not to get overinvested in their struggles. I have thought a lot about what graduate students are not: they are not my children; neither are they, I hope, my disciples or clones, because if they are, they have surrendered, and I have demanded, too much; nor are they my colleagues, not yet, though in time that is possible. Rather, I find it most useful to think of graduate students as apprentices learning the skills of a particular craft. I have a lot to teach them, but as in all good craft work, the final product is the result both of collectively generated and transmitted skill and of individual sensibility, taste, and ability.

Consequently, the mentoring relationship can't be all top-down and hierarchical, no matter how much I have skills to impart and experience to transmit. I have to hear as well as talk in order to be able to tease out from students the commitments and intuitions and insights that will be the decisive factors in their projects. I have never been able to figure out how one "gives" students dissertation topics, or why that would be a good idea if one is really preparing them for the open-ended world in which the content of their research is the one thing for which they bear ultimate responsibility. I see my role as helping to shape a project, to suggest materials that might refigure it, to probe the theoretical suppositions that propel it, and certainly to call attention to others whose work must be addressed. But "giving" someone a project seems to run counter to the ultimate aim of graduate training, which is not just to produce a PhD, but to prepare an individual to be a self-reliant, confident member of the profession. Sometimes the smartest students, the ones with the most ideas, have the most trouble settling into a dissertation. I have seen outstanding students try on three projects before settling on a final one, sometimes only after devoting some months to research and writing on one topic before abandoning it for a better choice. It's not pretty to watch, but sometimes it is the only way for a really lively mind to settle into its groove.

What then, specifically, can a mentor give to a graduate student? Hands down, the key thing is time. It is the best gift a mentor can give, and while there have to be limits to how many hours a professor gives to his or her graduate students, there is almost no way students can learn their craft from you if you are not regularly available to them. Craft work is exacting and time-consuming, and there aren't a lot of shortcuts. Sometimes you just have to sit in your office and hear a student out – listen to their half-formed ideas and try to coax out fuller ones or attend to their anxieties about the job market and give them help in preparing a first-rate dossier. As a standard part of my graduate teaching, I use graduate classes not only to teach a particular subject, but also to teach particular professional skills students will need as their careers advance. I invite them, for example, to give seminar presentations in the form of a 20-minute conference paper where the task is to learn how to deliver something orally that does not have to be read to be absorbed, and that can simultaneously engage an audience and convey an argument. This is an extremely hard task since many students wrongly think that being professional means being hard to understand. It's a perception that is unlearned only with difficulty.

Alternatively, I sometimes have graduate students write 1,000-word book reviews of major new publications in the field, teaching them how to define a book's central arguments and then to assess the most important of those arguments with tact and precision. It is a perfect occasion to talk not only about good new work in the field, but also about the ethics of critique. Again, students often think that criticizing everything is a sign of scholarly maturity. Critique they quickly learn how to do. What's harder is to help them figure out how to identify the positive good in an argument or a methodology and to criticize work with generosity as well as rigor. Over time graduate students can certainly learn how to do these common professional tasks better, and with more self-confidence, but not without trying them repeatedly and not without feedback and commentary from fellow students and from their professors.

However, the biggest demands on professors' time occur when classes are behind students. PhD exams, whether written or oral, provide a crucial opportunity for students to consolidate their knowledge of a field and to explore what might be possible dissertation topics. The exam itself is often something of an anticlimax. At Columbia it involves a two-hour oral exam in front of four examiners, and students often feel that the exam itself touches on about one 20th of what they know and are eager to discuss. Much of the real learning occurs in the work leading up to the exam, not in the actual moment of testing. Studying for orals can be a particularly lonely period, however, and meeting with students regularly during that time can both alleviate their sense of isolation and also provide wonderful opportunities to find out what really interests them about the material they are reading and how it might shape up into a dissertation project. Typically, I will meet with students from three to six times in advance of the oral exam, usually in blocks of an hour or more. It is a lot of time to commit, but it is a setting in which a real working relationship between student and professor can develop and where the faculty mentor can begin to let students take the lead in defining what is important and interesting to them in the material they are discussing together. Sometimes these are learning experiences for professors as well, especially if students want to address material that is off the beaten path. A student offering a field in Renaissance drama will seldom present me with more than a few texts I have not already read, but a field in Renaissance anatomies or travel books can be more of a challenge. One of the reasons to work with graduate students, however, is that they lead you down new paths. It would be impossible to say how much my own work has benefited over the years from the stimulation that comes from students wanting me to do a list with them on books I have not read before or wanting to do dissertations at one remove from my own central areas of expertise.

When students are actually writing the dissertation, the cycle of drafting and redrafting begins, each step in the process providing the mentor with a crucial opportunity to help students learn how to build and shape an argument. Sometimes chapters have to be rewritten three or four times before they click into their final shapes. The first chapter is typically the hardest because students inevitably try to put all the ideas they have for the whole dissertation into their first 50-page draft chapter. Winnowing out the debris, refining the central argument, staging ideas in sequence, interweaving literary readings with historical or philosophical or scientific material – these are all tasks that are hard to master, even for students who are very smart and who can write well. There is no way to learn them except to try them, again and again, repeatedly garnering feedback along the way.

I can't say often enough, then, that mentoring above all means giving time to students. Giving time to them is the only way they can benefit from the experience each of us has garnered as a member of the profession, whether we are sharing knowledge about teaching or publishing articles or finishing a long writing task, like a dissertation. But for me good mentoring also involves giving a certain *kind* of attention to the students who opt to work with you and be mentored by you. It means, in part, that you are honest in your responses to their work and their concerns. If a piece of work isn't good enough, at least not yet, the student needs to be told – not brutally, but straightforwardly. It's a cliché that criticism is a mark of respect, but it's one cliché that is true.

It's also important to have respect for their difference, which is perhaps the hardest part of mentoring, since the temptation to make a graduate student into a "mini-me" is seductive. Sometimes it's egotism, and sometimes pure impatience, that impels mentors to impose too many of their ideas on grad students, especially in the early stages of finding a dissertation topic and working it up into a serviceable form. It often takes a very long time for things to cohere, and sometimes the process just can't be rushed as students have to do more research, revise what they thought in light of what they discover, and so forth. Keats thought that "negative capability," the ability to be "in uncertainties, Mysteries, doubts without any irritable reaching after fact and reason" (Keats 1959: 261), was Shakespeare's defining characteristic. I think it is also a defining characteristic of many good mentors. They have to be capable of tolerating intellectual uncertainty on the part of their students because it is only by living through that uncertainty that students will find a meaningful path beyond it. This doesn't, of course, mean taking an entirely hands-off approach or letting students flounder; it does mean not rushing them to premature or unearned closure or to the closure you've already decided upon. It is always hard to discover that in the end you disagree with your own students' arguments, but that has certainly been true for some of my most lively mentees. Teach them what we will, in the end their work has to be their own.

Although graduate students are all highly individual and different from one another, working with them falls into fairly predictable stages, and the mentoring role changes from stage to stage, even though at each stage it requires lots of time, honesty, and mindfulness about the independence of the student with whom one is working.[2] At first mentoring centers on the acquisition of particular skills (both teaching and research skills), then on the more complex tasks of finding and developing the dissertation topic and sustaining an energetic argument over several hundred pages, and finally, with an intense burst of work, on the actual process of getting a job. The second phase is the really hard one where it is easy for mentees to drift away into isolation and depression before the enormity of the task they face. By contrast, the final burst of work around the job process can be a fairly manic one, with materials being written and revised at breakneck speed, adrenaline pumping.

At Columbia, the department has introduced two important innovations to make it easier for students to make it through the crucial dissertation-writing phase of their work. These innovations also collectivize the mentoring function about which I have been writing in very important ways. As my colleague David Damrosch has argued, parts of a graduate student's experience are extremely isolating (Damrosch 1995: 140–85). People often work alone when preparing for orals or writing their dissertation. While some thrive on this regime, others do not. A good mentor who keeps in close contact with the student can counteract the sense of isolation, but there are other mechanisms that can make this phase of graduate work more collaborative and provide the student with more than one mentor. At Columbia we have dissertation seminars for various fields. Our early modern seminar meets in the evening, usually every two weeks, and all the students in the field are members, with a special focus on those who have passed their qualifying exams and embarked on a dissertation. All faculty in the field are encouraged to come to the seminar at which advanced students present their dissertation prospectuses, major conference papers, their job talks, and, above all, their dissertation chapters. The seminar has various functions. First, it keeps all the advanced students in touch with one another and with the faculty. Wine and sandwiches are mandatory. Second, it gives students a rough timetable for producing work, as each student is expected to produce a piece of writing for the seminar every term. Third, it provides the students with a chance to vet their work before a number of people so that they get various responses on what is most valuable and convincing in their arguments and how to improve everything from the prose style to the organization to content. Fourth, it gets students used to public discussion and defense of their work, so that when they go on job interviews they can talk about their dissertations with confidence.

Of course, the primary mentors of the students who present their work in the seminar also meet with them after the session to debrief and to help them winnow and organize the feedback they received. The seminar doesn't replace the dissertation committee, but it augments its work in useful ways and provides students with a collegial context in which to try out their ideas. An unintended effect is often to "cool down" the relationship with the primary mentor, letting fresh winds into the conversation that has been developing for several years around the dissertation, mitigating some of the tendencies toward overinvestment that are so easy for a dissertation mentor to indulge.

Another practice, newly instituted, is to have one of the department secretaries schedule a formal meeting between the graduate student and his or her three-person dissertation committee within a month of the student's submitting a fresh dissertation chapter. In part, the practice is aimed at being sure that students have timely responses to their work and that all three members of the dissertation team are active. But the effect has been, again, to let students take part in a four-way conversation about their work that opens up the range of possible responses to it. At the end of the meeting, all four participants agree on a plan for going forward.

These innovations seem important to me, not because they replace the work of primary mentors, but because they offer students a fuller range of responses to their work and take some of the pressure off that highly complex relationship. If we want our students eventually to be the kind of independent colleagues we most value, lessons in letting go are part of what the mentor has to learn.

There is, then, a particular complexity and delicacy to the mentoring relationship between a faculty member and a graduate student. It is easy to get it wrong and no certainty that even if it is approached with intelligence and good will the result will be a student who loves the profession and goes on be a productive scholar and teacher at a school suited to his or her talents and interests. There are no guarantees on the mentor's considerable investments of time and energy and caring; and the academic job market is, as we all know, fickle and unforgiving. What we can do is give it our best shot and really pay thoughtful attention to the apprentice teachers and scholars who come into our orbit. If they go on to succeed in the profession and to become friends and colleagues, that is a sweet outcome. But even if they do not, it is a very special part of academic life to have worked with them and to have guided them as well as we possibly could.

Notes

1 All quotations from Shakespeare's plays are taken from *The Norton Shake-speare* (Greenblatt et al. 1997).
2 There is even a literature on the stages of mentoring, with one researcher talking about the passage from the "initiation phase" to the "cultivation phase" to the "separation phase" to the "redefinition phase," when mentorship ends and a collegial friendship can emerge. See Johnson (2003: 139).

References and Further Reading

Damrosch, David (1995). *We Scholars: Changing the Culture of the University.* Cambridge, MA: Harvard University Press.

Greenblatt, Stephen, Jean E. Howard, Katherine Eisaman Maus, and Walter Cohen (Eds) (1997). *The Norton Shakespeare.* New York: W.W. Norton.

Johnson, Brad W. (2003). "A Framework for Conceptualizing Competence to Mentor." *Ethics and Behavior* 13(2): 127–51.

Keats, John (1959). "Letter to George and Thomas Keats" (December 1817). In Douglas Bush (Ed.). *Selected Poems and Letters* (pp. 260–1). Boston: Houghton Mifflin.

King, Margaret (n. d.). "Directing the Research of Graduate Students: The Ethical Dimensions." Accessed 25 October 2007 from <http://www.chass.ncsu.edu/ethics/inst_mod/mentoring.pdf>.

Moore, Cindy (2000). "A Letter to Women Graduate Students on Mentoring." In Phyllis Franklin (Ed.). *Profession 2000* (pp. 149–56). New York: Modern Language Association of America.

Part II

Text

2

Planned Obsolescence or Working at the Words

Russ McDonald

I should begin by warning the reader not to be alarmed by my title, at least its first two words: a colleague feared that the phrase referred perhaps to a new administrative scheme for reducing the size of the faculty. In fact it is merely a nonthreatening metaphor. "Planned obsolescence," as some will perhaps remember, derives from the American automobile industry of the 1950s and 1960s. It refers to the practice of manufacturing cars so that they would be outmoded in four or five years and the consumer would therefore need and want the newer model. My argument in this essay plays with the phrase in a different sense: whereas the automotive industry sought to make its product obsolete, my aim instead is to dispense with the producer. The pedagogic process imagined and described herein reflects my conception of the Shakespearean classroom as a laboratory in which instructors engineer their own obsolescence, seeing to it that students absorb and develop the ability to read, interpret, and take pleasure in the plays and poems on their own, without professorial assistance. The teacher's ultimate goal, then, is to instigate a disappearing act in which the talents and capabilities of the instructor are transferred to, adjusted, and extended by the student. Cliché though it may be, the end of education is self-education.

My assignment in this collection is, I hope it will be agreed, uncommonly challenging: how to introduce students to Shakespeare's language or, more particularly, how to confront, not evade, the problem of the words. The discussion divides into three parts. The first section addresses the question of why I teach, and much of it is devoted to the attraction of the humanities generally, with Shakespeare and the humanities standing in for each other as needed. My primary aim is to identify what it is about Shakespeare's work that makes me want to transmit it to others. The second part is more polemical, diagnosing what I take to be a shirking of leadership in the twenty-first century classroom and urging a revised approach for instructors. The last section provides an alternative to the methods deplored in the second, consisting of some modest suggestions for helping students. This constitutes a kind of tool kit, the contents of which are dictated by what is to be built: in other words, how I teach is a function of why I teach what I teach. Throughout the three sections my goal should be perceived as the same – pedagogical self-annihilation.

Nothing but Fiction

When I was a college student, home for the summer and working as an electrician's helper, the journeyman I was assigned to help was my redoubtable Uncle Jack, a man of little education but immense intellectual vigor and tireless pugnacity. "What do you do all day at college?" he inquired, as we rode in the truck to the construction site. Perhaps with a half-conscious wish to provoke, I responded simply, "I read. That's it. That's what I do." "Hmph. And *what* do you read?" he persisted. "I bet you don't read nothing but *fiction*." He had a point. My happiest moments as an undergraduate were spent absorbed in the worlds of Austen, Pope, Keats, Faulkner, and, of course, Shakespeare. And in the good-natured contempt with which he mocked my vocation, Uncle Jack did me a service, forcing me early in life to articulate for myself the value of studying and teaching literature. He insisted that time spent with fiction was time wasted, that imaginative writing didn't put food on the table, that majoring in English was manifestly impractical. Why can't you be a naval architect? What are you going to do with a degree in English? Who is going to pay you to read?

Now I can report, *pace* Uncle Jack, that I have found somebody to pay me to read – my title as I wrote this essay was "Reader in Renaissance Literature" – although they don't pay me very much, which was his real point. But the basic argument is irrefutable, that the liberal arts are impractical, that they produce nothing tangible. In a militant version of this doctrine, the engineer father of one of my college friends – a talented musician who ought to have been a composer – forbade him to major in the humanities, flatly declaring that the family would not finance his wish to sit under a tree reading poetry. These hostile responses are hardly uncommon, as almost any of today's undergraduates can attest. The parental and sometimes peer opposition to a degree program in the humanities bears witness to a powerful antihumanist strain in Anglo-American cultural life, a disdain for the uselessness of the liberal arts, for the irrelevance of the literary. Worse, such antagonism sometimes arises from within the university itself.

Thus one of my unspoken motives in teaching Shakespeare is to promote the value of the immaterial. Artists themselves have long known the rewards of such impracticality. "What one seems to want in art, in experiencing it," said Elizabeth Bishop, "is the same thing that is necessary for its creation, a self-forgetful, perfectly useless concentration" (Schwartz and Estess 1983: 288). So my initial aim in these pages is to assert directly the value of arts and letters, to identify some sources of opposition to them, and above all to reassert the value of the perfectly useless. My comments also seek to encourage those of us who devote ourselves to the humanities, to establish some ways of thinking about our contribution, to devise a vocabulary for talking about what we do, about why we do it, and about how we might do it better.

The arts and humanities have always been imperiled to a lesser or greater degree, but at the beginning of the twenty-first century the threat seems to have returned in a mutated and pernicious form. We should hardly be surprised that the attraction to poetry or painting or music is regarded by the culture at large as at best irrelevant and at worst potentially dangerous. In a world committed to acquisition, societies historically grounded in entrepreneurship and commerce, and (most recently) a culture intoxicated with the new wine of technology, it is small wonder that the arts are neglected. If the business of America is business, then the arts aren't even in second place. That position would be reserved for sports. (Or, as we say in Britain, where it is no less central, "sport.") The humanities get what is left over when science and other paying enterprises have taken away all they can carry. In America this depreciation of the arts is a legacy of the Puritan heritage, with its antitheatrical strain, its distrust of images, its suspicion of most forms of play, its fear of femininity, and its irrepressible work ethic. The arts are offered lip service, tolerated rather than cherished, retained because they serve as proof of sophistication, a civic badge of honor. This is the reasoned position of the Dallas businessman at the turn of the last century who declared that, yes, he'd support the goddam opera as long as they didn't make him go.

Unhappily, the humanities are in danger not only from their natural ene-
mies in the realms of commerce and government but from opponents within
the academy as well. As almost every American and European university
is starved for funds, obliged to make itself pay, and reshaped according to
a corporate model, the humanities have become the stepchild, the indi-
gent orphan who must yield to those well-dressed, haughty disciplines that
can pay their own fare. If it doesn't attract grants, if it doesn't fit into the
"research foci," if it doesn't generate overhead or recoverable indirect costs
– in plain terms, if it doesn't pay – then it doesn't matter. Lurking behind
this academic pecking order is a profound historical misogyny, an economic
version of the prejudice that reading poetry or spending one's day practicing the piano might be permissible for girls, but that men, real men,
breadwinners, can't afford to waste their time in such inconsequential
activity. If you must major in English, at least go to Law School.

Such deplorable hierarchies are long-standing, but lately the familiar mis-
givings about art have enlarged their dominion to comprise not only commerce and science but the realm of the humanities themselves. Humanists
fret openly about their own irrelevance, about the remoteness of the ivory
tower. In Shakespeare studies, this self-laceration manifested itself first as
a robust antiformalism, a disapproval of attention to style or pattern or
beauty. Many of our colleagues in the 1980s and 1990s made their repu-
tations by arguing that criticism had to do social work, that all discourse
is political, that literary analysis therefore must be politically inflected. The
effort to understand the operation of aesthetic objects was considered outdated, quaint. Novels and plays and poems became primarily social documents: to see them otherwise was belittled as escapism or political quietism.
All this was bad news for the boy under the tree with his book of poems.

Although I believe that students, a category in which I include myself
and other literary critics, must be prepared to offer a reasoned statement
of why they do what they do, I also contend that the study of literature
and its artsy cousins – in other words, the analysis, preservation, and transmission of works of art – does not require apology. We must recognize and
admit that the humanities are never going to pay: rather than whimper
about the unfairness of this fact, we ought instead to set about showing
the culture that we shall not live by technology alone, that the arts and
humanities are also necessary. Whether or not the job of literature professor is more or less noble or justifiable than that of social worker or
medical doctor is not a question to be answered here, but I am persuaded
that we must recognize the products of the imagination for what they are

and not attempt to make them over into something else. This is what Stephen Booth deplores when he jests at those critics "who spent the 1980s trying to drive Mrs. Thatcher from office by reading Shakespeare" (Booth 1994: 44), or what Kenneth Burke warned of some 75 years ago: "we should not be driven by the excesses of our opponents into making too good a case for art. . . . One cannot advocate art as a cure for toothache without disclosing the superiority of dentistry" (Burke 1931: 90). There are more efficacious ways of achieving social change than the study of imaginative literature. Strictly speaking, the humanities are useless, and that is as it should be. Useless, but not worthless: the Shakespearean text, for example, is a source of limitless pleasure, and my aim as a teacher is to identify and pass along strategies for allowing others to partake of that pleasure.

Teaching Learning

As teachers of Shakespeare, we command the instruments essential for initiating this process, instruments which can be described in a variety of ways – historical information, expertise at reading, acquaintance with the critical tradition, skill at analyzing poetry, a capacity for synthesizing disparate details, familiarity with additional resources. Whatever we call it, or whatever method we elect to stress, the vital point is that such equipment affords the teacher a degree of authority – authority that should be acknowledged, exercised, and transferred to the student. Having spent several summers as Head Scholar in the Folger Library's Teaching Shakespeare Institute, I feel a certain heretical guilt about my pedagogical methods: my argument runs contrary to the current orthodoxy that the most effective way of teaching Shakespeare is to "get them on their feet," to make students speak the lines themselves. My style might be called "keep them in their seats." But whatever the method, I contend that teachers must not dodge the problem of the words, that the Shakespearean idiom is the irreducible feature that makes the plays and poems what they are.

My own best teachers were eager to impart information and modes of apprehension, were not discomfited by the fact that they knew more about their discipline than I did, and were not reluctant to share that expertise. Of course my convictions derive partly from the historical moment in which I was educated, when the fierce egalitarianism of the late 1960s flooded into every corner of the academy, sometimes with depressing results. I vividly recall an introductory English survey, a course in four authors – Chaucer,

Shakespeare, Donne, and Milton – in which the youngish instructor, a fiercely intelligent assistant professor in a first job, was so fearful of exercising authority or acknowledging any superiority of training or insight that she would enter the classroom, take up a casual position on the desk, and inquire, "Okay, what do you want to talk about?" The chairs were affixed to the floor, as I remember, or we would surely have been in a circle. Such insecurity made for a dismal hour, I can tell you, and thus it was a relief finally to pass into the second semester, where my instructor was the formidable Helen Bevington, mother of David. Mrs Bevington, whose modern poetry course was known as "Helen wheels," had no fear of intellectual self-assertion. I learned much from watching and listening to her read critically.

This need to exercise authority and to impart information is especially urgent in the case of the Shakespearean text, given the challenges of early modern English, and yet many of us are loath to employ the authority with which our training has furnished us. A primary symptom of the decline of pedagogical authority, especially in the North American classroom, is the desuetude of the lecture. Having recently taken up a teaching position in London, I can report that the British university retains its lecture system for many courses, and I have been reminded of its value by the brilliant performances of some of my new colleagues. My views, however, are informed by my experience in American universities, where small classes are by definition good and large ones indisputably bad and where the lecture is regularly derided, dismissed as old-fashioned, vilified as patriarchal and oppressive.

I wish to take this opportunity to contest the present orthodoxy. The lecture has suffered rather a lot from the rise of "new pedagogies," particularly those associated with the study of writing, or as we now rather grandly refer to it – since we no longer teach writing – rhetoric. A major source of this prejudice is easily traced: one of the culprits is Paulo Freire, the Brazilian educational theorist who expressed his views in his influential little book, *The Pedagogy of the Oppressed*. Regarding the teacher as the holder and abuser of authority and therefore the agent of the state, Freire seizes upon a convenient metaphor to impugn customary modes of teaching: traditional pedagogy, he argues, is based upon the banking theory of education.

According to this view, the instructor deposits information into the student as if into a bank account, and the student passively receives it. The transaction is one-sided, noninteractive, despotic:

The banking concept (with its tendency to dichotomize everything) distinguishes two stages in the action of the educator. During the first, he cognizes a cognizable object while he prepares his lessons in his study or in his laboratory; during the second, he expounds to his students about that object. The students are not called upon to know, but to memorize the contents narrated by the teacher. Nor do the students practice any act of cognition, since the object towards which that act should be directed is the property of the teacher rather than a medium evoking the critical reflection of both teacher and students. Hence in the name of the "preservation of culture and knowledge" we have a system which achieves neither true knowledge nor true culture. (Freire 1972: 67–8)

It is important to remember that Freire was writing from a distinct historical perspective, describing the experience of illiterate South American workers whose education was dominated absolutely by the state. Self-expression was out of the question. Whatever one thinks of American or British politics in the first decade of the twenty-first century, it must be acknowledged that university students suffer nothing like the tyranny Freire assumes. Thus the appropriation of his banking theory to represent traditional Anglo-American pedagogy is reductive, partial, and false. Its depiction of the instructor as active and the student as passive applies only in the physical sense. It ignores the possibility that the lecture may also function in affirmative ways.

The consecration of Freire, especially as his work has been taken up and disseminated by his North American boosters, has had a disabling effect on instruction in the humanities. This devotion to the principles of the so-called "democratic classroom" has been especially pervasive in composition programs, where principles of accurate, readable prose have yielded to the tyranny of unshaped self-expression, the dominance of journals and memoirs, the lure of anecdote and autobiography. "To dialogue," as the current phrase goes, is also a popular maneuver with new teachers or graduate instructors or those who are diffident about their own abilities and authority. We see mutations of this attitude in the familiar injunction that we should know where our students are coming from, that we should interest ourselves in what interests them. It is unimportant what the subject might be: what matters is the opinions of the participants. Expressivity trumps fact. We now practice, instead of the pedagogy of the oppressed, the pedagogy of the Oprah-esque – classroom as talk show.

Lest flippancy threaten to undo my argument, let me return critically to Freire, whose goal of democratizing the classroom errs in mistaking the authoritative for the authoritarian. When lecture functions properly, then its receivers are no less intellectually vigorous than the speaker. Ideally students' minds are even more active as the ideas presented interact with their own intellect and experience. The lecturer supplies a model of analysis, constructs and transmits a mode of comprehension, whatever the topic. Having devoted vast intellectual effort to mastering this material, the speaker invites the auditor to assimilate and share it, to master this methodology or that technique for reading so that the student can absorb, reproduce, and eventually surpass the model, ultimately advancing the cause of scholarship even further. Particular details may be forgotten, but information is required to fuel the student's mental machine; and while reading assignments and critical material may serve a similar purpose, the personal dynamic of the lecture, the appeal of human interaction and the benefits of concentration, can be both efficient and intellectually thrilling. Despite our laudable sensitivity to the Other, too often that model of receptivity is imposed only on the instructor, whereas students, who would benefit from Bishop's self-forgetfulness, from being transported beyond their own limited experience, are given a pass, permitted to ignore the available authority and to rely solely upon themselves. To relinquish the power of the lectern is to withhold necessary pedagogical nourishment: it is not too much to say that to dismiss the lecture is to deny the value of our own education.

In that disappointing sophomore English class, I in fact learned much about the four poets on the syllabus and about ways of reading poetry generally, although I learned neither from the instructor nor from my peers. Instead, I found critical exempla in the articles at the back of the Norton Critical edition of Donne. Noting that the linguistic root of lecture is "reading," I took as my lecturers that autumn C. S. Lewis, Joan Bennet, Helen Gardner, and other supremely gifted critics, and seeing them read taught me the rudiments of poetic analysis. When we read a text for our students, whether we do so in the form of a brief explication in class, a conference in the office, a written response to a claim in one of their essays, or a full-dress lecture, we create a model which may be emulated and then – we can hope – improved upon.

In fact, the process of lecture and reception might be considered a version of the principle on which early modern pedagogy was founded, the theory of *imitatio*. According to Roger Ascham, "All languages, both learned and mother tongues, be gotten, and gotten only, by imitation. For as ye use to hear, so ye learn to speak; if ye hear no other, ye speak not yourself, and whom ye only hear, of them ye only learn" ([1570] 1967: 114).

So, too, with the language of literary criticism. Students need model readers. Moreover, they need more than one: ancient and Renaissance commentators on imitation insist on the wisdom of emulating a variety of writers. That opinion is accompanied by another, more important principle, the necessity of transforming the model selected for imitation. Petrarch emphasizes this point by summoning the apian metaphor that pervades this discourse from the Greeks to the Italians to the English: "Take care that what you have gathered does not long remain in its original form inside of you: the bees would not be glorious if they did not convert what they found into something different and something better" (Pigman 1980: 7). All our most eloquent pedagogical predecessors insist upon the need for creative imitation. And so should we.

I've Got a Little List

Following the logic of my argument about embracing authority and supplying critical models, I ought now to present a dazzling reading of a Shakespearean passage to demonstrate how to help students confront the text. My plan is considerably more modest, however. I offer instead a series of practical suggestions, recommendations that can be subsumed under a single rubric: helping readers to engage with rather than ignore the language of the plays. To return momentarily to Uncle Jack, in whose Calvinist eyes it wasn't worth doing if it wasn't difficult, I am persuaded that it is the labor of struggling with the text that finally generates comprehension and satisfaction. Each of us has to develop personal strategies for meeting the challenges of the words, and the act of locating and developing these tactics will produce a more adept reader: the short-cuts that one finds on one's own are the most efficacious.

Nevertheless, what follows are some suggestions I have developed for myself and my own students. For me they are helpful when I undertake to read an early modern play for the first time – something by Dekker, for example – and I find that keeping this experience in mind helps me to imagine myself in my students' position as they sit down to read, say, *Love's Labour's Lost*. These recommendations take the form of a list, and after the last item I explicate and enlarge on each of them.

1   Lose the iPod.
2   Try reading aloud.

3   Work out your own method of using glosses and footnotes.
4   Read in manageable chunks, as skill permits.
5   Write a brief summary as you finish each scene.
6   Remember that you are reading dialogue.
7   Remember that you are reading poetry.
8   Forget that you are reading poetry.
9   Alter word order, adjusting syntax as needed.
10 Observe the logical pointers, particularly conjunctions.
11 Look for the antitheses.
12 Look for visible rather than hidden meanings.

Let me elaborate.

First, find a silent place to read a Shakespeare play, and don't listen to music when you do so. The text itself is music. If you attempt to read while listening to anything else, whether it be hip-hop or Handel, you divide your attention. Moreover, part of the experience of textual reception involves registering the rhythmic distinctions among different characters' speech. This is, to be sure, a fairly sophisticated effect to notice; often our cognizance of it will not be conscious, and some readers will be more alert than others to such rhythms and aural imprints. But however sensitive or insensitive the reader's ear may be, other music interferes.

Second, if you find it difficult to concentrate and hard to follow the sense of a passage, speaking the words aloud can sometimes clarify meaning. This recommendation may be applied to a whole text, but perhaps it is best employed occasionally, as a means of cracking an especially intractable or opaque group of lines. Reading aloud in a group can be instructive and diverting, and an audiotaped version can also be illuminating, but neither substitutes for solitary engagement with the words on the page.

Third, different readers will find different ways of approaching the para-textual aids provided in a modern text, particularly glosses and notes. The Norton edition, because it is single-column, is able to supply brief glosses of words and phrases alongside the lines. The British New Penguin editions print notes at the back of the book, a placement I find frustrating, and if I don't have the patience to flip back and forth between text and notes, my students certainly do not. Most editions place commentary at the bottom of the page. Some readers find the process of looking down and then up again every few lines hopelessly distracting, and thus they wait until they come to the end of the column or the end of the page before going back to look at glosses and notes. I usually recommend reading until the text doesn't make sense, that is, ignoring all notes until coming to an archaic term or an unfamiliar mythological allusion or some such obstacle that demands elucidation. Then, after finishing the scene, one can return to the notes and fill in details that may assist comprehension.

Fourth, no fixed rule dictates how much one ought to read at one time. Certain readers, depending on their familiarity with the early modern idiom, may find themselves able to read an entire play – say, *The Comedy of Errors* or another short text – in a single sitting, whereas others, with little experience, may be able to absorb no more than one extended scene. It is vital, however, to read enough at one time to achieve a sense of continuity or momentum. Reading *Antony and Cleopatra* in 42 sittings, one scene per session, will almost inevitably leach all sense of pleasure out of that text. Also, different kinds of readings require different levels of attention. An undergraduate reading *King Lear* for the first time will necessarily read at a different speed and with a different level of concentration than a graduate student reviewing the play in search of a paper topic. Generally speaking, it is best to read until one is conscious of not reading attentively, in other words, until one finds oneself skimming over the words instead of taking them in.

Fifth, the practice of writing a brief summary forces the question of comprehension. Do I know what happened in the scene I just read? Such a summary ought to be very short, no more than one or two sentences per scene, depending on the complexity of the episode. Limiting detail prevents the task from being too daunting, taking too much time, or breaking the momentum of the dramatic narrative. Moreover, creating such a plot summary also yields a convenient study document.

Sixth (but not lastly), it helps to remember that the lines we read are spoken by one character to another or others. This is obvious enough in stichomythia or witty banter, but in the middle of longer passages being mindful that a speaker is responding to what someone else has said can often elucidate a confusing stretch of text. If the sense of a passage is still elusive, it sometimes helps to reread the speech immediately preceding the difficult section, reminding oneself of who or what is being responded to. And certain fundamental guides to conversation can be applied: is the speaker agreeing with the other person? disagreeing? modifying an opinion? changing the subject?

Seventh, students (and perhaps colleagues) need to remind themselves that the words they read are usually dramatic poetry, and that its rhythms constitute an essential dramatic tool. (Sometimes, of course, they will be reading prose, and it is vital that they know the difference: while prose may exhibit a distinctive rhythm, it is of a different order than that of verse.) But knowing that Shakespeare's medium is dramatic verse may for many students be less a comfort than a source of anxiety. Most undergraduates suffer from fear of poetry, and our most diligent and compassionate efforts are rarely sufficient to cure them. Such fear – let's call it "poesophobia" – prevents the victim from liking verse, recognizing and appreciating its constituent properties, and in many cases even admitting that it exists. In short, if you don't acknowledge that it is poetry, you can simply talk about the characters and what they did and thought, not bother with the language, and skip over those bits that are hard to understand. My solution to this problem is to confront it directly, to call a spade, if not a spade, at least a dibble – in other words, to furnish the student with some tools for appreciating the contribution of the verse.

The way to begin is with vocabulary: the student who can put a name to a poetic feature that keeps asserting itself – "anaphora," for instance, or "image," or "slant rhyme" – is given power over the line that contains it and is much more likely to take pleasure in the effect of that feature. I often distribute a handout on explication, offering the student some 20 or so questions to ask about a speech or a poem, from metaphor to internal rhyme to tone to symbol. Handbooks are helpful in this case, such as Paul Fussell's (1965) *Poetic Meter and Poetic Form*, Richard Lanham's (1991) *Handlist of Rhetorical Terms*, or Gideon Burton's helpful website, *Silva Rhetoricæ*. Not all students will overcome their *poesophobia*, but it is worth trying to demonstrate the mechanics of poetic effects that readers and audiences have relished for centuries.

Having argued that we should acknowledge the poetic structure of Shakespearean speech, I come to the eighth recommendation, contradicting myself to suggest that we forget momentarily that we are reading verse. It helps to recall that we are reading English sentences, and we should not allow the structure of verse to obscure the fundamental communicative strategies of the language. In other words, Shakespeare's speakers all use conventional elements of expression: subjects, verbs, objects, complements. If a passage seems especially unyielding, it can be liberating to stop for a moment and try to discern the grammatical outline of the sentence, temporarily eliminating modifiers (simple adverbs on the one hand and lengthy dependent clauses on the other), prepositional phrases, and other forms of clutter until the basics of the main clause can be located and apprehended. Then the additional parts of the sentence can be reestablished and the complexity of the whole more easily appreciated. This method, of course, assumes that students know some basic units of grammar. While I suspect that no one alive, not even specialists, can diagram sentences like Miss McGee, my fifth-grade teacher, most students are not only ignorant of grammar but unable even to distinguish parts of speech: ask a student to identify the grammatical subject of a Shakespearean sentence and you're likely to get some complex, abstract paraphrase. Nevertheless, the principle that poems are composed of sentences, that the end of the poetic line in no way affects the semantic content of the passage, is worth reiterating and accessing.

Ninth, a related problem is that of syntax. The English language in the sixteenth century exhibits a word order that is mostly unfixed. Students need to be shown that our familiar pattern of subject followed by verb followed by direct object is a function of the narrowing of syntactical possibility over the eighteenth and nineteenth centuries, that Shakespeare and his contemporaries had access to a considerably greater variety of sentence structures than we have. The mobility of the major parts of the sentence allowed for specific verbal effects unavailable to the modern writer, and while those effects ought to be identified and enjoyed, students can be encouraged, once they know the difference among subject, verb, and object, to alter the order of the parts of a sentence in an effort to make the structure less initially mystifying and more like their own speech patterns.

Parts of a sentence and parts of speech lead then to the 10th hint, which is to follow the grammatical and logical pointers built into the poetic language. As Jonas Barish pointed out some 50 years ago about the prose, Shakespeare is an exceptionally logical writer: "One tends not to notice the logicality of Shakespeare's prose because it is managed with such virtuosity as to seem as natural as breathing. But by his constant invention of fresh logical formulas, his endless improvising of new patterns, Shakespeare, if anything carries logical syntax even further than Lyly" (Barish 1960: 23). Happily for the student, the logical fabric contains within it a series of guides to comprehension. Conjunctions are unusually revealing because, in structural terms, they promote our passage from one segment of thought to the next. The word "but," for example, signals logical reversal, negation, or at least modification of what has gone before. "Because," similarly, creates a recognizable and helpful integument between one statement and another. Becoming aware of such words and their logical functions affords an advantage in making sense of a difficult passage.

One of the most common of logical pointers is antithesis; it is also one of Shakespeare's determinative verbal structures. "His mind," says Helen

Vendler, "operates always by antithesis. As soon as he thinks one thing, he thinks of something that is different from it . . ." (Vendler 1997: 35). The stage director John Barton famously encourages his actors to look for the antitheses contained within their lines as a means of getting a purchase on the sense of the excerpt (Barton 1984: 55). Such oppositions are perhaps most readily apparent in the earlier plays, where the patterns are more numerous and more ostentatious, as in Queen Margaret's taunting of Queen Elizabeth in *Richard III*: "Decline all this, and see what now thou art: / For happy wife, a most distressed widow; / For being sued to, one that humbly sues . . ." (4.4.97–9)[1], and so on through four more paired lines. In the later works, although the patterns are subtler and less insistent, such antitheses are nonetheless fundamental and rewarding. Here is Coriolanus to the plebeians:

> You that will be less fearful than discreet;
> That love the fundamental part of state
> More than you doubt the change on't; that prefer
> A noble life before a long, and wish
> To jump a body with a dangerous physic
> That's sure of death without it –
>
> (3.1.150–5)

In both excerpts the broad antithetical frame is enriched with a series of more particular contrasting pairs over which the student might be encouraged to linger.

The final recommendation applies not only to Shakespeare but to the study and reception of imaginative writing generally. One symptom of the poesophobia I described earlier is the suspicion that poems and passages of dramatic verse contain hidden meanings, significance that the expert, the initiate, in this case the professor, has access to, but that ordinary readers have to struggle to discern. This prejudice should be countered explicitly and constantly: the reader ought to be seeking not recondite but available meanings. The Shakespearean text is not a puzzle to be solved, not a word game into which concealed meanings have been encoded so as to be spied out and extracted by the clever interpreter. It is, rather, a verbal structure calculated (among other things) to give pleasure, and we can never remind ourselves too often that that pleasure is on the surface, in plain sight and sound. This is not to say, of course, that the text is not an appropriate subject for analysis and further study. It is. But at the same time we must remember its more immediate claims.

No reader will fail to have noticed my omissions and amalgamations. I have not considered, for example, methods for employing film as a means of studying language. I have all but ignored the manifold possibilities of the internet for help with linguistic problems. Nor have I taken up the question of SparkNotes or other cribs and substitutes. (The metaphor I use with students is that reading a summary instead of the actual text is like going to a great restaurant and eating the menu: it's not the meal they're getting, but a verbal description of the meal.) Whereas in prelapsarian days teachers had to deal only with Cliffs or Monarch Notes, now students enter the classroom clutching editions of texts that have been "translated" into simplified, "modern" English. As one who values the words, I fear that to raise that topic is to court madness. Instead, I conclude by thanking readers for their attention to my lecture and, according to plan, making myself obsolete.

Note

1 All quotations from Shakespeare plays are taken from *The Riverside Shakespeare* (Evans 1997).

References and Further Reading

Ascham, Roger (1967). *The Schoolmaster*. Lawrence V. Ryan (Ed.). Charlottesville: University of Virginia Press for the Folger Shakespeare Library.

Barish, Jonas A. (1960). *Ben Jonson and the Language of Prose Comedy*. Cambridge, MA: Harvard University Press.

Barton, John (1984). *Playing Shakespeare*. London: Methuen.

Booth, Stephen (1994). "Close Reading Without Readings." In Russ McDonald (Ed.). *Shakespeare Reread: The Text in New Contexts* (pp. 42–55). Ithaca, NY: Cornell University Press.

Burke, Kenneth (1931). *Counterstatement*. New York: Harcourt Brace.

Burton, Gideon (Ed.). *Silva Rhetoricæ*. <http://humanities.byu.edu/rhetoric/silva.htm>.

Evans, G. B. (Ed.) (1997). *The Riverside Shakespeare*. Boston: Houghton Mifflin.

Freire, Paulo (1972). *The Pedagogy of the Oppressed*. Myra Bergman Ramos (Trans.). London: Sheed and Ward.

Fussell, Paul (1965). *Poetic Meter and Poetic Form*. New York: Random House.

Lanham, Richard A. (1991). *A Handlist of Rhetorical Terms*. Berkeley, Los Angeles: University of California Press.

Pigman, III, G. W. (1980). "Versions of Imitation in the Renaissance." *Renaissance Quarterly* 33, 1–32.

Schwartz, Lloyd and Sybil P. Estess (Eds) (1983). *Elizabeth Bishop and Her Art.* Ann Arbor: University of Michigan Press.

Vendler, Helen (1997). *The Art of Shakespeare's Sonnets.* Cambridge, MA: Belknap Press of Harvard University.

3

The Words: Teacher as Editor, Editor as Teacher

David Bevington

Textual scholarship can strike fear in the hearts of those who love their literature plain and simple, sunny side up. Tom Berger (himself a confessed editor) amused his audience at a Shakespeare Association of America conference some years ago by referring to that line of textual collations that one sees in scholarly editions, glaring at the reader either directly below the text or (more recently) at the bottom of the page, as "the band of terror." What is one to make of such telegraphic information, written evidently in a strange sort of code, and reading for instance as follows?

> 230 unchaste] *F*; vncleane *Q* 232 for want] *Q, F*; the want *Oxf (Hanmer)* richer] *F*; rich *Q* 234 That] *F*; As *Q* 236 to have] *Q*; t haue *F* 238 Which] *F*; That *Q* 239 do?] *Pope*; do, *Q*; do: *F* 241 regards] *F*; respects *Q* 243 a dowry] *F (a* Dowrie*)*; and dowre *Q* King] *F*; *Leir Q*; *Lear Q2*

I have chosen this sample from act 1, scene 1 of Reginald Foakes's admirable edition of *King Lear* (1997) simply to make the point that editing can seem dismayingly repellent and dry. The work of editing is, unavoidably, detailed, mechanical, and obsessed with minutiae. Indeed, the most careful editors in all ages have learned to embrace dullness in a creative spirit of intensive and detailed labor that can provide the only sure way to enlightened reading. "Let us now be told no more of the dull duty of an editor," said Doctor Samuel Johnson (1765: Preface), and he knew what he was talking about, having labored for years on his edition of Shakespeare. Johnson was fond of this kind of self-deprecating joke; he wryly put down his own extensive and tedious labors on his *Dictionary of the English Language* (1755) as the efforts of a "harmless drudge," a mere "lexicographer." What is there in such an enterprise that can be attractive to the teacher and the student intent on discovering the rich beauties of the Shakespearean text?

The daunting particularity and technical detail of textual editing seems strangely at odds with textual theory, which is a hot topic these days. Everyone resonates to the good news that *King Lear* exists in at least two texts, *Hamlet* in at least three, and so on; this seems of a piece with Michel Foucault's insistence (1977) that what we have is not a text but texts, and indeed what we have learned about Renaissance textual study in recent decades is that the story is multiple, constantly evolving. Texts refuse to stay put. What does one want to edit in an effort to represent what we call *King Lear*: the 1608 quarto, the 1623 Folio, or both, or a conflation? The idea of the definitive text now seems a will-o'-the-wisp at best.[1]

In what ways can the practices and issues of textual editing enlighten and enliven classroom teaching? I should like to argue in this essay that the task is not nearly as daunting or alien as it might seem. The pleasure of intimacy with drama comes by way of painstaking attention to the details of the text. Editorial investigation is much like close reading. The pleasure and intimacy of close reading are at the heart of teaching and of editorial practice. They are also close to what it is that actors and directors do in the theatre. Actors approach the language of their roles with the same close attention to textual detail as the editor. Close reading enables actors to take charge of their performances, giving them confidence in what they will be doing on stage. The teacher in the classroom, by showing students an up-close textual path into knowledge of the play, is passing along the same pleasure and the same intimate relationship with the playwright's words in action.

One direct classroom approach to the challenge of textual editing, of course, would be to teach classes in textual scholarship, at the advanced graduate level, for students who are at least potentially interested in becoming editors themselves, but admittedly the opportunities for this kind of teaching are rare and the candidates scarce. A broader approach to the teaching of textual analysis at the graduate level is to include some editing exercises in classes more inclusively concerned with Renaissance dramatic literature. I took a graduate course at Harvard with Alfred Harbage in the late 1950s that included some editing work as part of a larger approach to the pragmatics of Elizabethan theatre: the acting company, the use of the main stage and upper acting area, and so on. Other teachers, such as David Scott Kastan at Columbia University, put editorial practice into a larger theatrical context in this way. This approach can make editing seem exciting as an integral part of all that one wants to know about the early modern theatre, so that editing does not appear simply dry and technical.

What about applying one's presumed expertise as an editor to undergraduate teaching? I have no doubt that the subject of editing can itself be made as fascinating for undergraduates as for graduates, at least as part of a Shakespeare course rather than an entire subject for a quarter or semester. When I have occasionally devoted a class session to discussing what an editor does, I have felt no diminution of interest; quite the contrary. Here my impulse has been to discuss the subject not in theoretical terms but rather in terms of procedures and difficulties. We talk about what an editor does to work up a text for the modern reader, starting with the original printed copies and what they can tell us about printing history: how one goes about choosing among early printed versions for a "copy-text" to use as a base, how one reasons with textual variants as to how they may have been produced, and the like. The pleasure for students is likely to be in the intellectual game of inductive and deductive reasoning, as one wrestles with evidence that lies buried in these old texts.

More radically, teachers like Graham Holderness in the UK can generate a lot of excitement for theatre students by encouraging them to start from the very beginning in preparing a Shakespeare script for production, throwing out not only the commentary notes in modern editions but the editing itself, going back to the original quarto or quartos and/or Folio versions in the original spelling and punctuation and seeing what the students can make of the text for themselves. Part of the appeal in this is no doubt its energetic shouldering aside of scholarship and tradition in a manner calculated to make an editor like myself feel outmoded and unnecessary; it will almost certainly produce some far-out solutions, but the method has the immense potential advantage of encouraging students to learn by doing. I've never tried this teaching stratagem full scale myself, mainly because I am not in a theatre department and do not have the training to oversee an actual stage production. I organize a fair amount of dramatic reading of scenes in class, but this hardly provides the environment in which to go back to basics on the text. Another lifetime, perhaps.

An editor does many other things besides establishing a text through the processes of textual method, and here is where, for me, teaching and scholarship come most readily into productive interplay. As an editor of modern editions designed for students and general readers as well as scholars, I wrestle constantly with two main problems: what are the characters in Shakespeare's plays saying to each other or to themselves, and what is implied in the characters' speeches about spatial relationships and staging? Shakespeare's scripts are generally laconic about such matters. He does not give us long and detailed stage directions, as in Ibsen and Shaw, for example, specifying how the set is to be constructed, or what a character is wearing, or in what tone of voice a character speaks. Shakespeare wrote for the acting company to which he belonged, and was presumably on hand during rehearsals if any questions arose. In any case, his colleagues were trained professionals who needed little guidance in blocking their scenes or knowing what mannerisms to adopt in portraying certain character types. Other dramatists of the period similarly choose to leave such matters generally in the hands of the actors. The result is that Renaissance dramatic texts, including Shakespeare's, offer an endless variety of interpretive problems. The 400 or so years separating Renaissance vocabulary and usage from our own increases that need and opportunity for close reading that is historically informed but also free to explore multiplicities of meaning. This is what teaching is all about, or should be all about, and it is what an editor tries to do from dawn to dark.

One way in which we can observe the concurrence of teaching, editorial practice, and theatre is to consider the similarities between a lively classroom and a rehearsal for a production, especially early in the rehearsal process when the company is sitting around a table going through the script line by line. I have been struck again and again, as I have sat in on first readings of a script by an acting group, with the perception that what they are trying to do is essentially what a teacher should hope to bring to life in a classroom and what an editor should hope to embody in everything an editor does: clarifying spelling and punctuation, discreetly providing stage directions that help the reader visualize what is going on, and unpacking difficult language in commentary notes. In a first rehearsal, the director acts as the teacher, laying out his or her concept but also listening to what the actors have to say and orchestrating those comments into an interpretive conversation. Everything should be brought into question, interrogated, turned upside down to explore the range of possibilities.

Some modern editions pass right over thorny passages, preferring instead to gloss individual words or short phrases where the lexical meaning has shifted over four centuries of the development of the English language. I can understand the wish to leave interpretation of meaning up to the reader, and to allow for flexibility of interpretation rather than pinning it down to a paraphrase, but my own instincts, in editing and in teaching, are to keep trying to understand what is being said. Of course one wants to allow for multiple possibilities, but commentary notes can at least attempt to point in that direction. My experience in teaching is that many or most students need help getting started. To leave a difficult passage unexplained, in a text or in class, is to imply that its meaning is reasonably transparent. Very often, in Shakespeare, this is not the case.

Let me take, as an example, a passage from *King Lear*, from act 2, scene 2, at the point when the Earl of Kent, having arrived at the Earl of Gloucester's house with a message from the old king, quarrels with Oswald, who has also just arrived as an emissary from Goneril and Cornwall. Kent is plainly the aggressor in the legal sense of committing physical assault and battery, even though we understand why he is so incensed with the servile toadyism of Goneril's steward. We can see too why the Duke of Cornwall is quick to take charge of this breach of the peace. Kent is openly hostile toward the authority of the proceedings, and is anything but humble or penitent. When asked by Cornwall, "know you no reverence?", Kent replies, "Yes, sir, but anger hath a privilege" (2.2.70–1).[2] That answer intrigues the Duke, so much so that he argues with Kent, seemingly wanting to find out what has prompted such "mad" behavior in this "old fellow." What prompted you, he asks Kent, to tangle with Oswald? And, "Why dost thou call him knave? What is his fault?" When Kent insolently replies, "His countenance likes me not," Cornwall invites still more insubordination by his rejoinder: "No more, perchance, does mine, nor his, nor hers" (pointing perhaps to Gloucester and Regan). Kent obliges full tilt:

> Sir, it is my occupation to be plain:
> I have seen better faces in my time
> Than stands on any shoulder that I see
> Before me at this instant.
>
> (93–6)

In view of the fact that Cornwall has assumed the position of judge in the judicial proceedings that have been summarily assembled to try Oswald's accusation against Kent of assault and battery, Kent's answer is nothing less than contempt of court.

Before going on to Cornwall's reply, in the speech that seems to me most puzzling of all, let us go back over what has happened up to now in order to ask: what challenges does this passage pose for the teacher, for the editor, for the acting company? We need to ask ourselves what is at stake for ourselves, our students, and our readers. Getting students in class to read the parts of Oswald, Kent, and Cornwall can encourage the students in those roles to think as an actor might think, and also to ponder what an editor might decide to say by way of comment. What does the first stage direction mean when it specifies that Kent (in disguise as Caius) and Oswald are to enter "*severally*"? Once we have determined that "*severally*" means simply "separately, at separate doors," we then need to ask where each of them is coming from, and how they are dressed, and how, from the text, we can determine any of this information. Why does Shakespeare set the opening conversation between Oswald and Kent in the early morning? (Oswald begins, "Good dawning to thee, friend.") Oswald asks if Kent is "of this house?" to which Kent laconically replies, "Ay." Why does he say that? He is not a member of Gloucester's household. Oswald asks, "Where may we set our horses?" Kent flippantly replies, "I' the mire."

As the conversation goes around the classroom, one hopes as teacher that the students will agree that Oswald has just arrived by horse from some journey; presumably he should be outfitted for riding, with dusty boots and the like. Kent too has arrived recently, but he enters perhaps as though from inside Gloucester's house; the neutral stage doors in the Elizabethan theatre, in the absence of scenery, invite us to picture the entrances in this way. Or Kent may simply be coming himself from the stable yard, having only had time to arrange for his own horse's stabling. Thus Kent may also be costumed as though having traveled hard. The resemblance between these two men is useful: they are both in service to powerful or once-powerful aristocrats. They may be similar in age and build; this is a matter of choice, in the theatre or as one reads. Certainly the resemblances between the two are meant to accentuate the differences of temperament and moral fiber that have already manifested themselves in Scotland. The horses are not seen, but the references to them suggest that we are near a stable yard at Gloucester's house.

Oswald mistakes Kent for a member of the household at which Oswald has just arrived, and so naturally he asks for help. His addressing Kent as "friend" is intended to promote cooperation. We surmise that he does not recognize Kent, whereas we know they have tangled at Albany's palace in Scotland where Oswald serves as steward to the lady of the house, Goneril. Why does Oswald not recognize Kent, after the unpleasant incident in which Kent tripped up Oswald for speaking officiously to Lear? Perhaps Oswald is not good at remembering faces, unless he is pretending. At any rate, his inquiry as to whether Kent is a member "of this house" helps explain Kent's monosyllabic reply, "Ay"; Kent may be leading Oswald on, seeing whether this might lead to a confrontation. Kent is spoiling for a fight, while Oswald is apparently oblivious to the animosity, or at least wishing to appear so. He certainly is astonished to be dressed down by Kent in a barrage of splendidly inventive name-calling ("knave, beggar, coward, pander, and the son and heir of a mongrel bitch") and then beaten for his troubles. Kent does justify his anger as he is raining down blows on Oswald: it is because Oswald has "come with letters against the King," and has taken "Vanity the puppet's part against the royalty of her father" (35–7). Vanity the puppet is Goneril, here satirically fashioned by Kent into a debased character type from a morality play. Should the beating of Oswald be played for laughs? Or should it invite sympathy for Oswald for being pummeled by a man whom he thinks he has never met and to whom he speaks civilly at first? Is Kent a bully or a heroic defender of the innocent?

Similar questions and ironies arise when Cornwall arrives to take charge of the disturbance that has so suddenly erupted. What does Cornwall look like, and from where do we understand that he is coming? Again, the stage set offers little help, since no scenery is deployed; this is another way in which reading, editing, and mounting a production are so much alike, in that we as audience must fill out the script with our imaginations. We do know that Cornwall enters with Edmund the Bastard, who has his drawn rapier. Cornwall's duchess, Regan, and their host, the Earl of Gloucester, enter also, along with servants who proceed, at Cornwall's command, to part the combatants. The grouping is significant: Cornwall, attended by servants, is surrounded by the panoply and the perquisites of power. How is he dressed? Perhaps students will gather that he and Regan arrived a short time ago, having ridden hard from the west so as not to be at home to Regan's father. As we learn a short time later from Kent, Oswald traveled from Scotland to Cornwall with such speed, "reeking" and "Stewed in his haste," that he arrived there in time to warn the Duke and Regan of the need for their quick removal to Gloucester's estate (2.4.26–36). Since it is early morning, we may suppose that Cornwall and Regan and the rest look as though they have come quickly from their bedchambers, perhaps still dressed for sleep. The geographical particularity of their travels is essential to an understanding of what is going on, for students, editors, and actors alike: one needs to be clear that Scotland in the north and Cornwall in the south-west represent the portions of Lear's kingdom that he has given away to his two elder daughters and their husbands, having now lost his hopes of residing chiefly in Cordelia's "kind nursery" amid the comforts of the prosperous south-eastern part of England, the "third more opulent than your sisters'," as he characterizes it to her (1.1.86, 123–4).

Cornwall's role in this scene is suffused with an irony that needs to be studied in detail in our classroom discussion, all the more so because it opens up into an ironic pattern that is essential to the play as a whole. Cornwall is unquestionably a law-and-order person, and enjoys power because it enables him to be quite brutal in the exercise of it. Yet according to his own lights, and indeed as viewed by most persons in authority, he proceeds according to the law and with an intent of quelling insurrectionary behavior. Awakened in the early morning by a disturbance, he learns that the person called Caius who is brought before him has initiated an unprovoked attack on one who claims never to have seen this attacker before. The man standing at the dock, so to speak, is insolent. He refuses to explain his actions other than to say that he doesn't like Oswald's looks. Well, he does say more about how such dishonest rogues "bite the holy cords atwain / Which are too intrinse t'unloose" by abetting the violent proclivities of the lords whom they serve, bringing "oil to fire" and "snow to their colder moods" – in other words, exacerbating their masters' tendencies toward anger and heartlessness (2.2.73–82), but this too comes to Cornwall's ears as the ravings of a man who seems to think he can say whatever he pleases about anyone at all. Why should Cornwall not, as judge, deal severely with a troublemaker who refuses to explain himself? And especially when this accused man says to Cornwall's face that he regards Cornwall (and Regan) as just as bad as Oswald? What is an officer sitting in judgment to do with such flagrant contempt of court? If students are reading this scene out loud in class with feeling, or working on the scene for production, they ought to shiver with the anxious delight of what will happen next. It is a moment that calls for a stunning pause. Kent's caustic remark,

> I have seen better faces in my time
> Than stands on any shoulder that I see
> Before me at this instant,
>
> (94–6)

can only be taken as a direct and unprovoked insult. Did we hear him correctly? Good grief.

After savoring the gravity of a long moment's pause, Cornwall delivers a wonderfully sardonic appraisal of the troublemaker standing before him:

> This is some fellow
> Who, having been praised for rashness, doth affect
> A saucy roughness, and constrains the garb
> Quite from his nature. He cannot flatter, he;
> An honest mind and plain, he must speak truth!
> An they will take 't, so; if not, he's plain.
> These kind of knaves I know, which in this plainness
> Harbor more craft and more corrupter ends
> Than twenty silly-ducking observants
> That stretch their duties nicely.
>
> (96–105)

What are students and actors to make of this? What can an editor do to explain? How can a teacher steer a discussion about possible meanings? For a start, one can see if readers agree about certain words and phrases that have long lost their early modern signification: "affect" in line 97 means something like "adopt the style of"; "his" in line 99 often can mean "its" in early modern English. "An they" in line 100 means "If they" ("An they" actually reads "And they" in the Folio text; the editor has already made a choice for the reader, lest it be taken unwarily to mean "And" in the usual modern sense); "silly-ducking" in line 104 means "foolishly and obsequiously bowing." "Observants" in the same line are those who dutifully observe a law or fixed custom, as in "Observant Friars." When we consult the *Oxford English Dictionary*, as editors constantly do, we find that the word can take on the connotation of servants or attendants who behave obsequiously (*OED*, Observant *adj.* and *n.*, 3), and, sure enough, *OED*'s earliest citation in this pejorative sense is from *King Lear*, II. ii., 1605.

Another hazard in this speech is irony, or sarcasm. How does one know how to read sarcasm, and how does an editor or teacher or director help readers or actors know when something is to be read as meaning its direct opposite? "He cannot flatter, he," says Cornwall of Kent in the speech we are examining; "An honest mind and plain, he must speak truth!" (99–100). This is a persuasive candidate for sarcasm, since in context it seems evident that Cornwall is irate about Kent's duplicity, and duplicity of a particular sort: that of pretending to be forthrightly honest when one's secret intent is something entirely different. We begin to see how Cornwall is sizing up Kent's blunt speaking, not as honest candor but as an excuse for thumbing his nose at authority. "An they will take 't, so; if not, he's plain" (101). In context, this begins to make sense: If the authorities are willing to stand there and let Kent sound off, well and good; if not, at least he has had the pleasure of giving the authorities a piece of his mind.

At this point the rest of Cornwall's angry speech falls more or less into place: dropping his sarcasm, he says directly that he has had plenty of experience with troublemakers like Kent, whose guise of honest speech conceals or harbors more craftiness and dishonest intent than is to be observed in 20 obsequiously bowing attendants "That stretch their duties nicely" – that is, that exert themselves in their courtly duties with fastidious and attentive mannerisms. "Stretch" contains the idea of extending, directing, drawing out, and thus, figurally, exerting to the utmost (*OED*, Stretch *v.* 20). "Nicely" is rich with possible meanings; "nice" can mean foolish, stupid, wanton, lascivious, fastidious, dainty, precise, intricate, trivial, attentive, discriminating, and still more (*OED*, Nice *adj.* 1–13), all of which can hover over the word as Cornwall employs it. Sending students and actors to the *OED* (and other dictionaries; the *OED* is far from infallible) can be an illuminating exercise in seeing what is involved in editing and in understanding an early modern dramatic text.

How is Kent to respond to this cynical debunking of his motive in having spoken plainly? He chooses to speak in another key, one matched to the courtly parlance of hyperbolical flattery:

> Sir, in good faith, in sincere verity,
> Under th'allowance of your great aspect,
> Whose influence, like the wreath of radiant fire
> On flickering Phoebus' front –
>
> (106–9)

The excessive metaphors here ought to be a dead giveaway of insincere speech. Readers should immediately pick this up from the ways in which this utterance is so unlike Kent's normal way of talking, with the repeated and unctuous implorings and the comparison of the person being addressed to the gods of classical mythology. Even the alliteration of "flickering Phoebus' front," with its insistent "f" sounds, is not in Kent's usual idiom. Why is Kent speaking thus? One hopes that in discussion the students will see that Kent is doing just what powerful aristocrats like Cornwall expect and indeed demand: that their social inferiors address them in endless flatteries. This is in fact what King Lear expected of Cordelia in the play's first scene, resulting in her banishment when she insisted on speaking plainly; and we recall that it was for equally plain speech that Kent was banished also. Plain speech is something that Kent treasures more than his life or personal welfare; that idealism of his helps explain why he has so willingly endangered himself in this present scene by speaking his mind. He knows that Cornwall detests and mistrusts such plain speech, and he knows that Cornwall will comprehend that Kent's essay into fulsome flattery is meant as scornful parody.

Cornwall does indeed understand that, but he still does not grasp Kent's motive in being sarcastic. "What mean'st by this?" he asks. His question invites an answer that is, for me at least, the most difficult passage in the entire play:

> *Kent:* To go out of my dialect, which you discommend so much. I know,
> sir, I am no flatterer. He that beguiled you in a plain accent was a
> plain knave, which for my part I will not be, though I should win
> your displeasure to entreat me to 't.
>
> (110–14)

This begins easily enough, perhaps. Kent confirms what we have imagined to be true as he spoke, that his essay in obsequious flattery was indeed out of his usual dialect. He claims to have abandoned his usual plain speaking because Cornwall was so critical of it. We can hardly suppose, though, that Kent has changed his tune simply so as not to offend the Duke, since Kent has dared to insult the Duke more than once already; we hear sarcasm in this reply. "I know, sir, I am no flatterer" (111) can then mean, "I of course was only pretending to be a flattering courtier, praising you to the skies; we both know that I didn't mean it." But a further meaning, a deeply insulting one, may be imbedded here: "We both know that you are undeserving of flattery."

Let us move on. "He that beguiled you in a plain accent was a plain knave" (111–12). Who is "He"? This must be "some fellow" described by Cornwall in line 96 and following, who, "having been praised for bluntness," adopts plain speech as a persona that is in fact the very opposite of his inner nature but which then licenses him to speak plainly, whether people like it or not. Cornwall meant this as a highly critical characterization of Kent himself, but Kent now shifts the identity of this person away from himself to someone else, to some hypothetical person. Whoever it was that spoke to you in this seemingly plain manner but with hidden false intent, he tells Cornwall, was certainly not myself, it was some "plain knave."[3] Kent plays mordantly with the key word, "plain": in rapid succession here it means (1) "honest, straightforward, free from duplicity" and (2) "out and out, manifest." The word can also mean ordinary, common, lowly, flat, level, smooth, unobstructed, simple.

Kent is not finished. This seemingly plain fellow, he tells Cornwall, "was a plain knave, which for my part I will not be, though I should win your displeasure to entreat me to 't." We can readily understand why Kent does not want to be like the "plain knave" whose plain speech is a pretence licensing him to be critical; Kent wants to be a plain-speaking critic, though not for dishonest reasons. But why the rest, "though I should win your displeasure to entreat me to 't"? Perhaps Kent is suggesting that winning Cornwall's displeasure is something to be desired; Cornwall is such a thoroughly bad man that to displease him is to perform a virtuous act. Kent, then, sees what advantage and even pleasure he might gain by acting the part of that "plain knave" in that it would anger Cornwall, and yet Kent still refuses to be that "plain knave" (i.e., plain-speaking fellow) because that person is a "plain knave" (an out-and-out villain). The word "knave" begins to take on multiple meanings, too: it can mean a male child, a servant, a lowly person, an ordinary fellow, a rascal, a rogue.

Many are the advantages of close reading of difficult passages like this. Close reading illustrates the multiplicity of meanings in many of Shakespeare's words, especially those with thematic importance. It illustrates how brilliant Shakespeare really is: not just a sensitive poetic temperament with an astonishingly large and supple vocabulary, but incredibly smart. The logic of this taut exchange between Kent and Cornwall is of a density of intellect that one can only wonder at. It has the interesting effect of making both Cornwall and Kent appear to be persons of remarkably quick minds. Their exchange of dialogue also opens up vistas of the moral imagination that apply to the play as a whole. By his mocking way of suggesting that he can no longer speak plainly, since his honest utterances will only be interpreted as duplicity, Kent indicts the hypocrisy of a world gone massively wrong. Cornwall, along with Regan, Goneril, and Edmund, increasingly gains control over institutions and over language itself, to the extent that words like "knave," "plain," "honest," "loyal," "just," and "true" are turned inside out, like seeing and blindness, wisdom and folly.

Another assignment of the editor of an edition for today's readers, as for teachers and students, is to think about stage movement and gesture, with a view to determining when an added stage direction can be helpful. In the world of editing, a debate centers on the process: just as some editors are reluctant to explicate convoluted sentences in Shakespeare's texts, preferring to leave interpretation up to the reader, some editors are wary of added stage directions. Actors and directors are especially apt to be cautious, no doubt for good reasons: theatre people want to decide for themselves when an action occurs, and in what way. Certainly the editor needs to be wary of adding stage directions that might close off options. When one character bids another to "sit" or "kneel," does the character addressed actually sit or kneel, and if so, when, exactly, and when does that person get up? When Polonius, in *Hamlet*, wishing to emphasize the point that what he says is the undoubted truth (in this case, that Hamlet is mad for love of Ophelia), says, "Take this from this, if this be otherwise" (2.2.156), does the actor cut his throat with an imaginary knife, or gesture to the chain of office that hangs about his neck, or something else? An added stage direction can limit possibilities.

Yet the stage directions in Shakespeare's texts are sparse, and readers need help to get started. Critical and stage history offer many examples of ways in which stage action has been misinterpreted over centuries of time, and this again is where an editor, like a teacher or director, can encourage close attention to the script. A good example is to be found in *King Lear*, in the action immediately following the confrontation between Cornwall and Kent that we have been analyzing. Kent's punishment for insubordination and riot is to be placed in the stocks, to sit there "till noon" in Cornwall's sentence, to which Regan adds, with evident relish, "Till noon? Till night, my lord, and all night too" (2.2.136–7). Their wish is immediately translated into action: "*Stocks brought out*," reads the Folio stage direction. The Earl of Gloucester, in whose house this summary sentence is about to be executed, objects – not to the punishing of "Caius" as such, but to the inappropriateness of the sentence. The stocks are for offenders of the lowest social class:

> Your purposed low correction
> Is such as basest and contemned'st wretches
> For pilferings and most common trespasses
> Are punished with,

he cautions the Duke.

> The King must take it ill
> That he, so slightly valued in his messenger,
> Should have him thus restrained.
>
> (145–50)

The pronouns "he," "his," and "him" are a bit imprecise in this second sentence, as is often the case in early modern texts. Is "he" Cornwall, or Kent, or the King? At any rate, what Gloucester urges is that "Caius," whatever he may have done, is King Lear's emissary. The word "messenger" here carries its oldest and now obsolete meaning of "envoy, ambassador, representative"; often, in the early modern period, it signified "a government official employed to carry dispatches," especially "one employed by the Secretaries of State . . . who conveys messages to or from the Sovereign" (*OED*, Messenger, 1–3). For Cornwall to insult such a dignitary with ignoble correction is to insult the King himself, whose person the emissary represents. Cornwall accepts responsibility: "I'll answer that," I'll be answerable for the consequences. Cornwall and Regan both anticipate an imminent showdown with Lear himself, and are confident that they will not have to put up with any nonsense.

At this point, the passage of time becomes subject to theatrical illusion – an illusion that requires careful reading to understand. As this scene ends, Cornwall, his duchess, and his entourage leave Kent to his punishment; Gloucester offers apologies, giving as his only excuse that the Duke's disposition "Will not be rubbed or stopped." Gloucester will entreat for Kent, but cannot command. Kent, left alone, takes out a letter from Cordelia promising to seek remedies for the enormities that have now afflicted the state. The text of the letter is a little garbled, but does seem to offer a hint that she plans to return from France to aid her father, and that she is cognizant of Kent's "obscurèd course" disguised as Caius. Kent, in soliloquy, longs for the approach of day:

> Approach, thou beacon to this under globe,
> That by thy comfortable beams I may
> Peruse this letter.
>
> (166–8)

Some commentators have supposed that the "beacon" is the moon, since it appears now to be night and has been so for the duration of the scene: early in the scene, Kent bids Oswald to draw his sword and fight, since, "though it be night, yet the moon shines" (31), and now at the end Kent bids Fortune "good night" while he, Kent, sleeps (176). Yet the "beacon" certainly sounds more like the sun than the moon, and reading a letter in handwriting is impossible outdoors at night even at the full of the moon. What these editors were misinterpreting is a characteristic trick in

Shakespeare, of condensing time. The scene does indeed begin in darkness, or twilight, just before dawn (2.2.1). When Cornwall sentences Kent to be placed in the stocks "till noon" and Regan rejoins with "Till night, my lord, and all night too," they clearly are anticipating that Kent will remain in the stocks for the remainder of the present day and the night following as well. Through the condensing of time, nighttime arrives by the end of the scene, whereupon Kent spends the whole night in the stocks, as Regan has urged. Critics' search for the moon evidently stems from a neoclassical literalism about theatre that was omnipresent in eighteenth- and nineteenth-century productions: the stage should look at this point like an inn yard or courtyard of an aristocratic house, and time should proceed as it does in the world we perceive around us. Shakespeare's presentational stage, on the other hand, lacking painted sets or other ways of establishing the scene visually for the audience, leaves the audience's imagination free to suppose the stage a room and to understand that time can move forward by theatrical convention at whatever speed the narrative deems necessary. (*Antony and Cleopatra* is full of instances in which a quick transition from Rome to Egypt or vice versa covers a historical passage of some years.)

The bringing on stage of the stocks naturally raises the question as to when the stocks are to be removed. When King Lear, his Fool, and a Gentleman come on stage in what is marked in most editions as scene 4, having found no one at home in Cornwall and now having just arrived in Gloucestershire, they find Kent in the stocks still. But this occurs after an intervening scene, generally marked in modern editions as scene 3, in which Edgar is given 21 lines of soliloquy to describe how he has managed to escape his pursuers and is now about to disguise himself as a lunatic beggar. The Folio text and the early quartos have no scene divisions marked at these two points; indeed, the scene numbering does not appear in editorial tradition until George Steevens's updating of the Samuel Johnson text in 1773, though the idea had occurred to Alexander Pope in 1723–5. The idea is sensible enough, in one way: the Folio text does insert some white space in the column at both intervals, and we understand that Edgar does have a "scene" to himself, as it were; we have no reason to suppose that he has just happened onto the spot where Kent is in the stocks, and indeed such a place on the property of his enraged father, the Earl of Gloucester, would be most unsafe for him. Yet the stage is not cleared – not, that is, if we assume that Kent and the stocks are not removed for this short interval. There certainly is no indication in the early texts that the stocks were removed and then brought back on, and such moves would be intrusive and clumsy as a way of providing for such a short scene and thereby interrupting the flow of Kent's story.

Thus the most appealing solution, and one that seems even self-evident on modern presentational nonscenic stages, is to leave Kent and the stocks on stage throughout this sequence and suppose that nineteenth-century actor-managers and critics were too hemmed in by the tradition of scenic realism to imagine how Kent and Edgar could appear on stage at the same time. On the presentational stage, it is easy: Kent sleeps throughout "scene 3." The spotlight, as it were, shifts to Edgar. He darts in and then quickly out, having talked to us (also to himself) as if we are a kind of omniscient chorus – which we are. We grasp the theatrical convention inviting us to suppose that Kent is asleep in Gloucester's courtyard while Edgar, having recently fled for his life from this very house, lurks somewhere in the vicinity. The effect is almost that of a split screen. Since Edgar later joins Lear during the terrible storm, he cannot be imagined to have got very far. The location of the so-called "heath" where Lear and his companions are caught in the storm cannot be far away, either, since Kent comes to their aid by directing them to some "hovel" (3.2.61, 71) on Gloucester's estate where Gloucester is quickly able to find them. The "heath," by the way, is never named as such in Shakespeare's text (though it does sometimes appear in stage directions added subsequently by editors); it is another convention of realistic staging, as in the famous painting by Benjamin Wilson (1761), as engraved by Charles Spencer, of David Garrick in the storm, raging against the elements. Shakespeare does use the word "heath" elsewhere, in *Macbeth* and *The Tempest*, but not here. The locale for the storm in *King Lear* is better described as an open place.

Having Kent and Edgar on stage at the same time is actually an attractive idea. In class or in the theatre, one can invite discussion about this. Who are these two men? They are both fugitives from the law, threatened with death; they are both misunderstood and unjustly persecuted. Together with Cordelia, they represent the "fools" of this play who take risks for the sake of goodness and willingly accept the consequences. They are both stoics in the admirable sense of knowing that the worst may befall them, but that they can withstand the worst if they refuse to beg the favor of Fortune and accept their victimization with patient determination to persevere in being who they are. Once we understand the theatrical convention that on a presentational, nonscenic stage we can see them simultaneously while understanding that we are to imagine them in two different places, we can savor the juxtaposition for its rich thematic values about suffering and patience.

The hard decisions an editor must face are also those with which a reader or a teacher or a director must struggle. How is an editor to write commentary notes for this remarkable scene and provide stage directions in such a way as to illuminate what is so brilliantly metatheatrical about the scene, while at the same time leaving space for the reader to consider a multitude of possibilities? Certainly my own experience is that spending years of my life trying how best to edit texts for the reader and for classroom use, while at the same time being involved backstage with an acting company, has proved to be an unendingly profitable way to prepare for teaching.

Notes

1 For examples of the so-called "New" bibliography of the early and mid-twentieth century, see Pollard (1937), Hart (1942), Greg (1954), and Bowers (1964). For some more recent and revisionary studies of the subject, see Blayney (1982), McLeod (1994) Wells (1984), Werstine (1988), Urkowitz (1980), and Taylor and Warren (1983).

2 I quote throughout from *The Complete Works of Shakespeare* (Bevington 2003).

3 G. B. Shand (in a personal communication) offers another interpretation of this passage, positing that "He that beguiled you" refers directly to Oswald and his outrageous claim to have spared the life of poor old Kent, while "in a plain accent" might refer to the fact that Kent himself is now going to speak plainly, even bluntly. This reading requires different punctuation: ". . . He that beguiled you, in a plain accent, was a plain knave." As a way of learning the sense in rehearsal, one might offer the actor an inversion: "In a plain accent, he that beguiled you was a plain knave."

References and Further Reading

Bevington, David (Ed.) (2003). *The Complete Works of Shakespeare*, 5th edn. New York: Longman.

Blayney, Peter (1982). *The Texts of "King Lear" and their Origins*, vol. 1. Cambridge, UK: Cambridge University Press.

Bowers, Fredson T. (1964). *Bibliography and Textual Criticism*. Oxford: Clarendon.

Foakes, R. A. (Ed.) (1997). *King Lear*. The Arden Shakespeare, 3rd series. Walton-on-Thames, UK: Thomas Nelson and Sons.

Foucault, Michel (1977). "What is an Author?" In *Language, Counter-Memory, Practice* (pp. 124–7). Donald F. Bouchard and Sherry Simon (Trans.). Ithaca, NY: Cornell University Press.

Greg, W. W. (1954). *The Editorial Problem in Shakespeare*, 3rd edn. Oxford, Clarendon.

Hart, Alfred (1942). *A Comparative Study of Shakespeare's Bad Quartos*. Melbourne and London: Melbourne University Press in association with Oxford University Press.

Johnson, Samuel (1755). *A Dictionary of the English Language*. London.

Johnson, Samuel (Ed.) (1765). *Shakespeare's Plays*, 8 vols. London.

McLeod, Randall (Ed.) (1994). *The Crisis in Editing: Texts of the English Renaissance*. New York: AMS Press.

Pollard, Alfred W. (1937). *Shakespeare's Fight with the Pirates and the Problem of the Transmission of His Text*, rev. edn. Cambridge, UK: Cambridge University Press.

Pope, Alexander (Ed.) (1723–5). *The Works of Shakespeare*, 6 vols. London.

Steevens, George (Ed.) (1773). *The Works of Shakespeare*, 10 vols. London.

Taylor, Gary and Michael Warren (Eds) (1983). *The Division of the Kingdoms: Shakespeare's Two Versions of "King Lear."* Oxford: Clarendon.

Urkowitz, Steven (1980). *Shakespeare's Revision of "King Lear."* Princeton, NJ: Princeton University Press.

Wells, Stanley (1984). *Re-editing Shakespeare for the Modern Reader*. Oxford: Oxford University Press.

Werstine, Paul (1988). "'Foul Papers' and 'Promptbooks': Printer's Copy for Shakespeare's *Comedy of Errors*." *Studies in Bibliography* 41: 232–46.

4

Questions That Have No Answers

Alexander Leggatt

Most of this essay will be based on stories about students; but let me begin with two stories about colleagues. Colleague number one, a Shakespearean, is ideologically committed, with a definite set of principles based on the work of the last 20 or 30 years. In a departmental group discussion about teaching, having dismissed all Shakespeare criticism before that period as "350 years of naivety," he declared that his intention in teaching was to "win them over." He found it particularly satisfying when he persuaded his students to think the way he did. Colleague number two (not a Shakespearean), whose preference was to ask open-ended questions, to explore possibilities, and to refuse to give definitive answers, reported that a student confronted her at the end of a class: "What's the matter with you? My other profs *know* the answers." As my title implies, I'm with colleague number two.

Asking questions is a standard way to get class discussion going. Why does the character . . . ? How does this relate to . . . ? What do you think of . . . ? There is a way of doing this that is easy, tempting, and dangerous. That is to come in with the answer, and keep prodding the class until they find that answer. You meet their first attempts with variations on "Yes, that's interesting, but that's not quite it." Only when a student finally reads your mind and tells you what you're thinking can the class proceed. The problem is that the idea has not grown beyond the idea you came in with. But surely one has to come in with *some* ideas? Otherwise, the hungry sheep look up and are not fed. Well, do we really want our students to be sheep – especially sheep who have no idea how to feed themselves? Besides, hunger can be a good thing. Imagine a class at the end of which there is nothing left to say on the subject, and one never needs to think about it again. The feeling of unfinished business we all have when a class is over (didn't do this, should have thought of that) is a sign that the subject is still growing. One should always, in that sense, be hungry. One of my most satisfying experiences as a teacher was being told by a student in a Milton seminar that a number of class members who lived in the same house would sit on the porch in the evenings arguing about *Paradise Lost* – in other words, still hungry.

Of course to come in with no ideas at all would be desperately difficult: the old Russian mind-game – go into a corner and don't think of a white bear. By training and inclination we get ideas every time we read. Otherwise we wouldn't be in this business. The discipline we need is to ensure that those ideas always have a growing edge, and here is where the students help. The rest of this essay will be built on stories of how students over the years, instead of reading my mind, have read the plays and expanded the possibilities of the texts, I hope to their benefit and certainly to mine. I will use the present tense when I am conflating different classes over the years, the past tense when thinking of one particular class. It may appear that I am referring not to questions with no answers, but to questions with multiple answers. But in *The Cherry Orchard* Gaev declares that he has so many ideas for saving the estate that he has in fact no ideas at all. No one answer locks into place, solving the problem for good. Let me begin with a simple example (prefaced by a warning that there will be no endnotes identifying editions, since I want to preserve the oral quality of class discussion). In the wooing scene at the end of *Henry V* Henry promises Katherine, "And, Kate, when France is mine and I am yours, then yours is France and you are mine." Katherine replies, "I cannot tell wat is dat." The question is: why does she say that? Henry next tries to say the same thing in French, suggesting his own explanation: he's been too fancy, and she just doesn't get it. The suspicion I bring to this moment, and similar responses by Katherine ("I cannot tell"; "I do not know dat") is that she's stonewalling. She knows that sooner or later she will have to say yes, but she's not going to make it easy for him. She is not, as so many Katherines in performance are, charmed and flirtatious; she is being dragged into marriage and we should see the marks of her heels on the floor. Some students came up with variations on that answer, my answer. But one saw it very differently: she is provoking him to say more, not as a delaying tactic, but because she's interested and wants to hear him talk. That reading reopens the moment. Conventional academic criticism (including in this case my own) is concerned with power relations, and reads the moment accordingly. The student, however, saw another possibility: one person's interest in another person's words, not an assertion of power but the building of a relationship. The number of times this reading is taken in performance (the Olivier and Branagh films included) shows it is theatrically viable. And it keeps the scene open and enigmatic, and therefore alive.

In the middle of the sleepwalking scene in *Macbeth*, Lady Macbeth makes a reference to a character with whom the play has given her, so far, no relationship: "The Thane of Fife had a wife; where is she now?" Asking for comment on the line, I already had two ideas in my head: one was that it gives Lady Macbeth a relationship with another woman, linking it with the offstage cry of women that announces her death and allowing us a glimpse of a community of women the play never lets us see properly; the other was that "The Thane of Fife had a wife" sounds like a nursery rhyme. The students contributed more. Elsewhere in the play Lady Macbeth accuses her husband of lacking the resolution to kill; here, for the only time, she accuses him of killing. This is the one murder she cannot accept. It is also new information, a glimpse of a life outside a marriage in which she has been stiflingly fixated on him. Yet it is another sign of the rapport between them, in the question, "Where is she now?" Is she in heaven or hell? Macbeth told Duncan that the bell signaling his murder summoned him to heaven or to hell, and (with typical irresolution) did not decide which. He later makes a more definite statement: "Duncan is in his grave." Where do the dead go? As Macbeth hardens, his mind closes on a prosaic answer. For Lady Macbeth, who is not hardening but breaking, the question is open, and just for her to ask the question is something new. Concerned with the same problem, they pass each other in opposite directions. One student noted that the nursery-rhyme quality reminds us that Lady Macduff had children, who were also murdered. And Lady Macbeth has none. "The Thane of Fife had a wife": is Lady Macbeth singing a nursery rhyme to the child she never had – or to think of it another way, the child she would have had if she hadn't dashed its brains out? I came in with ideas about Lady Macbeth's relationship to another woman: the students pushed beyond this to relationships with Macbeth and with children, real and imaginary. The line opened out like a strip of paper that, when dropped in water, becomes a flower. It wouldn't have happened if I had stopped the discussion when someone, reading my mind, pointed out that the line is Lady Macbeth's only relationship with another woman. An instinct one has to develop is know-ing when to stop a discussion, and when not to. If it becomes rambling or repetitive, it needs to stop; but if one senses continuing hunger in the room, it needs to go on.

There are two interesting puzzles in *Hamlet*. (I mean, two that I have time for here.) When Claudius breaks during the play scene, we expect it to happen when the poison goes into the player king's ear – as in the dumb-show version in the Olivier film. This is what Hamlet thinks has happened, though his focus is on the words as well as the picture: "Didst perceive? . . . Upon the talk of the poisoning?" It is not what we saw. The poison goes in the ear. No reaction. Hamlet starts pushing: "'A poisons him i' th' garden for his estate." No reaction. "His name's Gonzago." No reaction. "The story is extant, and written in very choice Italian." (What's the matter with him? And what else can I think of saying to prod him? I'm getting a bit desperate here.) "You shall see anon how the murtherer gets the love of Gonzago's wife." Bang. "The King rises." A colleague once suggested to me that the delay is a sign of Claudius's control: he knows he is going to break, and he delays the moment until the reference to the second marriage, which is public knowledge. A good reading, and I have passed it on – though there is the difficulty that Hamlet's final taunt also identifies the second husband as the murderer of the first. Claudius is not altogether safe. In discussion a student developed the moment: it is a sign of the importance of Gertrude as the key motive for the murder. The reference to the mar-riage breaks Claudius because that, not the murder, is the raw nerve. Claudius will later list his motives as "My crown, mine own ambition, and my queen." Is "my queen" a trailing afterthought, or the climax of the line? My colleague saw Claudius the astute politician; my student saw Claudius the lover; the play sees both.

Why can't Gertrude see the Ghost? On occasions when I have been asked to talk about teaching I have used this as a classic example of a question with so many answers that it comes to seem unanswerable. I have asked this question in many classrooms over the years; here is a small sample of the results. She has been accused of spiritual blindness. (That was the expla-nation I learned in high school.) One student suggested she is not spiri-tually blind but simply realistic. The Ghost isn't there. It's a hallucination, which Hamlet and the audience share. We get sucked into reading the play from Hamlet's point of view, but he's not always right and this is one of those cases where we question him, and ourselves. We're wrong, Gertrude is right. A variation on this is that the Ghost has become more internalized, more a creation of Hamlet's mind. The next stage is for it to disappear altogether – as it does. Some answers are framed from the Ghost's point of view. It doesn't want to shock or upset Gertrude (this is consistent with the Ghost's advice to Hamlet to go easy on his mother). Alternatively, the Ghost, being a man's man, appears to soldiers but not to women. Is this deliberate on the Ghost's part? The First Quarto Ghost is in its nightgown, ready as it were to play the husband. Does it want to appear to Gertrude, and should it register chagrin that it can't? And there is of course a reading that nicely contradicts all the others: Gertrude can see the Ghost but can't or won't admit it. Gertrude in this case becomes not blind or realistic or bewildered but as rigorously controlled as Claudius, and with the same edge of desperation. When I raise this question, I let the answers come, and the one conclusion I allow myself is that this is characteristic of the play – we have many possible answers, all viable, none locking in as the truth. After all, this is a play that begins with a question, which is not answered but thrown back on the questioner. ("Who's there?" "Nay, answer me. Stand and unfold yourself.") In trying to answer its questions we find them recoiling on ourselves, as we become aware of ourselves as interpreters, while the play maintains its silence.

Claudius's delayed reaction and Gertrude's failure or refusal to see the Ghost provoke by surprise. We had expected the test on Claudius to be neater, and in act 1 the play establishes the convention that everyone on stage with the Ghost can see it. There are other moments that provoke by sheer strangeness. In *Titus Andronicus*, Titus places his severed hand in Lavinia's mouth with the command, "Bear thou my hand, sweet wench, between thy teeth." What on earth is going on here? My own tendency (as with *Henry V*) is to go political: it is an invasive act, a displaced rape, a sign of the disquieting resemblances between the atrocity Lavinia has suffered and the family's attempts to comfort her, which are also acts of control, this one being particularly coercive. But the moment allows for a much freer interpretive play than that, and students seize the freedom in various ways. Lavinia is biting the hand that feeds her, showing a lingering resentment at Titus's attempt to force her marriage to Saturninus. This shifts the focus from what Titus is doing to what Lavinia is doing, giving her a chance to be aggressive, even violent. (It is of course Titus who gives her that chance – wittingly or not?) On the other hand, she is like a dog being told to fetch. One woman student observed, "He talks to her as though she were a prostitute." I missed a chance here. I should have asked where that reaction came from: the element of coercion – do this, woman – or the skin-crawling endearment, "sweet wench"? I didn't, and the moment was lost. Another student saw in the image two essential body parts brought into unnatural conjunction. The advantage of that reading is that it preserves the strangeness, not trying to explain it. There is always a danger that explanations will kill the strangeness, and it may be that the strangeness is what we need. In fact, should one try to explain a moment like this? Another question that has no simple answer.

Desdemona, in her brief revival after her apparent death, makes two contradictory statements. One is logical and obviously just: "O, falsely, falsely murdered! . . . A guiltless death I die." But when Emilia asks, "O, who hath done this deed?" Desdemona replies, "Nobody; I myself. Farewell! / Commend me to my kind lord." The first statement is an implied accusation of Othello; the second exonerates him (with the possible ambiguity of "guiltless death" acting as a pivot between the two: her guiltlessness or his?). It is the second statement that raises questions. My own tendency has been to equate it with Cordelia's "No cause, no cause," no ordinary forgiveness but a grace that crashes through mere facts, treating guilt, real guilt, not as forgivable but as nonexistent. In a recent class, the students went beyond that. Some accepted the idea of forgiveness; others saw the moment as more ambiguous. In reducing Othello to "nobody" is Desdemona actually punishing him by wiping him out? Or is annihilating him another way of exonerating him – that wasn't the real Othello? This links with her earlier line, "My lord is not my lord." In a further reach, one student raised the question: who is "my kind lord?". We naturally assume it is Othello – but could it be Brabantio? In this reading she returns to the father she offended, the father she rejected in favor of Othello, apologizes to him and asks to be taken back. You're right, I never should have married this man. (She does not know that Brabantio is dead, and at this point neither do we; but Gratiano, bringing the news later in the scene, reminds us of him.) Another possibility: how literally can we take "I myself?" Is Desdemona saying, in effect, I brought this on myself? And does this mean that she herself is "nobody"? A line that I wanted to see as a simple, stunning outbreak of grace became more enigmatic, its multiple meanings leaving us uncertain about who is being accused, who is being annihilated, who is being sent Desdemona's last commendation. In a last assertion of independence, Desdemona is resisting interpretation. On the way back to my office after the class, another thought occurred to me, too late. What about Polyphemus and Odysseus? Who did this to you? Nobody.

Desdemona's apparent forgiveness of Othello is, like Titus's command to Lavinia, strange. Its strangeness forces us to examine it, and under examination it starts to break apart into multiple possibilities. A moment that is just as strange, in the opposite direction, is Edgar's command in *King Lear* to the blind Gloucester at what the latter thinks is the foot of Dover Cliff: "Look up a-height . . . Do but look up." The character Edgar is impersonating may not know Gloucester is blind, but Edgar does. At this point his multiple disguises are starting to wear thin, and we are becoming more aware of Edgar himself and his program of tending and guiding his father, leading him out of despair. Given that program, what do we make of the gratuitous cruelty of telling a blind man to "look up"? My suspicion is that Edgar bears a lingering resentment toward his father that comes out in this small flash of cruelty, and may be latent in the whole Dover Cliff experiment which, Edgar admits, could have killed Gloucester. Or is Edgar, as one student suggested, establishing his credentials, showing that as he can see the real world, he can put Gloucester in touch with it? This is complicated, of course, by our knowledge that the whole episode is a fake. Or is Edgar saying what Lear will later say to Gloucester: don't think of yourself as blind; there are still ways in which you can see? Gloucester will later take the point: "I see it feelingly." In his persistent asides, at once defensive and self-accusing, Edgar shows that he himself is bothered, even puzzled, by what he is doing. We should be puzzled too.

"Look up" is a small touch in passing, easy to miss if one is going too fast, looking for the main points. We need the capacity to say, "Just a minute. What did he just say? That doesn't make sense." In the reunion of the twins in *Twelfth Night* we may be so concentrated on the story conventions – "My father had a mole upon his brow" – and the general sense of wonder and resolution that we may not notice the details, some of which should give us pause. How many productions, for example, have paid attention when Viola says "Do not embrace me" and *not* let the actors do the predictable hug? For years I was interested in the fact that it was not just the memory of their father but the memory of his death that clinched the twins' mutual recognition, and I built on it ideas about the interplay of death and new life, their dependence on each other. It took me a while to notice the strangeness of Viola's line about that death: "And died that day when Viola from her birth / Had numbered thirteen years." The onset of puberty, the beginning of adulthood, and the passing of the old generation, connect logically. But she and Sebastian are twins. Why should we think of the day as *Viola's* birthday, not Sebastian's as well? In case we think Viola is merely self-preoccupied, Sebastian thinks in similar terms, calling the day of their father's death "That day that made my sister thirteen years." Asking a class for help on this one, I got back answers that made general points about women. Women in the mind of a male writer are always associated with trouble, and so it was on her birthday, not Sebastian's, that their father died. Women are more vulnerable to grief, and so it hit her harder. Women don't have lives without men. In a way these were stock ideas (or rather, stock ideas about what Shakespeare's stock ideas were), but they added a useful countercurrent to the generally positive view of Viola the play normally presents. Another student explained the focus on Viola in terms of the function of a recognition scene. Sebastian's identity is fixed; it is Viola's that is fluid. Her real name is spoken from the stage for the first time just before the reference to their father's death. Up to that point she is a nameless woman we know as Cesario, knowing that is not her real name. Now it is Viola's identity that needs to be created. The scene is about turning Cesario into Viola; in a sense this too is her birthday and she, not Sebastian, is the character who *needs* a birthday. What is at stake here? Overarching issues of gender, or the particular need of one character? And while we are at it, what do we make of Sebastian's willingness to see himself as not having had a birthday? As Viola's identity is created, does his vanish? Again we are haunted by the figure of Nobody. Or is that going too far?

I have been describing the sort of class in which one comes in with a couple of ideas and in discussion the ideas expand, sometimes adding to each other, sometimes pulling apart, but in any case accumulating so that no one answer is the right one, the one we were searching for, the end of the detective story. There are other classes in which an idea one brings in is flatly contradicted – bad for one's ego and good for one's mental growth. I had been comparing Lear's limited idea of what we now call social justice – "Expose thyself to feel what wretches feel / That thou mayst shake the superflux to them" (once you've eaten your fill, give the rest to the food bank) – and Gloucester's more radical idea of leveling: "So distribution should undo excess, / And each man have enough." I had just constructed this view of Gloucester as the real proto-Marxist when a student commented: "That's easy for him to say; he's going to kill himself." He would never have to face the consequences of his own theory. Two beats, and I had to reply, "Damn. You're right." This led to a homily about how the play never lets you settle on one reading or one idea, but pushes you on the way it pushes its characters on. But on reflection, was the student's idea enough to dispose of Gloucester as a true radical? I'm still thinking about that one.

I was curious to know how one particularly bright class reacted to the ending of *The Winter's Tale*, which I knew many of them were reading for the first time and with no prior knowledge. (*Epicoene* was coming up, and I wanted them to think about surprise endings.) I was ready for anything – one has to be – but I was probably expecting that Hermione's revival would produce a sense of wonder, mystery and relief at the return of life from apparent death. I asked, in a deliberately general way, what they thought of the moment when the statue comes to life. The first adjectives that came back in response were "creepy" and "spooky." She seemed not so much miraculously alive as undead. Hermione comes out of her grave; so does Dracula. Even the thought that she had been alive all the time, and could have ended Leontes's suffering much earlier, was disturbing. One student felt the ending didn't belong. Another found in the scene a sense of inertia: the story couldn't move forward, it had to move back. For others something seriously illicit had happened. They thought of the danger of raising the dead in *Doctor Faustus*, where the revived spirits are really demonic; only God can truly raise the dead. One student recalled the profound sense of disturbance when Hamlet's father returns from the grave. The most positive response was from a student who claimed the moment made her have to rethink the entire play. (I forget whether either of us drew the analogy with the film *The Crying Game*, where a surprise revelation transforms everything that has gone before.) But even that student was clearly disturbed. Instead of the perfect resolution the characters see, the students felt in various ways that something had gone seriously wrong. It is a sense I have sometimes had in production, and it picks up one moment in the text, when Paulina assures the spectators that she is not about unlawful business. It is a reassurance the audience may need, more than the stock responses acknowledge, and it may not be enough. Is this because we have been conditioned, not just by *Doctor Faustus* but by *Frankenstein* and countless works that have followed it, to see the danger of playing with life and death?

This raises another question: when asking for student reactions, can one let them bring in responses conditioned by their own world, not responses that accept the limits of the original historical context as we understand it? The answer may lie in that last reservation. We can only read from our world, and that applies to our sense of the history no less than our sense of the text. We have constructed the Renaissance (sorry, the Early Modern Period) that we need. One way to break out of that construction, and to see possibilities to which it might blind us, is to allow a free play of what may look like anachronism. The question is not whether anyone thought like that in 1603 but whether one can show that the text thinks like that. Is there an idea here that was present all the time, and just had to wait a few centuries to be released?

Even that latter question can be held in abeyance. One thing that survives from my Protestant upbringing is a tendency to say, "Prove it by scripture"; but I want to draw to a conclusion by reporting two cases in which I have called for responses that are deliberately free of the text. In the end we return to the play, but only after an excursion that may give us a fuller sense of what we may legitimately see there. I ask students to call on their own ideas, experiences and imaginations, independent of the fact that we're reading this particular 400-year old play by Shakespeare. Richard II breaks a mirror. What associations, independent of the play, are set up in your mind by the idea of breaking a mirror? Seven years' bad luck is usually the first response, but it does not stop there. You have broken yourself. You can no longer see yourself. You can no longer see the truth about yourself. Your face becomes a generalized blur. Your face is fragmented into different pieces; you become several different people. There is broken glass all over the place, and broken glass is dangerous. I ask for these ideas independent of the play; but it is a sign of the image's power that they all work within the play. (The idea of multiple identities returns in Richard's prison soliloquy.) The fact that they go beyond what Richard and Bolingbroke say about the act suggests that the image has escaped from the characters' attempt to use it; and drawing on our own instinctive responses helps us to see more fully the work the image is doing.

I like to begin *The Tempest* by asking students to forget they have ever read the play. Since it comes at the end of the course, I can never resist adding, "At this time of year, some of you may find that easy." The resulting laugh relaxes everybody and creates a free atmosphere in which the real work can be done. Forgetting *The Tempest*, let's play a word-association game. What comes into your mind when you hear the word "island"? A beach. Palm trees. Dark and scary – where are we? Escape. Abandonment. Constriction. The fear of loneliness. No man is an island. *Lord of the Flies, Robinson Crusoe, Swiss Family Robinson, The Island of Doctor Moreau, Star Trek*. Gradually the purpose of the game emerges: everything one can think of saying about an island is somehow there in *The Tempest*. In *Lord of the Flies* and the other works named (one could add More's *Utopia*, and I usually do) we see islands as laboratories in which to test the human species. How does it behave under controlled conditions? But *Star Trek*? I always like that response, because it allows me to launch into my pet theory that the planets of science fiction are really islands. Like islands they have only one climate, as one can see in *Star Wars*: the sand planet, the ice planet, the swamp planet, the redwood planet. In the past, someone would try to sabotage the game by invoking *Gilligan's Island*, but a generation has arisen that seems not to know that one. And of course it fits: Stephano and Trinculo.

Many of the same responses come back year after year. But in a recent class someone pointed out, for the first time in my experience of asking this question, that England is an island. (Strictly speaking, Britain is an island, but we didn't go into that.) This paid off in later discussion when we became alert to the fact that Prospero's island, unexpectedly, has horses ("Monster, I do smell all horse-piss, at which my nose is in great indignation"), church bells ("the solemn curfew"), and graves. All of these belong in England; what are they doing on what the Folio calls "an uninhabited island"? (Come to think of it, what are Prospero, Miranda, and Caliban doing on an uninhabited island?) The answer is that Prospero's island (sorry, Caliban's island) is also England. In the exotic location the first audiences could see images of their own lives, their experiences (and imaginings) of power, wealth, punishment, parent-child relations, love and sex – and, not living in Elizabethan England, so can we. The island is a mirror, not shattered like Richard's, but compounded like a fly's eye.

If one came in with a prepared answer to the question, "What is important about an island?" much of what I have reported would probably not have happened. I certainly had not thought of England. The sort of questions I like to ask have multiple answers, and no one definite answer. They are in a sense free of answers. And in being free, they free us (teachers and students alike) from our own preset thinking. We need that freedom. A physics professor once told me of the efforts he made to get his students to see that the experiments that don't work are the interesting ones. The point is not to cook the books so that they appear to work but to understand the failure of the expected answer, and push on to a new discovery. Similarly, I learned from one of my undergraduate teachers that the important line in a poem is the one that doesn't fit the interpretation you've just constructed. You need to use it to work to a new and fuller interpretation. In the teaching of Shakespeare this involves a close reading of the text, and you will have noticed how many of my examples involve brooding on single lines. This is part of the freedom; the text is the common ground on which teachers and students meet. Your privilege as a teacher may be that you have read *King Lear* dozens of times. Their privilege as students is that they may be reading it for the first time. But you have the same text in front of you. To limit the texts to what a particular ideology or a constructed historical context will allow is to cut off that freedom, giving the instructor privileges that stifle discussion. (This is not to say that history should not be acknowledged; but there are times when it should be thanked and sent on its way.) To bring in common experience (even *Star Trek*) is to suggest why the plays still matter in a world far removed from the world in which they were written. This, together with close textual work, is the sort of thing actors do. Shakespeare was an actor, and wrote for actors. In the end, actors have to make choices about moments readers can leave open. But there is a stage of rehearsal where the choices are open, and free exploration takes place. A class needs to be like that kind of rehearsal, a place where ideas can live and grow, not a place where they are frozen and stored, never to stir again.

Part III
Text and Performance

5

Teaching the Script

Anthony B. Dawson

As my title makes clear, I have been asked to talk in this chapter about "teaching the script." My approach to the challenge implied in that phrase has changed over the years, in tune with developments in Shakespeare studies and what we mean by terms like text and script. These are richly rewarding things to be allowed to talk to young people about, not least because it is a way to interest them in the work of the most wonderful (in the literal sense of that word) of all writers. I consider myself lucky that university authorities are willing to pay me to stand in front of (or beside) a group of people and talk about Shakespeare – I would almost (but not quite!) do it for nothing. And of course, with Shakespeare, that consummate man of the theatre, it isn't only a matter of talking about, it's also a matter of performing. A great thing over the years of teaching is that I've got to play all the best Shakespearean roles, both men and women, and without a critic in sight (except of course for my always exacting, but also partial, students).

Years ago, when I first began teaching, the challenge was to show the students that Shakespeare's plays *were* "scripts" or, at least, that they were designed for playing in a particular kind of theatre and their full meanings could only be realized in performance. Moreover, the fact that they were initially designed for Elizabethan stages gave them their specific forms, allowed for the connections they were able to generate between scenes, and conferred on individual scenes their unique shape. I often began (and still do begin) the first class with a demonstration on reading theatrically, focusing on a scene that most of them are already familiar with – part of the ball scene in *Romeo and Juliet*. In it, Juliet's father and his old cousin observe and greet the newly arrived maskers, Capulet teases the girls, then calls for music and orders his servants to turn the tables up and quench the fire; it's a busy scene, with dancers moving into positions, servants scurrying around, and, once the dancing starts, two old men chatting at the side: "Nay, sit, nay, sit, good Cousin Capulet" (1.5.30).[1] We pause over this unremarkable line to consider why "nay, sit" is repeated – elderly garrulousness, or is there a little game of polite deference as to who should sit first? The two reminisce about masking in their early days, and the dance moves past and around them. The scene offers opportunities to discuss implicit stage directions, multiple points of focus, the importance of silent characters, different stage actions taking place at the same time; we pay attention too to abrupt changes of register, such as when the old men's comic interchange ("Will you tell me that? / His son was but a ward two years ago") is suddenly interrupted, the rhetorical heat turned up, by Romeo's "What lady's that which doth enrich the hand / Of yonder knight?" (39–42). The servant's hurried and careless response ("I know not, sir") is strange; why, I ask, would he not know the mistress of the house in which he serves? Is he inattentive, indifferent, too busy? His mind, perhaps, is on the urgent business of waiting on the guests. But the scene moves quickly forward to Romeo's song in praise of the unknown girl's beauty, which is accompanied by Tybalt's staccato movements – Tybalt has heard something alien, and works himself into a rage. Audience attention is drawn to him and his reproaches, and then to his uncle's pacific response which (we note the irony *en passant*) suggests the possibility of reconciliation between the jarring families. On the stage the 60-odd lines pass by quickly, but how much is going on! It takes us most of a class period to work through, since the aim is to get them to read imaginatively, to attend to everything that is happening on the crowded stage in order to take the full measure of the scene.

As I said, I have been "teaching the script" for a long time. When I began 30-odd years ago, my voice was a relatively isolated one, though there were of course others making the same point. Back then, "performance" had not yet come to pervade the vocabulary of Shakespeare criticism; indeed it was at best a peripheral concern, the province of a few pioneers like Harley Granville-Barker, John Russell Brown, and J. L. Styan. By now, of course, all that has changed. One would be hard pressed to find a recent edition of Shakespeare or a book about him that does not mention performance, and many editions and books put performance at the center. Furthermore, the notion of what "performance" is has now expanded, so that the term covers not only what happens on stages, in the normal theatrical sense of that word, but also (in a move no doubt influenced by Shakespeare's own metatheatrical concerns) on the broader stages of the world, where performance can refer to any utterance or any act spoken or carried out, more or less consciously, as part of the intricate pragmatics of everyday interaction. And also, famously, "performative" no longer refers primarily to what happens in theatres, but now, in the vocabulary developed by J. L. Austin (1962), names a particular kind of speech act (such as those that make things happen in the world) and a particular form of self-making, as in the performances of gender discussed by Judith Butler (1990).

Back when I started, however, when the so-called "new criticism" still held sway (though the strain was beginning to show), it was by no means the norm to insist on the performative nature of Shakespeare's plays. Still, students being relatively amenable creatures then as now, it wasn't a major chore to interest them in what it might mean to consider *Hamlet* not strictly as a poem but as a script. A way to do this was to subject the script to theatrical scrutiny as we did with the ball scene in *Romeo and Juliet*. Another way was simply to read parts of the text aloud, with precise feeling and careful attention to the shifting rhythms of speech and thought (avoiding, in other words, fine elocution). One of my teachers when I was a graduate student had been Daniel Seltzer, himself a superb actor and a man thoroughly at home in the theatre. Working as his teaching assistant, I learned the value of approaching character as embodied in the language and, mysteriously, in the body of the actor as well; and I discovered the delights to be found in a nuanced reading of many a forgotten line when rendered as something spoken on a stage. So I had a superb model. But true to other sides of my training and the reasons I took to the study of literature in the first place, I was fascinated too by aspects of the plays that didn't connect directly to performance – with the ways, that is, that they were not, expressly, scripts. These were more "literary" matters such as patterns of language opened up by the "new" criticism, or generic structure, or metatheatrical adventurousness – ways of bringing thought and feeling together, of giving ideas life. So I didn't want entirely to neglect such ways of reading, even while emphasizing the theatrical.

Nowadays, the situation is reversed. The performance people (us) seem to have won – we have succeeded in convincing our colleagues that the stage does matter, that Shakespeare's plays are indeed scripts, and that to imagine otherwise is somehow to miss the point. That this is part of a larger intellectual movement, in sociology, anthropology, linguistics, and so on, is certainly true, so we can hardly take credit for having alone shifted the direction of Shakespeare studies, though our efforts have certainly had an effect, not least through the influence we have had on students who themselves have gone on to work in the field. But with the change in attitudes toward performance, with its move from the margins to the center, comes a different pedagogical challenge. Now, it seems, one needs to show students how the plays are not only scripts, but literary works with a long history, poems as well as plays. To be sure, this is verging on heresy, but it's now the *relations* between these works as scripts, and as something more than just scripts, which need emphasizing.

Still, I like to begin on the performance side, with a question for my undergraduates: having established, through our work with *Romeo and Juliet*, the importance of reading theatrically, we can move on to the more general question, "What exactly is a Shakespearean script?" Their answers are various and fruitful, but typically open up new questions. One possible answer: "It's the 'text' that's in the anthology"; or another: "It's what Shakespeare actually wrote." The dialogue continues:

—Is [I ask] *Hamlet* a script?
—Of course *Hamlet* is a script.
—Is a script the same thing as a text?
—Well, not exactly [someone replies], the "script" is the text when it is used as the basis of a performance.
—So what we have in the anthology [the *Riverside*] is not strictly a script?
—Right, not exactly, though it could be.
—When it's not a script, what is it?
—A play, a text, a tragedy [these thoughts from different corners of the room].
—When it's a script, does it stop being those other things?
—Well, no, obviously it's still a tragedy, whether it's a script or not.

And so the discussion has landed us quickly in a lexical slough, one that highlights the difficulties of sorting out the relations between text, script, and performance, This is something we can then go on to explore, though perhaps not really solve (the aim is to confront such puzzles, not eliminate them). Indeed the issue of what a text is has arisen over recent decades in the course of the very developments that have put performance at the center, and the two matters are closely related. One of the reasons why Shakespeare's texts are now typically regarded as plural and unstable is precisely that performance has intervened: the stage, once maligned as a source of contamination threatening the purity of the text, is now seen as an essential element in the collaborative process that produced the plays as we know them.

Thus the business of the "script" can start us talking about how we know, or rather how we don't exactly know, what Shakespeare actually wrote; about how the theatre, from his own time till now, has collaborated with, and yes, even at times contaminated, what he wrote. One recent year, beginning the course with *Hamlet*, I decided to dive right into the textual problems associated with script. I had ordered both *The Riverside Shakespeare* and G. R. Hibbard's (1987) Oxford edition of the play. The majority of the students were using the latter, but there were enough *Riverside* texts scattered around the group of 45 or so, that we could have a little fun. I directed them to 4.4. With their different texts in front of them, the students could easily spot the discrepancies. Those using the *Riverside* text found Hamlet on his way to England, accompanied by his treacherous friends Rosencrantz and Guildenstern; en route, they come across the Norwegian army as it marches toward Poland under the command of the stalwart Fortinbras. In the Oxford text, however, Hamlet does not appear at all at this point; in it, 4.4 is an eight-line scene consisting of Fortinbras's instructions to his Captain (parallel to the first eight lines of the scene in *Riverside*). Thus the conversation between Hamlet and the Norwegian Captain, and the prince's ensuing meditation on the mysterious reasons why he continues to delay his "dull revenge" ("How all occasions do inform against me . . .") drop out of sight. Instead of being faced with yet another self-lacerating soliloquy, those using the Oxford text would pass quickly on to Gertrude's fears and the disturbances of Ophelia's mad scene.

The result was what I hope was a fruitful form of consternation. One student actually wondered aloud whether Prof. Hibbard had not made a hideous mistake and forgotten to print the long soliloquy that he (the student) could plainly see in the text held by the young woman beside him. He clearly had not read the preliminary section that explains the origin of this particular text; but then again I hadn't asked the students to do so either, since I was hoping for a bit of perplexity as a way into the problem. Of course it didn't take long to point out that the speech in question is indeed printed in Hibbard's edition, but only as part of an appendix, which prints the 18 passages that occur in the second quarto (Q2) but are omitted from the text of the play in the Folio (F). So Hibbard has clearly not made a mistake – he is simply following a different early version. Once the discrepancy was noted and explained, we could proceed with our discussion of script with a concrete example before us – one that raises the specter of instability and makes the search for a single text just a little chimerical. We could speculate on why the Folio omission might have occurred, especially of course the idea that it seems to reflect theatrical practice, cuts made for a particular performance. This led us into the matter of copy-text, why different editors have chosen to base their editions on different early texts, and what those decisions might mean for a consideration of what a script is. Later in our discussion of the play we could also consider, referring back to this discovery, how Hamlet's character might appear different with or without this final soliloquy. And we could add to that a discussion of how the two texts present us with a somewhat changed Laertes, and, together with the more radical Q1, suggest alternate ways of understanding and playing the relationship between Hamlet and his mother.[2]

One important effect of our discussion was to bring the work of editors to the students' attention. The idea was to move editing as a practice to the foreground, to make the students conscious of what is at stake when we talk about plays, texts, and scripts. In producing a text of a play such as *Hamlet*, modern editors make hundreds of choices, large and small, that of their "copy" or control text one of the most crucial. Evans, in preparing the *Riverside Shakespeare*, chose Q2, because it seemed to him, as it has to many editors, to be closer to Shakespeare's original, untouched by what appear to be theatrical cuts and changes – the very elements that led Hibbard to choose F. My point, in raising this issue as in some ways foundational, was first to alert students to the existence of such different early texts, and then to complicate their assumptions and presuppositions about what "Shakespeare" actually is. It helps them see that to think about the differences between texts of the same play is not to engage in dusty antiquarianism, but rather provides a way of confronting major interpretive issues. But more important than that, they could take note of how, from the very beginning, performance has affected what we think of as "the text." They could see how someone, maybe Shakespeare, maybe his fellow actors, thought improvements could be made to the rhythm of the show by, in this case, trimming and speeding up the fourth act.[3] We could note as well that, since the part of Hamlet is a very long and demanding one, giving the main actor a bit of a break at this point might help him swing more energetically into the final scenes. The students, frequently held back from such considerations by a feeling of awe before the cultural standing of the bard and the sacredness of his texts, come to see the malleability of the script, the ways in which it is subject to the most mundane circumstances (weariness on the part of audience or actor, for example).

This allows them to feel just a little liberated, and thus prepares them for a major project that they will take on later in the year, where they have to produce their own scripts. The project's purpose is to have them become directly involved in mounting Shakespeare's plays. Over the years I've developed a way of doing this that is scary for them at first, but which inevitably gets the best marks when they come to writing their course evaluations. I divide the class of about 45 into seven or eight groups, and make each group responsible for a particular play on the reading list. They have to do a full, but significantly cut, version of the play for which they are responsible (one that will fit into a 50-minute class period with time for set-up and a bit of discussion). I have the luxury of teaching at an institution that still offers full year (two semester) courses in certain "big" subjects such as Shakespeare. This means the students have lots of time to pull their performance together – almost all their shows take place in the second term.

In general, despite their shyness about actually performing in front of their classmates, and their terror about remembering their lines, the students love doing this. Sometimes they even fall in love doing it. I've seen at least one wedding and quite a number of relationships grow from the intense collaboration that the project demands. And even when there are not such dramatic consequences, members of the groups usually bond with each other and can be seen in the weeks that follow their presentations, slipping off together for an after-class coffee or beer.

Their first task, once they begin working as an ensemble, is to prepare the script, working from the texts they have. Our thought experiment with *Hamlet* comes into obvious play here: knowing they are participating in a long tradition of adapting and recasting the plays in response to theatrical exigency, the students rise to the occasion with zest, if also with trepidation. Furthermore, because several students do not buy either the assigned individual text or the *Riverside*, they are used to meeting with other discrepancies and differences between various texts as these have arisen; they thus are ready for battle over variants when it comes to sorting out their own scripts. They've learned that tinkering with the texts is an age-old practice, but now they have to cope with a hands-on experience that confronts them willy-nilly with the shifting nature of theatrical scripts and the role of collaboration in the production of such scripts. Usually two or three members of the group take on this task – it isn't a great one that needs a committee of the whole. But they need to ratify their version with the others, and be ready for disagreement. They quickly find out how difficult it is to decide what parts of the play are essential, what can be reluctantly let go, what seems fairly peripheral. Sometimes, with particularly long or complex plays such as *Troilus and Cressida* or *King Lear*, they can concentrate on one of the plots more than the other(s), but it's never easy, since the links between elements of the narrative need to remain salient. I remember one impressive version of *Antony and Cleopatra* that used inserted dumb shows to move the story along quickly (the battle of Actium represented by tiny model ships!). Naturally, the process of refining and stabilizing their script extends over the rehearsal time. As they begin to work on their production, they realize that some stuff can go, other bits need to be reinstated, transitions need to be included, and so forth.

This has turned out to be a fruitful way of inducing a certain strategy of discovery, whereby the students must perforce confront the *fact* of "script." It "teaches the script," but in a pragmatic, experiential fashion. Their task is to come up with a workable theatrical document to serve as the basis of their performance. I ask them to hand in their "book," to use the Elizabethan word for it, so I can remind myself of the shortcuts they took, and the links they allowed for or missed. Some groups, of course, are better than others at providing a smooth running script, but all of them are forced to come to grips with the practicalities of theatrical presentation. They also are encouraged to think about the relation of their script of a particular play to that of others. With *Othello*, for example, we may have discussed in class some of the differences between the quarto (Q1, 1622) and the Folio versions of that play. But what began as a relatively abstract issue becomes brutally concrete when they must produce their own actors' version; they must indeed ponder the ways that their text represents this object called "Othello," which is at once both fluid and stable, both many and one. Such are some of the vexed questions that arise around the script, and become the basis for class discussion more broadly.

The next step is to begin rehearsing, and memorizing their parts. I rarely intervene in this process, and they usually want to keep secret whatever surprises they might have up their sleeves. In fact the only intervention on my part that is sometimes called for is if there is a student who is slacking his or her responsibilities, or some other kind of conflict in the group. Almost always, a couple of meetings in my office will sort this kind of thing out, and while it's true that some students put more into the project than others, the level of cooperation and collaboration within groups is typically impressive and fair. (I assign the same mark to the whole group – and it's normally a high one since they put so much imagination and effort into the project.)[4]

Their work on developing their text conduces to an understanding of what a theatrical script is – and what it is not. At the same time, I also stress the literary side of Shakespeare's achievement. Hence while their preparations are going on, my lectures on the plays will sometimes range far from performance itself, often taking in historical and cultural contexts: issues as diverse as early modern attitudes toward sex and gender, tragic structure, or the ethics of revenge. (The performances usually take place near the end of our classroom consideration of a particular play.) As I said earlier, the view that Shakespeare's texts are scripts meant for performance is now commonplace; but that is only half the story. They are also literary works, shaped, in their creation and reception, by traditions both ancient and modern. I don't think these two elements are extricable from one another, or even fully distinct, and my teaching no doubt reflects this conviction. And not only my teaching; in some of my recent writing as well (2006, 2007), I have been arguing for a bridging of the unnecessary split that recent criticism has carved between the literary and performative aspects of Shakespeare's texts.

So, in the rest of the chapter I would like to pursue the question of the convergence of these two supposedly opposed ways of coming to understand Shakespeare. Something that arose in connection with one of the student performances provides an excellent starting point. I recall a particular moment that was strongly theatrical and embodied, but rich in literary suggestiveness as well. Like that famous scene in theatrical history in 1610 when Henry Jackson was moved by the young actor playing Desdemona on her death bed (his account appears in Evans 1997: 1978), this too involved Desdemona, and in particular her outstretched hand. Just as her husband moved toward her with murderous intent, she reached out, and that simple gesture helped me see the text, both as script and as poem, differently. Picture the scene: an ordinary industrial classroom with hard linoleum floors, desks from the 1970s, fluorescent lighting; but transformed into Desdemona and Othello's bedchamber by the simple addition of a few props – a candle, the pedagogically burdened front desk moved to the middle of the room, canopied with a gauzy curtain and spread with a white duvet, the intrusive house lights turned off. Desdemona prone: "Who's there? Othello?" – "Ay, Desdemona." – "Will you come to bed, my lord?" (5.2.23–4). And out through the diaphanous curtain she reached her hand, lingeringly, the same "liberal hand" she had extended to her distraught husband just minutes before (in a sequence from 3.4, but remember this is a cut version). That earlier gesture was here repeated in a lovely moment of grave theatrical embodiment. We discussed this afterwards: they had planned the repeated gesture, so they recognized a pattern, or intuited one anyway, a pattern that I had never paid a lot of attention to, but which I was led to think more about: a linkage of hearts and hands throughout the play.

At the next class, after a hurried look through the play, I could expand on their insight, hooking it into what might be regarded as a more literary kind of analysis, reading the play's obsessive preoccupation with the problem of knowledge and evidence in relation to this little motif of heart and hand, and tracing some of its transformations and ramifications through a series of passages, beginning with the dialogue to which they had deliberately referred with the repeated movement:

> *Othello*:   Give me your hand. This hand is moist, my lady.
> *Desdemona*: It yet hath felt no age nor known no sorrow.
> *Othello*:   This argues fruitfulness and liberal heart;
>   Hot, hot, and moist. This hand of yours requires
>   A sequester from liberty: fasting and prayer,
>   Much castigation, exercise devout,
>   For here's a young and sweating devil here
>   That commonly rebels. 'Tis a good hand,
>   A frank one.
> *Desdemona*: You may, indeed, say so;
>   For 'twas that hand that gave away my heart.
> *Othello*:   A liberal hand. The hearts of old gave hands;
>   But our new heraldry is hands, not hearts.
>
>   (3.4.36–47)

Clearly the gesture here is crucial, as Desdemona extends her hand in the same act she made when she gave away her heart, and when she sealed that gift in marriage; but Othello's present reaction to her hand registers a very different reading of the physical evidence from the one we are encouraged to imagine as having taken place before the play begins. The meaning of Desdemona's seemingly straightforward gesture has been rendered ambiguous to him, difficult to interpret correctly, by the action and insinuations of the play thus far. Recall that earlier moment when Iago mocks Roderigo's reading of the "blessed" Desdemona: "Bless'd pudding! Didst thou not see her paddle with the palm of his [Cassio's] hand? Didst not mark that?" (2.1.253–5). We, like Othello, are encouraged to read differently by such revisions of the meaning of what we see, to let our erring imaginations range. This raises the awkward question of how we react to, and are implicated in, performance. The idea and the image, both physical and verbal, reappear in *Winter's Tale*: "This entertainment / May a free face put on . . . / 't may – I grant. / But to be paddling palms and pinching fingers, / As now they are, and making practic'd smiles . . ." (1.2.111–16). There too someone is reading gesture against the grain, interpreting according to a screen that is etched both by what has been said and done and, more immediately, by the fact of performance itself. Shakespeare's plays are scripts, but they also, as the link with *Winter's Tale* suggests, form one large *oeuvre*, with cross-currents that bind the performed and the literary in a network that *is* theatrical, though it is a theatre that is not confined to any singular space or time. The heraldry of hands and hearts, the possibilities of devotion and betrayal in figures as different as the Virgin Mary and Jason, is an ancient one and deeply embedded in the European literary imagination. What we see in Shakespeare is one more embodiment of that ancient theme.

In *Othello*, the complex relations between knowledge, love, and hands, opened to view by these images, are thickly woven: Iago, for example, resists Othello's importunity, his insistence on knowing his ancient's thoughts, by replying, "You cannot, if my heart were in your hand, / Nor shall not, whilst 'tis in my custody" (3.3.163–4). He owns his own heart – no one else can know it. That is the very thing he implies about Desdemona when he says of her *hand*kerchief: "Why then 'tis hers, my lord, and being hers, / She may, I think, bestow't on any man" (4.1.12–13). Again, when he fabricates Cassio's dream for Othello, we find the same connection between hand and heart: "In sleep I heard him say, 'Sweet Desdemona, / Let us be wary, let us hide our loves'; / And then, sir, would he gripe and wring my hand" (3.3.419–21). A few minutes later, Iago is vowing: "Witness that here Iago doth give up / The execution of his wit, hands, heart, / To wrong'd Othello's service!" (465–7). So many extended hands, so many impenetrable hearts. It is the density of this recurrence, the way it is sedimented into the language, that gives it literary valence, but that doesn't stop it from being theatrical as well. It is no wonder, then, that when Othello steels his determination to destroy his wife, hand, heart and all, he puts it in metaphorically resonant terms: "No, my heart is turn'd to stone; I strike it, and it hurts my hand" (4.1.182–3). There is no separating the literary from the performative here, no detaching the poetic and metaphorical from the gestural, as Othello no doubt strikes his own hardening heart. Climactically, the combination of word and *gestus* creates a special poignancy in Othello's last speech: "Speak of me as I am . . . one whose hand / (Like the base Indian) threw a pearl away / Richer than all his tribe" (5.2.342–8).[5] Does his gesture somehow recall hers?

Looking more closely at the "liberal hand" sequence, we noticed how the perceptions of both Desdemona and Othello are given voice, but don't meet: the "moist" hand saying to Desdemona merely that she is young and happy, *green*. But to Othello, the hand's message is more twisted and uncertain: "liberal" and "good" suggest fruitfulness, but that good hand is "moist" in his imagination with the sweat of lust, harboring a "devil" that requires sequestering. That the "devil" has other roles in the play goes almost without saying; but at this point in our class discussion I might turn briefly to the end where Othello looks down toward Iago's feet, "but that's a fable. / If that thou be'st a devil, I cannot kill thee" (5.2.286–7). This kind of lateral move is something I find myself doing frequently, telling the students to flip quickly to another reinforcing moment, while keeping a finger on the spot we've left. So with the metaphorics of Iago as "devil" briefly noted, the discussion returns to that earlier scene where the "sweating devil," mark of Othello's "possession" by Iago's imagination, finds a chimerical embodiment in Desdemona's extended hand. The point of course is to register as precisely as possible how physical performance, the movement of bodies on stage, concretizes a set of relations identified as literary and teased out through critical analysis.

At this point our discussion can move in several directions. Trying to follow Ariadne's thread through the textual/performative maze, I would favor moving to how, in the dialogue from 3.4 that stands at the center of the discussion throughout the whole 50 minutes, Desdemona ignores, or doesn't see, her husband's more ominous meanings; the two of them talk at cross purposes, the communication gap becoming too readily an abyss. "For 'twas that hand that gave away my heart": it is a "frank" avowal, but she misses the loaded meanings in Othello's use of that word – "frank." From there, to give weight and "thickness" to this interlocutory pattern, we can shift to their little dialogue in 3.3, when Desdemona begs a favor for Cassio, "That came a wooing with you" (71). Othello's response is a repeated "I will deny thee nothing" (76, 83), which sounds like compliance but fails to recognize what *she* sees so easily, that she makes her request for his sake: to reinstate Cassio is no "boon" for her, but a way to do himself good – "I will deny thee nothing." Somehow, sadly, he is unable to hear her, even at that stage. Their interchange is in turn the prelude to the long "temptation" scene in which Iago successfully introduces Othello, through indirection and insinuation, to what is in *his* head, and offers "The execution of his wit, hands, heart, / To wrong'd Othello's service" (466–7).

And the same mishearing or misprision, with the tragic temperature now significantly raised, occurs climactically in the final scene:

Desdemona:	Send for him hither;
	Let him confess a truth.
Othello:	He hath confess'd.
Desdemona:	What, my lord?
Othello:	That he hath us'd thee.
Desdemona:	How? unlawfully?
Othello:	Ay.
Desdemona:	He will not say so.
Othello:	No – his mouth is stopp'd;
	Honest Iago hath ta'en order for't.
Desdemona:	O, my fear interprets. What, is he dead?
Othello:	Had all his hairs been lives, my great revenge
	Had stomach for them all.
Desdemona:	Alas, he is betray'd and I undone!
Othello:	Out, strumpet! weep'st thou for him to my face?

(5.2.67–77)

Comic misunderstanding, of the sort one frequently meets in the speech of Shakespeare's clowns, is turned in this passage to poignant horror. They again talk at cross purposes, and Desdemona, frightened as she is, falls into an unfortunate choice of words with "Alas, he is betray'd and I undone," which only confirms Othello's worst fears when she means to exculpate herself; Cassio really has been betrayed, but not in the way Othello understands her phrase.

I am trying, in detailing our attempts to follow the intricate weave of patterns and connections, to describe something of the process of teaching this complex thing called the script. In this case of *Othello*, the student performance has provided a way in, a starting point, with that extended hand. It was an invitation for me to develop their insights, get them to explore the aesthetic dimension of the play, with its dense layering of motifs that can find expression both onstage and in the "study." (And, as I hope is clear by now, these two interpretative spaces reinforce each other.) This led us to focus on the short dialogue in 3.4, which both thematizes the interplay of heart and hand and provides a performative center, a stage image, for some of the most salient and moving aspects of the whole play; that little sequence, then, proves an anchor, a kind of ballast for our subsequent move-ment across the surface of the text and, we hope, into its depths as well.

This is to some extent a matter of improvisation. I find, as I gather more and more experience as a teacher of Shakespeare, that the best way to pre-pare is to keep immersing oneself in the texts, to be ready for lateral moves, for explorations that may take you to a place you hadn't really visited before, or perhaps more frequently to places you hadn't at that moment planned to visit. Teaching is, for me, often an improvisatory enterprise, in the sense that jazz is improvisatory – the riffs that emerge in class derive from long experience and a deep acquaintance with the possible harmonies of what I know (even if I don't always know that I know!). Improvisation is at the heart of teaching because it is a way of responding to one of the funda-mental elements of the encounter between student and teacher: the imperative of meeting and speaking to the student(s) in the places they occupy, and bringing them somewhere else. Of course there can be dan-gers in improvisation (Iago after all is a master improviser). One can ride a wave of associations without settling down, dazzle without illuminating. But in general, I have found that, having lived with these marvelous plays for such a long time, their resonances float around in my mind like remembered melodies, and (at least some of the time) I'm able to call on them to give weight and density to a given interpretive moment.

What, finally, am I after in teaching Shakespeare? What do I most want to achieve by enabling a relationship between his work and generations of students? I suppose it's a mix of things: long-term acquaintance, a lifelong ease with this formidable cultural figure; the power of performance to illu-minate and etch into the mind an image that is a kind of truth; the sheer delight of a flash of insight, of a pattern seen and traced. Perhaps more than anything, a complex *empathy* that involves entering into the minds and worlds of brilliantly realized other persons, into a distant historical place, and into a rich and difficult language, one that both is and is not the English that we know today (an immersion that may even be – vain hope – a means of revitalizing, in some minds at least, that homogenized and instrumen-talized code that the world uses today for international "communica-tion"). Often those of us who teach the humanities are confronted by our more practically minded colleagues with questions about the usefulness of what we do. There are many answers to such questions, but perhaps they boil down to empathy and awareness: an attuned, alert, and compassion-ate self-positioning in the world. Shakespeare's mind, as Virginia Woolf writes of it, is a model of such an awareness:

All desire to protest, to preach, to proclaim an injury, to pay off a score, to make the world the witness of some hardship or grievance . . . was fired out of [Shakespeare] and consumed. Therefore his poetry flows from him free and unimpeded. If ever a human being got his work expressed completely, it was Shakespeare. If ever a mind was incandescent, unimpeded, I thought, turning again to the bookcase, it was Shakespeare's mind. (Woolf 1972: 58)

It has been a privilege and frequently a joy to act as a conduit between that mind and those of hundreds of young and not-so-young students, who have arrived in my class from a thousand backgrounds and mental places and who, I hope, emerge a little readier to meet the world as it is; for the readiness, as Hamlet saw, is all.

Notes

1 All Shakespeare quotations are taken from *The Riverside Shakespeare* (Evans 1997).
2 On this matter, see Werstine (1988).
3 Scott McMillin (2001: 9–10) has shown how what seem to be theatrical cuts in several of Shakespeare's two-text plays occur mostly in the third and especially the fourth acts, as though the players were aware of a possible sag at that stage in the performance and wanted to move things along a little more forcefully.
4 This matter of evaluation is a vexed one, but my approach to it is as straightforward as possible. Since ours is not a theatre class, there are no expectations about fully accomplished acting skills. But I do require good command of the text – repeated failures of memory will affect the mark. Basically I look for imagination and panache, a thoughtful condensation of the script (one with reasonable coverage and in which the transitions make sense), inventiveness in staging, and solid *effort*. I tend to be quite a bit more generous with "A"s for this project than for the standard written ones.
5 In *Winter's Tale* too, the culminating, in this case redemptive, gesture is an extended hand: "Nay," says Paulina to the dumbstruck Leontes, "present your hand" – and he does, helping Hermione down off the pedestal (5.3.107–11).

References and Further Reading

Austin, J. L. (1962). *How To Do Things With Words*. Cambridge, MA: Harvard University Press.
Brown, John Russell (1969). *Shakespeare's Plays in Performance*. Harmondsworth, UK: Penguin.

Brown, John Russell (Ed.) (1976). *Shakespeare in Performance: An Introduction Through Six Major Plays.* New York: Harcourt Brace Jovanovich.

Butler, Judith (1990). *Gender Trouble: Feminism and the Subversion of Identity.* New York: Routledge.

Dawson, Anthony B. (2006). "Priamus is Dead: Memorial Repetition in Marlowe and Shakespeare." In Peter Holland (Ed.). *Shakespeare, Memory and Performance* (pp. 63–84). Cambridge, UK: Cambridge University Press.

Dawson, Anthony B. (2007). "What Editors Do and Why it Matters." In Laurie Maguire (Ed.). *How To Do Things With Shakespeare* (pp. 160–80). Oxford: Blackwell.

Evans, G. B. (Ed.) (1997). *The Riverside Shakespeare,* 2nd edn. Boston: Houghton Mifflin.

Granville-Barker, Harley (1927–37). *Prefaces to Shakespeare.* 3 vols. London: Sidgwick & Jackson.

Hibbard, G. R. (Ed.) (1987). *Hamlet.* Oxford: Oxford University Press.

McMillin, Scott (Ed.) (2001). *The First Quarto of Othello.* Cambridge, UK: Cambridge University Press.

Styan, J. L. (1967). *Shakespeare's Stagecraft.* Cambridge, UK: Cambridge University Press.

Werstine, Paul (1988). "The Textual Mystery of *Hamlet.*" *Shakespeare Quarterly* 39, 1–26.

Woolf, Virginia (1972). *A Room of One's Own.* Harmondsworth, UK: Penguin.

6

A Test of Character

Miriam Gilbert

Many years ago, when I first started teaching, I discovered – almost by accident – the central strategy that I've used ever since. The course was an undergraduate Shakespeare course, in my second semester of full-time teaching; the play was *Macbeth*. So we must have been more than halfway through the semester, and I was trying to begin discussion of the play with some kind of elaborate statement about "inversion of nature" (obviously thinking of "foul is fair" and the witches). But my students simply weren't interested in thinking about that kind of abstract idea. Rather they were absolutely riveted by – or, to my ears, fixated on – questions such as "Why does Macbeth let Lady Macbeth push him around so much?" and "Isn't she really responsible for his decision?" After a few more attempts on my part to interest students in my questions, the light suddenly dawned: couldn't I get to the same issue via *their* questions? After all, couldn't the wife telling the husband what to do be seen as an inversion of traditional household order? Doesn't 1.7, when Macbeth is considering the assassination, lead directly to the problem of violating natural law, on both personal and cosmic levels?

The more I listened to student questions, and the more I encouraged students to help frame and organize the discussion through those questions, the easier discussion became. No longer did I agonize over the question of whether to start a discussion of *Othello* by asking about Iago's motivation or Othello's race, but I accumulated student questions so that I could see which of those problems seemed most prominent for that particular class; after all, I quickly realized, we could always get to the other issue later. No longer was I working against the barrier of unspoken questions/concerns or unvoiced bafflement, but instead was able to utilize the energy of the students' interest. The technique of asking students to write down the major questions they've got and to bring them up as we begin talking about a play, not only assigns a certain level of responsible preparation, but sets out the major issues for the class, and, along the way, tends to reassure people that the questions they've had are not stupid or irrelevant.

What I've also learned is that, for many students, questions begin with characters (as the example from my abortive *Macbeth* discussion shows). That is, what grabs students – and what bothers them – is what the characters are like, and why they are behaving as they are. Speculating about why students so immediately ask about characters may point in many directions, including towards generations of high school teachers trained by teachers who read A. C. Bradley's *Shakespearean Tragedy*, but I think the real reason is that characters seem easier to grasp than anything else in the play – more immediate than questions of structure and more accessible than the language. While for some students, questions of source and origin (what *did* the Elizabethans think about Jews or Moors?) seem to offer possible solutions to difficult characters, there is still a tendency to want the plays, and therefore the characters, to make sense right now. Generalizations about attitudes towards women, children, "others," only go so far.

So, based on my experience with teaching – and my long-time interest in studying theatre performance, whether trying to reconstruct past performances or commenting on current ones – I want to raise again the notion that talking about characters is a valid and a highly useful thing to do in the classroom. I'm not trying to redo the A. C. Bradley/L. C. Knights conflict, or to engage myself in the question of whether we ought to read Harold Bloom or not, but rather to suggest why this seemingly outdated approach may still be relevant. Laurie E. Maguire makes the same point in her recent book, *Studying Shakespeare: A Guide to the Plays*: "I am not advocating character study, and its companion, situation, as the aim of Shakespeare criticism, but I want to insist on their usefulness as a point of entry into all Shakespeare plays" (Maguire 2004: 8). Like Maguire, I'm talking about *teaching* the plays, not about finding the single lens through which to read them. And talking about character has been – for me and my students – the most visible and the most useful point of entry, a way to find a coherent path into texts that seem baffling.

Though students turn to character study because it is familiar and offers explanations that pull together disparate elements, some scholars are still uncomfortable with such an approach. One of the most powerful attacks on this kind of criticism has come from Alan Sinfield (1992) precisely because he sees many characters as resisting such unification. In the chapter "When is a Character Not a Character? Desdemona, Olivia, Lady Macbeth, and Subjectivity," Sinfield argues that "Desdemona is a disjointed sequence of positions that women are conventionally supposed to occupy" (1992: 53), Cressida "is organized to suit her role in the story of the men" (p. 54), "Lady Macbeth is a fantasy arrangement of elements that are taken to typify the acceptable and unacceptable faces of woman, and the relations between them" (p. 56), and Olivia "proves to be not a continuous consciousness (let alone an autonomous essence), but a strand in a far wider cultural argument" (p. 66). Although Sinfield accepts that characters may be seen "not as essential unities, but as simulated personages apparently possessing adequately continuous or developing subjectivities," he also insists that "the presentation of the dramatis personae must be traced to a textual organization in which character is a strategy, and very likely one that will be abandoned when it interferes with other desiderata" (p. 78), especially the stereotypes created by a patriarchal system.

What Sinfield overlooks, to my mind, is the fact that these characters, who seem to begin as strong, even powerful, women and who end either in silence or in submission, are written to be played by an actor, and in that actor's body – by which I mean the expression of voice and movement and response – lies a unity that cannot disappear. Moreover, even when actors talk about playing individual moments, not necessarily searching for links between one scene and another, the very fact that the same actor keeps reappearing leads the audience to create explanations, to find the connections. Looking only at the lines on the page, and not at what happens in the spaces between the lines – spaces that on stage are often highly memorable – may lead to a theoretically sophisticated notion about the nonexistence or the centrality of a particular character, but such looking/reading/listening seems inescapably limited. To assume, for instance, that "the final Desdemona" is one who "submits to Othello's abuse and violence" (Sinfield 1992: 53) is to ignore performance history or to fail to imagine the Desdemonas who have fought back against Othello's attack, both verbally and physically. The number of times she finishes Othello's lines suggest a quick response to his accusations in 5.2 and while Desdemona always dies on the bed, she doesn't necessarily stay there; my most recent viewing of the play, at the Globe, featured a Desdemona who struggled with a locked door and who had to be picked up and carried, still struggling, to the bed. To speak of Desdemona's silence without mentioning Emilia's speaking up, albeit too late, is to overlook the way in which both women have been transformed by the play's events, so that Desdemona loses her eloquence and Emilia finally gains the determination to speak. One might even argue that such transformation happens to male characters as well. If Othello is first characterized as "the Moor," but also with racial slurs equating him with animals, he then becomes "Valiant Othello" (1.3.50) for the Venetian senators, and the audience, and over the course of the play keeps changing, so much so that Lodovico asks "Is this the noble Moor?" (4.1.271). And Iago, standing third on the list of longest Shakespearean roles, becomes progressively less voluble as the play continues, and ends with a defiant vow of silence, "From this time forth I never will speak word" (5.2.312).

Students' fascination with character motivation helps explain why teaching the tragedies often seems so much easier, since those plays are usually dominated by a central character that one *has* to talk about. What I've often read as student respect for the tragedies may, in fact, simply be a response to problems they easily recognize. By contrast, the comedies often seem less accessible, even trivial, until questions about character motivation and the implications of behavior and action get raised. Teaching *The Merchant of Venice* is actually much easier than teaching *A Midsummer Night's Dream*, because Shylock so threatens and challenges my students. I might add that one strategy that does work with *Dream* is to ask why we need the performance of "Pyramus and Thisbe," a question that often leads to discussion about the mechanicals and why we can't dismiss them as mere "comic" characters. The history plays are, at first, even more remote, filled as they are with names that seem literally place-holders: Gloucester, Northumberland, York. But once students recognize the personal dimension of the history plays, especially the conflict between family members, they then tune in quite quickly to the political dimensions

Take, for instance, 1.3 of *Richard II*, a scene to which my students almost always respond with bafflement: what, they wonder, is going on? Why does Richard stop the fight between Mowbray and Bolingbroke? Why does he banish them both? Why is he, to use a word that I hear almost every time I teach the play, so wishy-washy? My approach here is to get students to look at what Richard says when he banishes the two men – and, more importantly, *how* he says it. I use an exercise I call the "telegram" in which I ask students to look at the 17 lines beginning with "Draw near" and ending with "Therefore we banish you our territories"

(1.3.123–39). "If," I ask, "you had to condense the speech down to the fewest number of words that would convey the message, what would those words be?" Not surprisingly, most students will opt for the last line cited – "Therefore we banish you our territories" – skipping over the elaborate metaphors that Richard uses. "Fair enough," I say, "so what are all those other – extra – words doing there? What do they tell us?" And now, having tossed out approximately 16 lines of text, the students have to consider what those lines might mean. They come up with a variety of explanations: Richard is justifying the banishment, Richard is showing his power (they note the number of times the first person plural pronoun appears), Richard is being a politician (which seems to be a way of saying he's covering up stuff). And when I ask "Who is Richard's audience?" students then begin to see that the justification and power-language and even cover-up might be aimed not merely at Bolingbroke and Mowbray but at everyone else on stage. Occasionally students will come up with even more possibilities: perhaps Richard is nervous about what he's doing and therefore needs to set up the justification more fully; perhaps he is spinning out the suspense, making Bolingbroke and Norfolk wait for his decision. The point is that once students take the language seriously as something that reveals character and that an actor can *use*, they begin to see the scene as a much more complex display of power politics than they originally thought. And then when asked to consider what Richard gains by banishing both Mowbray and Bolingbroke, they can see that Richard is not being wishy-washy at all, but is actually making the move that will remove two powerful threats from the kingdom. Mowbray, the more dangerous because he is actually the person involved in the death of the Duke of Gloucester, is sent away for the rest of his life; Bolingbroke, whose accusation of Mowbray is actually a veiled threat against Richard himself, is sent away for 10 years. Moreover, the reduction of Bolingbroke's sentence to six years takes place after Mowbray leaves the stage, and thus may imply a gesture calculated to make the king look merciful, as if he's giving a special dispensation to Bolingbroke because of his aged father, John of Gaunt, who is, of course, the King's uncle.

By considering this scene in terms of choices that a character might make, students not only revise their opinions but gain a way of thinking that helps them understand other difficult moments in the play. Most of these concern Richard: why does he yield at Flint Castle, without even offering a fight? What is he doing in 4.1, the deposition scene? But such an approach also focuses attention on Bolingbroke who, in contrast to Richard, doesn't often offer long speeches of explanation or even evasion. Richard's epithet for Bolingbroke – "silent king" (4.1.291) – is at moments maddeningly true, and students come to see that Bolingbroke might be read as deliberately not revealing what he's thinking. One such moment is the beginning of 4.1, a scene that is both potentially comic (with men hurling gloves at each other) and seemingly cuttable (the BBC production of *Richard II* cuts the scene altogether). In 1990, Charles Osborne, reviewing the RSC's production for the *Daily Telegraph*, bemoaned the inclusion of "that ludicrous scene in which virtually the entire cast keeps flinging down gauntlets or slapping one another in the face with them" (Osborne 1990).

When I first started thinking about this scene, I saw it in terms of structure. In large part, my reading was influenced by John Barton's 1973–4 production, a production that insisted on parallels between Richard and Bolingbroke, even to the extent of casting Richard Pasco and Ian Richardson for both roles and asking them to switch back and forth on different nights (Gilbert 1979). So the scene was, both in my mind and on a mental stage, a scene about Bolingbroke facing the same problem that Richard had faced at the play's beginning, namely, accusations about who killed the Duke of Gloucester. I read the scene as one revealing Bolingbroke's lack of power, his inability to deal with the situation which, when not king, he had initiated. But a later production – perhaps it was Ron Daniels' 1990 version at Stratford-upon-Avon – introduced a very different possibility. When Bolingbroke said, in the scene's first line, "Call forth Bagot," he gave a little nod to one of his followers, a nod that seemed to suggest "You know what to do." When Bagot was brought in, he had a hood over his head, which got whisked away, but we immediately knew that he was a prisoner, and someone who was being produced for a special purpose. Thus Bolingbroke's command, "Now, Bagot, freely speak thy mind" (4.1.2), sounded both ironic and threatening, and the subtext seemed to be, "Speak the lines that you've been told to speak and maybe you'll be allowed to live." Now the scene was a demonstration of Bolingbroke's power as, one by one, nobles stepped forward to accuse the hapless Aumerle, still Bolingbroke's cousin, but clearly in a lot of trouble for having supported Richard. The whole scene was staged by Bolingbroke to trap Aumerle, and the nobles joined in, either because they had been primed to do so, or were quick to pick up the implication that accusing Aumerle would win brownie points with Bolingbroke. When Aumerle had accumulated enough gages and thus enough possible fights to make his life-expectancy extremely short, Bolingbroke then calmly stepped in to take command, his silence during the scene the silence of a man watching his scenario unfold.

I can only guess at the source of this powerful staging. Had the director pondered over the implications of "Call forth Bagot," and thus come up with the idea that "producing" Bagot could actually make a point, rather than simply having the character appear, or step forward? Did the actor playing Bolingbroke discover the little nod that implied the preplanned scenario? Maybe the actor playing Bagot, using his extended absence from the stage to imagine what might have happened to him between 2.2 where he plans to go to Ireland to meet with the king and 4.1 (his next textual appearance), had come up with the notion that perhaps Bagot, the only one of the "caterpillars of the realm" to survive, had done so by offering Bolingbroke a deal; "Let me live and I'll do whatever you want, including fingering Aumerle for the death of Gloucester" is an imaginary but possible offstage line. Whatever the background for the choices, they resulted in a moment that I've never forgotten, an interpretation that has illuminated the play for me, and that has led to questions helping students to make sense of a scene that otherwise seemed opaque.

And those choices – originating from a stage production – lead me to the other major reason for an emphasis on character in teaching Shakespeare. Simply put, by thinking of lines as evidence of a character's thoughts, feelings, motives, and so on, you find production after production creating new ideas. Actors in roles both large and small become your allies in the classroom, stimulating you to think of possible interpretations, functioning as examples that make such interpretations immediately clear to the class. For me, the basic source for such an approach goes back to the writing (and teaching) of J. L. Styan, especially in *Shakespeare's Stagecraft* and *The Elements of Drama* (Styan 1967, 1969) and in writing from John Russell Brown (Brown 1966). But perhaps I understood the connection to character most sharply from the work of John Barton, as made clear by actors he had worked with at the Royal Shakespeare Company and from his 1984 London Weekend Television series, *Playing Shakespeare*. In 1975, I watched several workshops with RSC actors rehearsing scenes and they all spoke about the way in which the language gave them clues about their character. Barton's television series of rehearsal-like sessions with actors, and the accompanying text (Barton 1984), made the same point repeatedly. In the opening program, "The Two Traditions," Barton talks about the modern tendency towards naturalism, which he defined as "the acting style and the kind of text which is the norm in the theatre and film and television today. The deliberate attempt to make everything as natural and lifelike as possible" (Barton 1984: 11). Naturalism might seem opposed to the Elizabethan theatrical tradition with its outdoor theatres, its short rehearsal time, the way in which actors had only their individual parts (rather than the entire play), and, above all, the richly elaborate and poetic language. But Barton's point is that one could use that language, which he referred to as "heightened," to help find the character. Thus, when looking at the opening lines of *The Merchant of Venice*, he focuses not simply on Antonio's speech, which seems "relatively naturalistic" but on Salerio's which "is actually much trickier for an actor because it's full of images and metaphors and similes" (pp. 16, 17). Asking the actor reading Salerio (David Suchet) what he thought Salerio was trying to do, what was his "intention," Barton got the response "to cheer Antonio up. Probably by sending him up" (p. 17). So then the question becomes how does the language support that intention? And the answer is central to all of the work Barton and his actors did with language:

> Heightened speech must be something that the actor, or rather the character he's playing, *finds for himself* because he *needs* those words and images to express his intention. So you, David, need those words to cheer up and send up Antonio. We can put this idea in various ways; we can say you've got to *find* them or *coin* them or *fresh-mint* them. We can use any word we want to describe the idea of inventing a phrase at the very moment it is uttered. The vital thing is that the speaker must *need* the phrase. He must not think of such phrases as simply words that pre-exist in the text. They have got to be words that he finds as he utters them. (Barton 1984: 18)

The idea that the character chooses the language can also suggest the reverse – namely that the language defines the character, that everything we know about the character comes from the language itself, not from some "character" preexisting somewhere. Peter Brook made the point in *The Empty Space* (1969: 13) when he wrote about the deadening effect of labels when acting. Brook recounts the episode when he found a woman in his audience "who had neither read nor seen *King Lear*" and asked her to read aloud Goneril's first speech:

> She read it very simply – and the speech itself emerged full of eloquence and charm. I then explained that it was supposed to be the speech of a wicked woman and suggested her reading every word for hypocrisy. She tried to do so, and the audience saw what a hard unnatural wrestling with the simple music of the words was involved when she sought to act to a definition:

> Sir, I love you more than words can wield the matter;
> Dearer than eyesight, space, and liberty;
> Beyond what can be valued, rich or rare;
> No less than life, with grace, health, beauty, honour;
> As much as child e'er loved, or father found;
> A love that makes breath poor, and speech unable;
> Beyond all manner of so much I love you.

Anyone can try this for himself. Taste it on the tongue. The words are those of a lady of style and breeding accustomed to expressing herself in public, someone with ease and social aplomb. As for clues to her character, only the façade is presented and this, we see, is elegant and attractive. (Brook 1969: 14)

The example has stayed with me because it seems so "right" and yet so difficult to achieve. But while students are often willing to reach quickly for labels and definitions, actors are, I think, more likely to try to find the character without those labels. Perhaps that's because the actor is looking for the way in which the play is about his or her character; one thinks of Ralph from *Shakespeare in Love* who, when asked about the play he's in, begins with "Well, there's this Nurse," since that's his role. While one can see the limitations, as well as the comic absurdity, of the "It's all about me" approach, I'd like to suggest its value as well.

When an actor focuses on a character, he or she may well invent a backstory, finding details that are congruent with the text, but not necessitated by the text. So, for instance, generations of actors playing Peter Quince in *A Midsummer Night's Dream* have suggested that Quince is not only the director of "Pyramus and Thisbe," but perhaps the playwright as well. Such a "backstory" then underpins Quince's repeated insistence on getting his precious words absolutely right, and I have seen a number of Quinces who not only correct Bottom's "odious savours sweet" (3.1.77) in rehearsal, as the text dictates, but then add a silently mouthed "odorous, odorous" when Bottom/Pyramus gets the same line wrong in the same way during performance.

While Quince's "backstory" has become very familiar in productions of *A Midsummer Night's Dream*, I've seen only one production of *Much Ado About Nothing* that has reimagined a character who usually seems merely part of the plot. It's difficult to think of any criticism that considers why Borachio comes up with the plan to slander Hero, other than his association with John the Bastard and, presumably, his obligation or willingness to participate in whatever evil John wishes. But in 2006, the production of *Much Ado* directed by Marianne Elliott in Stratford-upon-Avon quietly set up the possibility that Borachio was a potential rival for Hero's affections, and might actually be interested in Hero for himself. Set in 1950s Cuba, with soldiers dressed in reasonably look-alike khakis (only small epaulets at first distinguished Claudio's uniform from Borachio's), the production first focused on Borachio when he "magically" produced a flower (description from RSC rehearsal notes, April 25, 2006) and handed it to Hero as she followed her father offstage and she blushed and smiled. Borachio was young, personable, and likeable (Jamie Ballard also played Mercutio that season and understudied Benedick); his report to Don John in 1.3 about what he had overheard became less simple exposition, and more an indication that Borachio was personally interested in the news that Hero was going to be married to Claudio. In 2.1, where all the men appeared wearing elaborate masks, with Don Pedro in a lion's mask (thus emphasizing his leadership role) and Benedick in a monkey's mask, Borachio's was that of a "sad clown" while Claudio's mask is described in the rehearsal notes as "a Jester, with 1 horn." Borachio danced with Hero before Don Pedro cut in on the line "Lady, will you walk a bout with your friend?" (2.1.80–1) and the audience could see (1) that Hero was having a lot of fun dancing with Borachio, and (2) that Borachio felt outranked and upset when Don Pedro took over as the dancer. Hero seemed genuinely taken aback by being wooed by Don Pedro, who was clearly older and stiffer in manner than either Claudio or Borachio. Both of the younger men were picked out in spotlights, watching Hero during her dance with Don Pedro. Borachio's sense of exclusion increased when he began dancing with Margaret only to have Benedick cut in on him (the promptbook shows that Margaret's exchanges, 2.1.94–105, with Benedick and Balthasar, in both Q and F, were reassigned, so that Borachio got the first three and Benedick took over with the last two). Thus, by the time Borachio reappeared in 2.2, he had a fairly large chip on his shoulder, and his reason for "crossing" the marriage was the revenge of an enlisted soldier on a man of similar age but higher rank and lots more privilege. Even his drinking in 3.3, where he tells Conrad what he has done, seemed to be a result of his feeling hurt, rather than simply a visualization of his name.

The payoff for this reading came much later in the play, first in 4.2 when Borachio heard that Hero had died, and was obviously very upset (one might note that he doesn't speak in the last part of the scene while Conrad attacks Dogberry as a "coxcomb" and an "ass"), and then even more tellingly in 5.1 when he confesses what he has done. Twice in that speech (5.1.226–38) he refers to himself as a villain, he asks at the beginning for Claudio to kill him, and concludes by saying "I desire nothing but the reward of a villain," probably death. If Borachio is merely an extension of Don John, then this kind of repentance makes little sense (although one might imagine a Borachio smart enough to realize that a show of repentance might be helpful); but if he is, like Jamie Ballard's Borachio, someone who has acted out of hurt feelings and now sees the consequences of his behavior, so much so that he even insists "by my soul" (5.1.295) that Margaret was innocent, then his long confession becomes a way for him to unburden himself of the secret he has been carrying, and the sincerity of Ballard's delivery underlined that interpretation. Such a reading is, admittedly, a minor point in the play, so much so that none of the newspaper reviews even mentioned it. But that reading of Borachio lingers in my mind, offering a way to make sense of what otherwise seems merely a plot necessity, and increasing the extent to which we see the privilege-based callousness of both Don Pedro and Claudio.

While we may not know exactly how such interpretations come about – Borachio's flower doesn't appear in the original prop list although as early as February 10, 2006, the rehearsal notes indicate "Borachio should have a very sad face on his mask" – the rethinking of any role may come from the director, or from a moment in rehearsal, and often from the actor's own personality and experiences. Roger Allam, writing about the Mercutio he created for John Caird's 1983–4 production of *Romeo and Juliet*, recalls, "I began to recall my own experience when I was Mercutio's age (late teens I decided, a year or two older than Romeo) as a pupil at a public school called Christ's Hospital," and goes on to describe the "strange blend of raucousness and intellect among the cloisters, the fighting, the sport, and general sense of rebelliousness, of not wishing to seem conventional (this was the sixties)." From that background – admittedly one that he may have reconstructed or even mythologized – he also found a sense of male relationships: "The real vessel for emotional exchange, whether sexually expressed or not, were [*sic*] our own intense friendships with each other. ... What I was seeing in Mercutio was his grief and pain at impending separation from Romeo, so I suppose I sensitized myself to that period of my life when male bonding was at its strongest for me" (Allam 1988: 109).

In addition to this illuminating through-line for the character, sensing Mercutio's fear that he is losing Romeo's attention (and affection) led Allam to find a way to play the Queen Mab speech, not as Mercutio "being somehow taken over by his own extraordinary invention," but as Mercutio's attempt to "get some response" from Romeo (Allam 1988: 112, 113), goading him with the images, pushing him to respond, even though that response was actually a rejection that left Mercutio "very hurt and angry." As Allam puts it, "once I had perceived Mercutio as being hurt and indeed jealous of Romeo's love for Rosaline, I did not then find the Queen Mab speech isolated, but part of a continuing and passionate argument, and therefore possible to make sense of" (p. 114). And Mercutio's feelings for Romeo also led Allam to construct a rationale for intervening in the duel – getting rid of Tybalt so as to "bind Romeo to himself still further" (p. 117). Even though I didn't get to see this production of *Romeo and Juliet*, the ideas that Roger Allam's essay presents have become part of my under-standing of the play, especially when students ask about the Queen Mab speech. My response – or sometimes a paper topic – is to ask "What is Mercutio trying to do here?", not to get students to recreate Allam's essay, but to think about the speech both as a reaction to and a persuasion of Romeo.

A similar rethinking of a major character – and an even more problematic one – came with Juliet Stevenson's portrayal of Cressida in the 1985 RSC production of *Troilus and Cressida*, directed by Howard Davies. Stevenson was aware that her reading of Cressida might have been provoked by a defen-sive reaction in the rehearsal room, something she saw that happened to female rather than male actors: "You react against the way tradition and prejudice have stigmatised them – Cressida the whore, Kate the shrew – and every time they're judged you feel protective. Perhaps too protective. So you might end up playing a Cressida who is above reproach and a Kate who's neurotic, not shrewish" (quoted in Rutter 1988: xviii). But, speak-ing about the production in a talk to the RSC Summer School in the summer of 1985, Stevenson explained her sense of Cressida as someone who became aware that she had been used – and she based her argument not on defensive stereotypes but on the play's language. She spoke of Cressida's "maxim" in her first soliloquy, "Therefore this maxim out of love I teach: / Achievement is command; ungained, beseech" (1.2. 294–5), lines so seemingly confident or knowing or even cynical that generations of critics, working from this line (and indeed from the entire soliloquy) have argued that Cressida is a dissembler from the beginning of the play. But Stevenson reminded the audience that after Troilus spends the night with Cressida and then hears from Aeneas that the Trojan lords have decided to give Cressida to the Greeks in exchange for Antenor, his reaction is "How my achievements mock me!" (4.2.71). Is that all she is to him, asked

Stevenson, an "achievement"? Even though Cressida isn't on stage to hear Troilus's words, she may easily figure out that she is something he's won (and now lost), but not important enough to fight for. Stevenson's words have stayed with me, forcing me to look again at how Cressida is treated, how surrounded by men at all times (there is never another woman on stage with her), how little choice she has once she's been turned over to the Greeks.

Both Allam's essay and Stevenson's talk stand out for me as moments when an actor, thinking about a character, made me rethink that character, and his or her place in the play. And, importantly, both actors connect the ideas about character directly to the language: Allam moves from personal images and experience to dealing with a major speech, while Stevenson juxtaposes two lines, one by Cressida, one about Cressida, to raise questions about who is betraying whom. So, too, for students – starting with questions about characters leads them inevitably to paying more attention to language. Long speeches cease to be impenetrable blocks on the page but rather moments when characters might try to overwhelm their listeners or wait for answers. *Troilus and Cressida* 1.3 is almost a case-study of language as deliberate obfuscation when Agamemnon, Nestor, and Ulysses use lengthy speeches to cover up/repress unpalatable truths about the Greek failure to take Troy. Henry V's threats to the citizens of Harfleur include the repeated line "What is it then to me" (3.3.15, 19), perhaps not merely as a rhetorical device but as a way of trying to get an answer – a playing I remember from Iain Glen's 1994 Henry V. Single lines can become amazingly charged, as witness the variety of readings possible for Shylock's "I am content" (4.1.391) from Olivier's strangled scream to David Suchet's deliberately cheerful delivery, ending in a question mark, as if to indicate, "Is that what you want me to say?" to Henry Goodman's long pause before he returns to the reality of the courtroom and whispers his response to Portia's worried question; all of these readings are visible on videotape, Olivier's and Goodman's from National Theatre productions, and Suchet's in Barton's *Playing Shakespeare*. Seeing what actors can do with lines – and learning, through class performance, to interpret the lines themselves, both with voice and body – students become excited explorers of the multiple levels of the text. They learn not what the text means – in an absolutist way – but what it *can* mean. With actors for colleagues, with theatre performances always suggesting new possibilities for thinking about characters, and with students sensing their power to collaborate in making meaning as they talk about or rehearse the text, is it any wonder that I am drawn, like my students, to ask questions about the people of the plays?

References and Further Reading

Allam, Roger (1988). "Mercutio in *Romeo and Juliet.*" In Russell Jackson and Robert Smallwood (Eds). *Players of Shakespeare 2* (pp. 107–19). Cambridge, UK: Cambridge University Press.

Barton, John (1984). *Playing Shakespeare.* London: Methuen Drama.

Bevington, David (Ed.) (2003). *The Complete Works of Shakespeare.* New York: Longman.

Brook, Peter (1969). *The Empty Space.* New York: Atheneum.

Brown, John Russell (1966). *Shakespeare's Plays in Performance.* London: Edward Arnold.

Gilbert, Miriam (1979). "*Richard II* at Stratford: Role-Playing as Metaphor." In Philip C. McGuire and David A. Samuelson (Eds). *Shakespeare: The Theatrical Dimension* (pp. 85–101). New York: AMS Press.

Maguire, Laurie E. (2004). *Studying Shakespeare: A Guide to the Plays.* Oxford: Blackwell.

Osborne, Charles (1990). "Review of Richard II." *Daily Telegraph*, November 9, 1990. Reprinted in *Theatre Record* 10:23: 1553.

Rutter, Carol (1988). *Clamorous Voices: Shakespeare's Women Today.* London: The Women's Press.

Sinfield, Alan (1992). *Faultlines: Cultural Materialism and the Politics of Dissident Reading.* Oxford: Clarendon Press.

Styan, J. L. (1967). *Shakespeare's Stagecraft.* Cambridge, UK: Cambridge University Press.

Styan, J. L. (1969). *The Elements of Drama.* Cambridge, UK: Cambridge University Press.

7

The Last Shakespeare Picture Show or Going to the Barricades

Barbara Hodgdon

A day or two before my first class as a teaching assistant for the required English 101 course, I went to the English department chair: "I've never done this before . . . ," to which he replied, "I don't worry about you at all: you're an actor." But how was I to act on that first day, facing 30 first-year students who were probably resistant writers and readers? The role had no script; I badly needed one. A more experienced grad student instructor saved the day: all I had to do was smile, introduce myself, hand them a syllabus, give out an assignment, smile, and leave the room. How sensible! After all, I did have a syllabus (painstakingly constructed in a workshop), and smiling (twice, book-ending my performance, so to speak) seemed an especially good idea: I might even pretend to pose a question or two, open up a conversation. So armed, I walked into the classroom, seized the lectern (to still my shaking hands), and, performing my first smile, looked out to see a blur of faces and bodies. I dried. Handing out the syllabus was not possible: I couldn't let go of the lectern. Although I may have mumbled something about the first assignment, all I remember is that after the room had emptied, I was still there, frozen to the lectern. "Fail again. Fail better": Beckett's line drifts through my head. Just as the persistence of this memory of high anxiety suggests teaching's existential risks, so too does writing about teaching: putting oneself, quite literally, on the line seems potentially hazardous.

So how to begin? How to start? I need another cup of coffee . . . another script . . . another story.

"We tell ourselves stories in order to live," writes Joan Didion in *The White Album*, speaking of how, given the events of the 1960s, suddenly the script that she knew, the one she was meant to follow, no longer made any sense. Reading Didion, I encountered my own history; to adapt Alan Bennett in *The History Boys*, it was as if a hand had come out and taken mine. We also tell ourselves stories in order to teach – murmuring interior monologues about our love/hate relationships with why and how we do what we do, justifying ourselves to ourselves. But there have been many moments – and we live in one as I write – when, as the world outside the academy seems urgently to need my attention and commitment, I wonder about spending my life teaching 400-year-old plays. Plagued by twinges of white liberal guilt, I worry that I should be going to the barricades. But since I'm not exactly sure where they are or what I might do to change the world when I get there, in the meantime I'll say what I can, from the place where I sit.

There is always a dream of the perfect class, perhaps existing in some parallel universe: I've yet to find it, though once I came close. It was not a Shakespeare course but an introduction to theory, and thinking back on it from a distance, I did very little except generate a reading list. From the beginning, this group of 25 students took control of their own learning: often, I'd come into the classroom to find them eagerly talking with one another – not about the latest hot item of campus or personal gossip but about the day's readings. Everybody read everything; everybody argued through and around Barthes, Foucault, Derrida, Freud, and Butler – and begged for more; they exchanged and edited one another's written work. So now, when preparing classes, I sketch out three possible scenarios, the first of which is modeled on my memories of that experience, recollected in tranquility. I walk in (avoid the lectern), smile, say good morning – and ask what they've discovered, sometimes playing off a question I've previously posed, "priming the pump," in Miriam Gilbert's apt metaphor. I then become auditor to a conversation that may or may not include me, one in which the students are doing intellectual work, making knowledge, finding out what they do and do not know. I call it silent, or invisible teaching – something I learned from one of my children. As a third-grader, he'd become fascinated with Greek gods and heroes and asked to go to Boston's Museum of Fine Arts, where his teacher had said he could see them. For some reason, rather than pointing to objects I thought important or reading out captions, I just followed him from "the Greeks" to "the Egyptians," where, after just a few moments, he said, "The Greeks thought of themselves differently than the Egyptians" (the start of an on-going conversation).

The second scenario leans towards (loosely) Socratic dialogue, building not from a proposition, but from a question that spurs a train of thought – one that (ideally) leads, not to the "right answer" but to a response that provokes another question (finding questions trumps knowing answers, or even having *Hamlet*, Freud, Foucault, or Greenblatt in one's hip pocket). This class features occasional minilectures – fleshing out a point, bringing early modern contexts, as well as critical and theoretical perspectives drawn from secondary readings, to the table. If neither of these strategies works – if none of the questions goes anywhere, if the longueurs seem to stretch towards infinity and the room goes dead – the fall-back position is "all about me" – or all about me + Shakespeare: I do stand-up routines, Shakespearean improvs. On the one hand, this class panders to the student who wants to be taught, to the passive learner, the student-as-client who is paying for professorial performances (I'm not a good teacher for this version of the Gentleman's C student). On the other hand, it's not pedagogically empty, for not only does it offer an opportunity to forge a direct connection to performance but it also models the end result of the process Skip Shand calls "actorly reading." And after all, there's a long history of anecdotes about famous teachers of Shakespeare who, Bottom-like, continue to enchant student-audiences by playing all the parts, doing the words in different voices, playing to – and for – pure pleasure. Even for our information-age students, talking constantly on cell phones or plugged into iPods, attuned to their own voices or those of other media, there's something mesmerizing about the *sound* of Shakespeare. It's compelling for me, too, as I wait out the time (two lines? four?) for the room to go still (at best), listening to a little touch of Henry V or Lady M or Hamlet in the early afternoon. Nobody knows that it's not really me showing off: I'm ventriloquizing all the performers I've ever heard. It's playback time.

Walking to my office after a class, and on throughout the day, it's also playback time: the instant replay of what, exactly, worked and what did not. Even when I sense a vague smell of success, when the verbal tap-dance seemed to be a hit, I recall the (perhaps apocryphal) story about Laurence Olivier, sitting in front of his dressing-room mirror after playing Othello, deeply depressed. Told that it had been amazing, he replied that he knew it was but didn't know why. It's different, though, when the carefully imagined plan or the script goes limp – rather like the bouquet of dandelions painstakingly picked for your mother but wilted by the time you get home. None of the questions seems to be the right question, the one that unlocks one idea, another, and then another, starting a chain reaction. Next day (or via email), I offer footnotes or outtakes to previous classroom performances, backing and filling, returning to points that had seemed to fly by everyone's left ear. What is it, exactly, that will invite students to linger longer in front of the words, convince them that close reading is rather like gossiping with a close acquaintance, where you have an opportunity to say what's what and to think about what it might mean. How to convey the idea that one's impressions become more vivid in direct relation to the trouble one takes with that lingering? How to give – or even package – the gift of discovery? Yet even if I bank a particular trick of the trade, it may not be repeatable, for the next term's students will constitute an entirely different classroom dynamic: the course may have the same title and number, but it's always a "new" course. The urgent questions remain.

So how to begin – again? Who said it first: "If Shakespeare were alive today, he would be writing screenplays." My colleague Jim Burnstein, the scriptwriter for *Renaissance Man* (1994), credits Russell Fraser, his teacher, but it may have been Laurence Olivier who first remarked that if Shakespeare were around now he'd be writing new television comedies, or soap-opera cameo parts for aging actors. Certainly by the late 1960s and early 1970s, the idea that Shakespeare wrote "cinematically" was circulating in academic culture, spawning courses titled "Shakespeare *on* Film" or (eventually) "Shakespeare *and* Film." Although "Shakespeare" stands as the primary term, both historically and as the "source" for the films, there is, I believe, an important distinction between viewing the films as illustrative footnotes to Shakespeare's text (and/or performance) and tilting the binary to privilege that somewhat slippery and elusive genre, the Shakespeare film. For "Shakespeare and Film," the most recent incarnation of an upper-level course cross-listed in Screen Arts and Cultures and English at Michigan, course-work focuses on considering Shakespeare's plays as pretexts (rather than prescriptions), on tracking and attempting to theorize the various processes of adaptation at work in each film text, and on directing attention to how the specific textualities and technologies of two performance media work together to generate historically situated cultural meanings.[1]

Just as the show at the local cineplex opens with adverts and trailers, the first class meeting features previews of coming attractions – "clip art," in Laurie Osborne's neat phrase. First, I juxtapose Herbert Beerbohm Tree's death scene from *King John* (1899), the first Shakespeare film, to a recent

30-second Nextel TV commercial, *Romeo and Juliet* on cell phones (the major plot points are there; it's high on romance and action – arguably, what the play has become, post-Baz Luhrmann). Not only do both advertise different Shakespeares, they also map historical territory, from silent films and films that record stage performance to sound films that play with or erase Shakespearean language and open onto digital culture, including video games as well as the realm of YouTube, FaceBook, and MySpace where today's students live. Then I pose several global questions. To what extent do film and television adaptations of his plays express and determine our culture's rewriting/rewrighting and reading/misreading of Shakespeare? What influence does this have on how we respond to and write about both the plays and the films? Is it, perhaps, after years of serious moviegoing, that we inevitably imagine Shakespeare filmically – that is, instead of speaking of *adapting* Shakespeare to film, are we already embedded within a discursive world that conceives easily, even "naturally," of a cinematic Shakespeare?

Harking back to that first, long-ago class plan, I could stop here, remind students of the next day's screening and follow-up writing assignment, smile, and leave the room. Instead, screening a second set of clips – the opening sequences of Orson Welles's *The Tragedy of Othello, the Moor of Venice* (1952) and Tim Blake Nelson's *O* (2001) – tracks another historical move: from art-house film to mainstream mass-culture product aimed at a niche audience, the teen market. Now it's time to put the students to work, to find out how they think, and to urge them towards understanding that this course is "about" bringing something to the course materials, about their learning *process*. This also keys into what I want students to take away with them: a degree of expertise and ownership that has to do with becoming a responsible and responsive reader of several kinds of texts – the film text and Shakespeare's playtext, the play on the page – and with the ways each interfaces with the other. This "real" work, then, begins with an adaptation of Miriam Gilbert's brilliant opening exercise, "What's Going On Here?" – the most perennially successful move I know, the base and pillar of my thinking about teaching, not just Shakespeare, but any dramatic, literary, lit-crit, theoretical, performance or film text.[2] *What*, I ask, are you seeing and hearing? *How* do these sequences invite you to see and hear? And how does image/music/text (tucked away in the course pack, essays by Roland Barthes are in their future) invite you to construct meanings? "Invite" is an important verb choice here: all I can do is hand out invitations, put materials on offer; whether or not the invitation solicits a forthcoming RSVP, so to speak, is not in my control. At best, initial responses to these questions lay down the foundation for what, ideally, will be a collaborative endeavor: film majors will begin teaching English majors how to use the vocabulary of film language; English majors will keep reminding film majors of "words, words, words." There is, of course, a built-in trick here – for although neither opening sequence is scripted by Shakespeare, each not only "comes from" the play but also sets up particular frames for looking and for the look.

This initial diagnostic exercise in looking opens onto two others. The first two films track the history of Shakespearean histories: two *Henry V*s, Olivier's (1944) and Kenneth Branagh's (1989), reiterate the move from art-house to "popular," mass-market film. Punning on Norman Rabkin's (1977) title (his essay is also in the course pack), I named it "Ducking and Rabbiting." To begin with Olivier's film, of course, is to begin with what many consider "authentic" – that is, British – Shakespearean acting, right in Shakespeare's own theatre; to imagine what a performance looked like "back then"; and to cast a critical eye on how, over half a century ago, theatre historians and popular myth conspired to create an early modern theatre filled with eagerly responsive (at least to Falstaff) groundlings. Even more significant, however, was the extent to which students immediately became invested in decoding the relations between theatre and cinema, between "fairy-tale" worlds (the French court) and cinematic realism (Agincourt eve, the battle), "stagey" performances and naturalistic acting. Moreover, the US's current engagement in a political, religious, and military conflict outside (as well as inside) its borders offered an ideal opportunity to get students thinking – and talking about – parallel ideologies. Certainly they had only to see Olivier's Henry to know instinctively what ethical luggage he was carrying: the freight his image took on made the point that the settled morality/ideology and accepted beliefs which lay behind his 1944 film are as much over now as the set of beliefs and assumptions that circulated in Elizabethan culture around 1599–1600. Not only, then, did Branagh's post-Vietnam Henry push another history, as well as different textualities and configurations of King Henry, into view but also connections students made among histories, images, ideology, and performance carried forward to frame the next film, Orson Welles's *Chimes at Midnight* (1965), where Welles's signature stylistics – long take, tracking camera, deep focus, simultaneous movement of actors and camera – and, of course, Falstaff's inimitable presence, reimagine "Shakespeare-history."

In this course, students view 12 films (screened outside of class time), write six one-page, single-spaced responses to films of their choice (three before and three following a midterm break), two papers (c. 2,000–2,500 words) and an end-of-term project they fashion themselves, which may be a short film, a compilation/collage, or a substantially longer paper. Conceived as practice in close reading/formal analysis, the short responses (ideally) generate material that travels into and can be expanded on in the two short papers. Due at class time the day following a film screening, they (also ideally) serve to energize classroom discussion the next day, when, throwing a sequence up on the screen (I'm lucky to have a projectionist who plays all the clips), I say, "Talk to me" – and if they don't, it becomes an occasion to model (ever-deepening) analysis, focusing on elements of mise-en-scène, then editing, then sound. An example:

> Where is Shakespeare in this film? How does Olivier's film use, manage, adapt, ignore, use up Shakespeare's play? Focus what you want to say on a single sequence or moment – a small slice of the film. Try to discern how camera position and movement as well as diegetic and extra-diegetic sound engage in meaning-making.

The "brief" for ensuing responses follows this basic model but is particularly gauged to each film; the most challenging of the writing assignments, these also were the most successful: inviting (even forcing?) students to make every word count not only engages them, from the outset, with editing their writing but also models writing as process, as rewriting. In this particular course, nearly everyone wrote about Kurosawa's *Throne of Blood* (1957), Tim Blake Nelson's *O* (2001), and Michael Almereyda's *Hamlet* (2000). The final response put the pedagogical ball, so to speak, in their court: "As one part of a final examination for this class, you are inviting students to write about a sequence from Taymor's *Titus*. In particular, you want responses which will engage with the idea of 'cinema as subject' that we have been exploring these last few weeks. What sequence would you choose and why?"

So far, I have been concerned with strategies for showing students how the vocabularies of film language mediate Shakespearean "appearances" – working, so to speak, "outside," or slightly at an angle to, Shakespeare's writing. Perhaps it's time to acknowledge a pedagogical heresy. I used to invest heavily in "covering the play" – at least until I asked, "What, exactly, am I covering it with?" Now, while I expect that students will read each of the plays, "the text" is not where we begin but, rather, the place to which we (repeatedly) return. Although doing so risks substituting visual for verbal complexity, at least to some extent this reverse trajectory takes pressure off the fear of the words – a fear that, even among the most articulate students, sometimes can strike them dumb. For *Macbeth*, "the text" comes at them through Trevor Nunn's film of the 1978 RSC small-scale production, starring Ian McKellen, Judi Dench, and others – a film that's very much "about" speaking Shakespeare (among other things). Although it is usual to consider the cinematic image as all-powerful, that is less the case with a Shakespeare film, in which vocal performance constitutes one of the central facts of the film experience: arguably, it is sound that makes the "Shakespearean body" whole. Moreover, there's a further charge here beyond listening to masterful actors: for students who know McKellen primarily as Gandalf in *The Lord of the Rings* trilogy (2001–3) or as Magneto in the *X-Men* films (2000–6), watching him perform Shakespeare not only is nothing less than revelatory but also provides an opportunity to explore how actors make the words do work. "Work" is a rehearsal verb – and that's appropriate here, for what we're investigating, after all, are the processes of complementarity and exchange between verbal and visual image.

Teaching *Macbeth* long ago, I mixed up a gallon or so of stage blood and had everyone dip their hands in it – an experiment that took metaphor too far: after two or three minutes, several students bolted from the room to wash their hands. Now I let Roman Polanski's film (1971) – and Jim Burnstein's account of his own romance with Shakespeare and how he learned to write film scripts by reading Polanski's – drive home the sensual links between word and sight.[3] In Polanski's opening scene, a blood-red sun rises over an empty beach, a gnarled stick appears in right frame, and the witches gather: digging a hole in the sand, they bury a noose and a severed hand, in which they place a dagger, then pour blood over it. Burnstein tracks the next few appearances of the noose: the chain of office Ross brings to Macbeth, the iron ring around Cawdor's neck as he jumps to his death, Duncan's empty crown, rolling across the floor in the murder room. Later, "Follow the noose" becomes a course mantra – a game to play with any number of films, whether tracing the cage/net images in Welles's *Othello* or the repetitive religious iconography in Luhrmann's *Romeo + Juliet*. For just as Shakespeare lays down ideas, images, and actions in an opening scene or scenes that continue to resonate or detonate throughout, filmmakers lay down image and sound tracks that repeat and repeat in the brain, become hard-wired onto narrative. Established through working at Polanski's *Macbeth*, that idea travels forward to energize looking at Akira

Kurosawa's *Throne of Blood* (1957), where the beauty and economy of image and the haunting strangeness of the sound track invite students to look and listen with a difference: all of the students who wrote brief responses fixated on the image of Lady Asaji, the swish of her dress as she moves across the floor, the eerie shot where the camera, holding on the door, waits for her to emerge from darkness.

So juxtaposed, these three *Macbeth*s illustrate, and riff on, the various modes of compromise that undergird adaptational processes: Shakespeare with his language, Shakespeare transformed through an autobiographical lens, Shakespeare without his language, translated through the spatial conventions and performative disciplines of Japanese theatre. Adaptation, transformation, translation, tradaptation (Michel Garneau's useful term): however one names it, it's not new. After all, it's a kind of neo-humanist endeavor. Just as Tudor humanism brought together sixteenth-century intellectuals in a project of excavating, and reusing, the classics, turning their gaze towards stylistic as well as ethical matters, so too might study-ing Shakespearean adaptations be considered as somewhat like that pro-ject. The operative phrase here is "somewhat like" – for there's no direct one-to-one relationship between sixteenth-century humanism and present-day academic humanism, except, perhaps, that both focus on linking edu-cation to civic virtues. Does it matter what this archeological process of rereading is called? In some sense, yes, it does. Linda Hutcheon (2006) calls it "palimpsestuous recreation" – a term that neatly captures the sense of multiple overlaps and erasures that mark the tensions between several media, several sites of cultural capital, and so generate a "product" which is both authoritative and original. Students picked up the idea, spoke of the presence or lack of "aura" (Walter Benjamin's famous term) or agency in particular films. Increasingly, and especially towards the end of term as they began working on final projects, they began to see themselves as pretending to "be" Shakespeare – or at least working like him, repeating his practice of raiding Plautus, Boccaccio, Sidney's *Arcadia*, Gascoigne's *Supposes* (itself translated from Ariosto's *I Suppositi*), Chaucer, Holinshed's *Chronicles*. As though imitating the Shakespeare of Marc Norman's and Tom Stoppard's knowing and witty screenplay for Madden's *Shakespeare in Love* (1998), who picks up bits and shards of phrases overheard on the street, gets advice from fellow-actors on titles and characters' names (and decides to leave out the dog), students raided the films they had seen, incorpor-ated, replayed, and reenvisioned flashes of the sights and sounds they had admired in their own recompositional practices.

Pretending to "be" Shakespeare – a version of Stephen Greenblatt's desire to speak with the dead, a phrase that rehearses humanistic aims (Greenblatt 1988: 1) – has its dangers. At least to some extent, those androcentric aims, focused on humans and human possibility, inflect and infect teaching, so that the idea of the individual – or, in the case of Shakespeare, the character – becomes paramount. In a worst case understanding of this scenario, what students hear and all too easily latch onto is that adaptation's virtues have to do with making Shakespeare "relevant" (I cringe when I hear it or see it appear in a paper, and try to outlaw the 1960s mantra), for where that leads is to "Shakespeare really is all about me." But to some extent students are right about that. Taking place in recognizably postmodern worlds, a number of recent Shakespeare films, aimed precisely at the 15–25-year-old prime market niche, seem designed to close the great gap in time between an early modern Shakespeare and the newest reinvention of Jan Kott's (1965) Shakespeare as our contemporary. Students viewing Baz Luhrmann's *William Shakespeare's Romeo + Juliet*, Tim Blake Nelson's *O*, or Michael Almereyda's *Hamlet* can see avatars of themselves "playing" at and with Shakespeare. What is it like to be Juliet, Desdemona, Othello, Iago? If I were Hamlet, what would I do? Students want to know: it's a way for them to explore alternate identities at a time when their own are still in flux.

Confronting this phenomenon head on, I devote a class to *Hamlet*-ing – screen an archive of actors performing "To be or not to be." Once again, I remind students that clip art constitutes a practice that does a disservice to film by using it to illustrate another argument – exactly what I rail against in other settings about using performance to illustrate text. I'm not sure there's a responsible way around this, but I do think we need to be aware of how we're doing what we're doing with film clips – and to make students aware of it. Once again, I'm advertising, offering trailers for films other than those we look at in detail. And once again, one objective has to do with inviting students to think historically – to engage with a double history: one that looks back to look forward, Janus-faced, like "Shakespeare-history." This "history" begins with a hook in the form of two jokes: the moment from *Last Action Hero* where Olivier's Hamlet gets transcoded by the bored boy in the classroom into Arnold Schwarzenegger, who solves the riddle of something rotten in the state of Denmark by blowing up Elsinore and "takin' out the trash"; and the audition sequence from Branagh's *A Midwinter's Tale*, where the actor auditioning for Hamlet announces that "Hamlet is not just Hamlet – oh no . . . Hamlet is Bosnia . . . my grandmother . . . geology." Going to a silly place is one way of calling attention

to the accumulated baggage that has adhered to this famous soliloquy, perhaps perceived as the most "authentically Shakespearean" of all utterances.
What, I ask, are the specificities of each actor's behavior? How does each
actor make the words do work? And how does each film invite us to look
and hear: how are we pulled close to or pushed away from "the character"? The performance compendium begins with Olivier: the famous shot
right through the head that opens onto a languorous reading in voice-over,
one of the most powerful speaking positions in film. It's all "about"
Shakespeare – all about the words, floating outside of the body, outside of
history. Then Richard Burton, throwing the words away, his performance
hasty, marked by a single gesture – brushing his hands across his face as
though to efface presence on "shuffled off this mortal coil" – that tells it
all. Mel Gibson, down in the catacombs, his active body moving through
his grief as he leans into his father's tomb; Kenneth Branagh, mirrored three
times; Adrian Lester, writing the words back onto his body; Ethan Hawke
(from Almereyda's 2000 film), where "To be" happens twice – once on
Hamlet's video diary, as he holds a gun to his mouth; again as he roams
the "Action" aisle of a Blockbuster video store. One student remarked, "That
speech is so loaded with previous performance . . . by remembering previous performances we form an intertextuality which we bring into our
viewing of each version."

Riffing on Almereyda's film, one of the last three screened in the course,
together with Luhrmann's *Romeo + Juliet* and Julie Taymor's *Titus*, films
in which cinema itself becomes a subject, working at times to trump
"Shakespeare," another student wrote:

> The video confessions are an electronic adaptation of soliloquies. . . . Video
> is Hamlet's weapon: exposing and documenting is the action Hamlet takes
> and his final triumph: as the main players perish, the memories left on video
> which we again see at the end, are his alone, a visualization of the story that
> he asks Horatio to tell – that is, Hamlet has co-opted the space of the future.
> And the final shot of the teleprompter, scrolling the words just spoken
> onscreen, effectively places Shakespeare himself in the role of "prompter"
> for the film. While this in itself seems fairly obvious (that Shakespeare's
> words from the page dictate what we see and hear onscreen), the prompt's
> specificity as part of an electronic medium – the medium of the future –
> seems to suggest that that very mode may dictate life itself.

I'm bragging a bit now, and omitting to mention students such as Cut-
and-Paste Carrie, whose writing came straight from Wikipedia and who
(after repeated urgings) finally came to my office in the last week of classes

and informed me that she hadn't understood anything all term. It's never an absolute win: failing better also can mean failing to measure, or even cross, the distance between the front and back of the room. Nevertheless, the above example of the kinds of thoughtful work students can generate remains one of the rewards of teaching. So do off-hand comments, which read less like applause for a successful performance than as appreciation for a good dinner. What I once thought might be acting has become more like cooking: assembling and ordering the ingredients that will produce intellectual pleasures. "Taking this course," one student remarked, "made me realize that I want to become a Shakespearean film actor or direct and produce a Shakespeare film." As Hector says in Alan Bennett's *The History Boys*, "Pass it on."

But where to conclude? Perhaps most appropriately, with the question of how to end a course – adapting current pedagogical jargon, how to measure outcomes. Long ago, I gave up giving final examinations, largely because I always hated them but also because the exam, which presents an obstacle that looms in the student's future, plays primarily to one set of skills: the ability to remember facts and dates (I was deeply frightened by time lines in the third grade), match passages to speakers, write short or long essays on command. Exams test whether students have "done the reading": they imply completion, closure. To be sure, some students are absolute ace test-takers, but I'm not convinced that the examination situation invites them to do their best thinking. Moreover, I don't want to close off students' thinking, give them the sense that they can chalk up Shakespeare and put him into a convenient compartment: I want them to take away a sense of accomplishment, yes, but I also want them to continue thinking – to ask more questions and to make connections not just to other coursework but also to their experiences outside the university. Teaching Shakespeare and Film also has made me rethink the efficacy of the long paper as a culmination for the course. Some students did choose to write them – and to try their hand at the single rider attached to the final assignment: a self-reflexive component in which they assessed their critical practice.

What was striking, however, about this particular course was the number of students who chose not to write "an English-paper paper" for their final project but to play with Shakespeare, to do in some way, shape, or form what we had been doing all term: adapt Shakespeare, use, use up, or discard his texts. There's something about giving students the freedom to get rid of that text, which studying film invites, that, somewhat ironically and magically, not only sends them right back to it but also provides an open invitation to go beyond it. When I asked one of the most thoughtful students what she thought the difference was between writing a paper and doing something else, she said, "It's the connection – the opportunity to make something, not just to tell about it." Making. Doing. Showing – or showing off – not Telling. Some wrote film scripts: in an update of Macbeth, titled *An Election to Die For*, the Macbeth figure was running for president, aided by three witches named William, Walter, and Wendy, execs at Scotland Petroleum, Inc., "a very large (and very secretive) oil company." There was a short Kaufmanesque film, *Being Hamlet*, theorized through Georges Baudrillard, that attempted to link Shakespeare to "a world of new media in which *everything* is an adaptation" (Hamlet met the Ghost in a graffiti-crazed alley in broad daylight); a video game, using Halo language, that played primarily with characters but also, ironically, included a "monologue moment" as part of its climactic battle scene; and *Exeunt*, a series of interviews with Montague, Lady Montague, Lady Capulet, and the Nurse – after the play was over. In the latter, all were seeing the same therapist, represented by the camera, to whom they spoke directly; in an ironic commentary on parenting (Shakespearean? their own?) all were deeply concerned – not with the deaths of their young but with themselves.

Given the eager, thoughtful classroom conversations about *Macbeth*, *Throne of Blood*, *O*, and *Hamlet*, I was fully prepared for these to be the hits of the season. But the play that trumped them all was *Henry V*, and the first films we had studied. As though fixated on the play, its central figure, and the St Crispin's Day speech, students used it to play out their obsessions with (and attitudes towards) the war in Iraq, its domestic and public faces. Several students collaborated on a short film using Sonnets 55, 71, and 147, each spoken as a voice-over, to trace a young soldier saying goodbye to his lover, then crouched in a foxhole writing her a letter and, finally, arriving home to find her with another man. Another student mounted a seven-minute film, titled *All hell shall stir for this* (Pistol's line).[4] Collaging footage pulled from YouTube (the image databank that stands beside Shakespeare, which students also use as a data bank) to accompany Branagh's delivery of the St Crispin's Day speech ("he changes his tone to give the audience a more intense experience of 'being there'"), he mixed together six different songs to convey "a complete story of changing emotions." "What's he that wishes so?" is keyed to an image of George Bush, shot from behind, addressing an audience of soldiers: it's followed by a parade of coffins, a father weeping over his son's combat boots. At "He that outlives this day, and comes safe home," the image track shows soldiers kicking open doors, rows of body bags, a painfully young soldier crying over a comrade's body. Henry's phrases echo over shots of corpses littering Baghdad's streets in the wake of yet another suicide bomber, leveled cityscapes, teenage soldiers pointing huge weapons at the camera, a child with no face left, a bloody hole where once there had been an eye (in memoriam for the young boys viciously murdered in *Henry V*), mouth open in a silent scream. "This story shall the good man teach his son" through to the end of the speech ties to an image chain that begins with a pool of blood, shows prisoners led in single file, a row of empty helmets set on rifles, soldiers crying, flag-draped coffins, a soldier saluting with his prosthetic arm.

As the film was screened at the last class meeting, you could feel the room go quieter and quieter, a silence that lasted for a few minutes after the lights came up. Then somebody said, "It's like Falstaff never died, or it's a different Chorus than Shakespeare's – a chorus of images, speaking Falstaff and Williams back to Henry." To the extent that this stood as a lightbulb moment, it also represented an instance of conversation, adaptation, translation, and transformation in which the student had engaged with Shakespeare's words, made them his own, put them to use to do political work. If this is what a Shakespeare play can accomplish in a time of seemingly permanent national and international upheaval, speaking back to terror and loss, perhaps the barricades are right here, in the classroom. Will something like this happen the next time? There's no way of knowing for certain. But just in case, I think I'll stay where I am, with Shakespeare, on the front lines, hoping that another such sudden mysterious rush of meanings will come again.

Notes

1   With thanks to all the students enrolled in Screen Arts and Cultures 455/ English 467 during Winter 2007 and with deep thanks to Matthew Cherette, William Couch, Alex Funt, Katie Magill, Lynne May, Kevin McCarthy, Michael Miner, Neda Mirafzali, Sharif Nasr, Eric Pierce, James Rourke, Jeffrey Segal, Alyssa Torby, Jillian Walker, and Jeffrey Zeman.
2   Gilbert has never published a description of this strategy – an instance of how many of the most successful teaching strategies come from oral traditions.

3   As a graduate student, Burnstein spent two years asking for a copy of Polanski's script; finally (so he claims), Polanski's agent tired of hearing from him and sent him a copy. Dog-eared and slightly yellowed, it remains one of Jim's most prized possessions.

4   This film, by Michael Miner, can be accessed at *http://www.youtube.com/ watch?v=JydQ6GtUnEo*

References and Further Reading

Barthes, Roland (1977). "The Death of the Author" (1970); "From Work to Text" (1971). In *Image/Music/Text* (pp. 142–8; 155–64). Stephen Heath (Trans.). New York: Hill and Wang.

Benjamin, Walter ([1955] 1968). "The Work of Art in the Age of Mechanical Reproduction." In Hannah Arendt (Ed.). *Illuminations* (pp. 217–51). New York: Schocken Books.

Bennett, Alan (2006). *The History Boys*. New York: Faber and Faber.

Didion, Joan (1979). *The White Album*. New York: Simon and Schuster.

Foucault, Michel ([1977] 1979). *Discipline and Punish: The Birth of the Prison*. Alan Sheridan (Trans.). New York: Vintage Books.

Freud, Sigmund ([1915] 1989). "The Unconscious." In Peter Gay (Ed.). *The Freud Reader* (pp. 572–83). New York: W.W. Norton.

Garneau, Michel (1989). In "Préface" (by Eugène Lion) to *Coriolan de William Shakespeare* (pp. 7–8). Michel Garneau (Trans.). Montréal, Québec: VLB Éditeur.

Greenblatt, Stephen (1988). *Shakespearean Negotiations*. Berkeley: University of California.

Hutcheon, Linda (2006). *A Theory of Adaptation*. New York and London: Routledge.

Kott, Jan (1965). *Shakespeare Our Contemporary*. Boleslaw Taborski (Trans.). London: Methuen

Osborne, Laurie E. (2002). "Clip Art: Theorizing the Shakespearean Film Clip." *Shakespeare Quarterly* 53: 227–40.

Rabkin, Norman (1977). "Rabbits, Ducks, and *Henry V*." *Shakespeare Quarterly* 28: 279–96.

Filmography

Chimes at Midnight (1965). Directed by Orson Welles. Internacional Films Española/Alpine, videocassette.

Hamlet (1996). Directed by Kenneth Branagh. Castle Rock/Columbia, videocassette.

Hamlet (2000). Directed by Michael Almereyda. Miramax/Buena Vista Entertainment, DVD.

Henry V (1944). Directed by Laurence Olivier. Two Cities Films Ltd, DVD.

Henry V (1989). Directed by Kenneth Branagh. Samuel Goldwyn Company, DVD.

King John (1899). Directed by William K. L. Dickson. British Mutoscope and Biograph, videocassette.

Kumonosu jo [*Throne of Blood*] (1957). Directed by Akira Kurosawa. Toho, DVD.

Last Action Hero (1993). Directed by John McTiernan. Columbia, DVD.

Macbeth (1979). Directed by Trevor Nunn and Philip Casson. A&E Home Video, DVD.

A Midwinter's Tale (1995). Directed by Kenneth Branagh. Castle Rock/Midwinter Films, videocassette.

O (2001). Directed by Tim Blake Nelson. Lions Gate, DVD.

Renaissance Man (1994). Directed by Penny Marshall. Cinergi Pictures Entertainment/Touchstone, DVD.

Shakespeare in Love (1998). Directed by John Madden. Bedford Falls/Miramax/ Universal, DVD.

Titus (1999). Directed by Julie Taymor. Clear Blue Sky Productions/Twentieth Century Fox, DVD.

The Tragedy of Macbeth (1971). Directed by Roman Polanski. Playboy, DVD.

The Tragedy of Othello: The Moor of Venice (1952). Directed by Orson Welles. Mercury Productions, DVD.

William Shakespeare's Romeo + Juliet (1996). Directed by Baz Luhrmann. Twentieth Century Fox, DVD.

Part IV

Contexts (Institutional, Cultural, Historical)

8

Dancing and Thinking:
Teaching "Shakespeare" in the
Twenty-First Century

Kate McLuskie

Dancing and Thinking

In the first act of *Waiting for Godot* (Beckett 1956), the endless tedium of Vladimir and Estragon's wait is interrupted by the arrival of Pozzo and Lucky. Pozzo suggests that Lucky might perform for the other two. The performances offered include dancing, singing, reciting, or thinking. Vladimir is surprised that Lucky can think and is assured "He even used to think very prettily once, I could listen to him for hours." Estragon, however, concludes: "I'd rather he dance, it'd be more fun." In the event, Lucky's dance is painfully dragged out of him by Pozzo's violence, and his thinking is a parody of academic discourse that should make scholars blush. Neither activity, moreover, is allowed enduring significance, even for the pair who had welcomed the distraction. After Pozzo and Lucky have left the stage Vladimir and Estragon muse:

Vladimir: That passed the time.
Estragon: It would have passed in any case.
Vladimir: Yes, but not so rapidly.

In these exchanges, Beckett, with characteristic brilliance, identifies and dramatizes the twin poles of artistic and intellectual endeavor. One can dance or one can think: in either case, time passes, as it would have done if neither activity had taken place. There is no hierarchy of value between dancing and thinking: Estragon suggests "he could dance first and think afterwards, if it isn't too much to ask him."

Nevertheless, the characters still try to assign meaning to both kinds of event. When Lucky has completed both dance and encore, Pozzo asks "Do you know what he calls it?" He ignores Estragon's pretentiously abstract suggestion: "The Scapegoat's Agony," and Vladimir's more scatological interpretation: "The Hard Stool." He suggests instead a title that invokes both the movement of Lucky's dance and a possible route into the ideas that it might represent. The dance is called, he says, "The Net. He thinks he's entangled in a net." In spite of offering a title that is also an interpretation, Pozzo refuses to allow Vladimir to respond to or develop the idea. He moves straight on to the thinking, which itself can only be initiated by the physical action of giving Lucky his hat, and is accompanied by silent but violent reactions from all the characters on stage. The thinking cannot produce meaning. Its endless citations and lists and reservations prevent the core sentence around which they hang from ever being completed. Moreover, any meaning it might convey is violently upstaged by the other characters' frenetic physical activity.

Lest the impossibility of making meaning out of performance-events is misunderstood, Beckett repeats the sequence in the second act. The rich physical comedy of the first presentation is replaced by the play's single elegiac moment that briefly connects the time of human activity with a larger sense of inescapable repetition that transcends time itself: "They give birth astride of a grave, the light gleams an instant, then it is night once more. (*He jerks the rope.*) On!" At the risk of falling into the pretentious meaning-making that is mocked in this episode, I would like to suggest that the encounter between Vladimir, Estragon, Lucky, and Pozzo dramatizes the comic misalignment between the experience of the physical arts and the discursive meanings that we demand of them. Beckett offers an absurd version of an aesthetic conundrum that also seems to have preoccupied Shakespeare (and a number of his contemporaries).

In his search for a new "purpose of playing," Shakespeare has Hamlet insist that performance must transcend the mere experience of speeches and clowning in order to "hold, as 'twere, the mirror up to Nature; to show Virtue her feature, Scorn her own image, and the very age and body of the time his form and pressure" (3.2.21–4). Hamlet elides the distinction between experience and reflection (in both senses of the word) by proposing that the right sort of playing would create the desired symbiosis between the two instantaneously. If the clowns did not speak more than was set down for them, and if the lines were delivered by neither a periwig-pated fellow nor the town crier, then the experience of playing would simultaneously create the desired ethical and intellectual effect.

Nevertheless, as Hamlet's adapted version of the Murder of Gonzago showed all too well, this effect could not be guaranteed. Ophelia is baffled: "What means this, my lord?"; the Queen opines that the lady protests too much and even the King is "frighted with false fire." The meaning of performance, whether miching mallecho or the puppets dallying, is in the control of neither performer nor author – least of all beyond the grave.

Hamlet's words about the purpose of playing have, in modern times, provided continued reassurance about the lasting purpose of playing (or working on) "Shakespeare." Teachers of Shakespeare daily manage the complex oscillation between the literary works, the performed plays, and a discursive activity that seeks to translate both objects and events into meaning. They must acknowledge that a theatrical event takes place in real time (it would have passed anyway) and they must manage, more or less self-consciously, its contested relationship to the literary "work" in order to produce meanings that are communicable, repeatable, and can be assessed and debated.

The tragic or comic struggle over the contingency of meaning, the relative significance of Lucky's dance and his thinking has, in the twenty-first century, provided the terms for a contest over pedagogic practice that polarizes reading the plays and performing them. The historical fact that Shakespeare wrote for two companies of players has hardened into a consensus that the plays that form the curriculum of Shakespeare teaching were "written for performance," a common assertion that entirely begs the question of the relationship between performance and meaning or even the plays' early modern performance and the extant printed versions of the texts (see Erne 2003). In educational circles, the idea that Shakespeare "wrote for performance" has supported the view that the experience of Shakespeare in performance is critical to the appreciation of his plays and that that experience will in and of itself produce educational value. The progressive shifts in educational focus from content to experience, from assimilating received knowledge to creative interaction with it, have also restated Estragon's simple reaction to Lucky's dilemma: "I'd rather he dance, it'd be more fun."

Teaching Practice

As part of the 2006–7 Complete Works Festival, the Royal Shakespeare Company's education department, RSC Learning, worked with Warwickshire County Council Arts Zone to mount a "Schools Mini Complete Works of Shakespeare Festival" that allowed 2,300 children to participate in a week-long series of performances, managed entirely by the youngsters themselves, supported by RSC training for both teachers and children. The event was an extraordinary achievement of logistics and leadership that was undoubtedly memorable for children and teachers alike.

The representation of the event in the media emphasized its core educational values. For example, Reg Pogson, Director of Warwickshire County Council's Arts Zone, said:

> There were dozens and dozens of examples of schools of all sizes, with children of all ages, embracing Shakespeare and using it as the basis for some fascinating creative work. We had children as young as five appreciating Shakespeare's work and interpreting it for a 15 minute performance. Almost every school in Warwickshire did some form of Shakespeare work during this period including the special schools [i.e., schools for children with physical and learning difficulties] who staged their own successful drama festival. (Pogson 2006)

The educational and social aims of the event were clear. The enthusiastic engagement of a significant number of children was the cause for festive celebration but the association with Shakespeare was especially significant. That connection allowed the event to fulfill the educational objectives of the National Curriculum, which itself assumed, created, and recirculated the value of "Shakespeare." The participation of the children and the inclusion of the whole state school sector, including schools for children with special educational needs, were at the heart of the enterprise. Particular social categories (small children, special schools, socially excluded young people) were identified as the project's beneficiaries combining the values of "Shakespeare" with the values of universal access that are at the heart of progressive educational policy. "Shakespeare" was the occasion for education, not merely its subject matter: the plays (or at least their narratives and most famous lines) became the locus of creative experience that transcended meaning.

The Warwickshire Schools Festival was part of a larger education project, launched during the Complete Works Festival, under the banner "Time for Change." However, in spite of this announcement of a radical break with the deadly educational thinking of the past, the project was the culmination of a complex set of relations between critical thinking about Shakespeare and the politics of education that had been changing for the previous 20 years.

Bardbiz and Time for Change

One of the more entertaining episodes in the late twentieth-century culture wars over Shakespeare in the UK was the six-week exchange of correspondence on the state of Shakespeare studies that came to be known as "Bardbiz."[1] It began with a review by Terence Hawkes (1990) of a number of important English and American books about Shakespeare. Hawkes mocked the capacity of the English to be "unhinged by doublet and hose" and he linked the books (that were the culmination of new directions in Shakespeare scholarship begun in the 1980s) to the discovery of the Rose theatre and the general revival of Shakespeare as the site of values that transcended commerce and spoke unmediated through history.

In the ensuing controversy, Hawkes was supported by the scholars who had established cultural materialism as the strongest oppositional voice in English Shakespeare studies. He was challenged, surprisingly, by a young journalist, James Wood, who had no special position in the line-up of academic controversialists but claimed to speak for a common-sense appreciation of Shakespeare's greatness that might rescue it from academic in-fighting. A new flank was opening up in the intellectual battle against a complacent admiration for Shakespeare as a marker of enduring human and artistic values. It was an attack on the newly claimed political and historical Shakespeare on behalf of an anti-intellectual aesthetic of appreciation.

Some of the participants have presented this battle as one of the heroic conflicts in the liberation of Shakespeare for politically inflected and historically informed educational and intellectual work (Hawkes 1992). However, another of its effects was that it reified the particular educational, theatrical, and intellectual practices associated with individual plays and poems written by an early modern dramatist, into an abstraction called

"Shakespeare," that could be usefully invoked as a signifier of value, regardless of the exact content of the signified that it stood for. This signifier, "Shakespeare," appeared in the moral panic in the media about the decline of compulsory Shakespeare in university English departments.

The national, intellectual, and educational politics that lay behind those debates were more complex still. The Bardbiz correspondence was published in *The London Review of Books*, a journal whose launch in 1979 coincided with a long-running and bitterly fought dispute between Times Newspapers and the labor unions over new production facilities that would eventually change the traditional structures, location, and technology of the London printing industry. It would be strained to assert any systemic correlation between the traditions of Shakespeare and the traditions of the printing industry.

The debate in the *LRB*, moreover, crossed and recrossed the domain of "tradition" that was being debated in other, more materially significant, terms in the conflict occasioned by the strike at *The Times*. This was one of a series of industrial disputes that not only challenged changing technologies and working practices in the print industry but also acted out the determination of Margaret Thatcher's Conservative government (1979–90), to reduce the power of organized labor in the industrial and commercial relations of the UK. From the government's point of view, "tradition" in UK industrial relations was to be rooted out, to be replaced by a more flexible workforce who could more easily be directed by market conditions.

An additional aspect of this change in industrial relations involved creating a more vocationally focused and instrumental system, imposed on all levels of education from primary schools to universities. A key factor in those debates was the discussion of the place of "Shakespeare" in the National Curriculum that was introduced into schools in 1988. Its aim was to ensure that the experience of education should produce clearly identifiable knowledge, established by testing and producing the same "learning outcomes" for children across the whole state system of education in the UK. The policy was highly controversial and contested, in part because of the authoritarian way in which it was introduced, and because teachers' unions were concerned that the additional work involved would not be adequately resourced.

Those political issues, however, were often subsumed into more general discussions about education in the arts (there was far less disagreement about the need for a National Curriculum to improve performance in mathematics). The domain of tradition that the government wished to see rooted out of labor practices was to be reasserted in the traditional education which included, in the list of the then Conservative Prime Minister, John Major's, stated educational values: "Knowledge. Discipline. Tables. Sums. Dates. Shakespeare. British History. Standard English. Grammar. Spelling. Marks. Tests" (King 1993). For those who wished to distance themselves from the reactionary ideological use of "Shakespeare," the imposition of "Shakespeare" in the National Curriculum was a matter for concern. However, as the policy was implemented, it became increasingly difficult to express those concerns clearly in the discourses of "tradition" and "innovation" or conservative and progressive approaches to education.

Those binary oppositions were increasingly being cross-cut by a different, though equally long-lived, invocation of the needs and rights of the individual child. Though the political ideologues who championed the National Curriculum deplored what they saw as the unsystematic and unaccountable nature of "child-centered" education, the rhetoric of child development and children's rights proved extraordinarily difficult to dismiss from educational policy and practice. Laying out his principles for educational research in a 1985 application to the Leverhulme trust (currently in the archive of The University of Birmingham's Shakespeare Institute), the distinguished English educator, Rex Gibson, wrote:

> All pupils have a *right* to Shakespeare. That right is echoed in the recent words of Cicely Berry: "he is not the exclusive property of the educated middle classes" (*Guardian* 11 January 1986); and in the words of his fellow actors and editors John Heminge and Henry Condell "to the great variety of Readers, from the most able to him that can but spell" (Preface to the First Folio 1623).[2]

This stirring statement is extraordinary in its ability to align generalized "pupils" with a generalized "Shakespeare" via a language of rights. It was given a carefully limited class significance that was slightly distanced by being associated with someone other than Gibson himself, the influential voice coach of the Royal Shakespeare Company, Cicely Berry. The reference to class was, however, immediately disconnected from contemporary class struggles and linked back to the universalist (though actually commercial[3]) invocation to the reader of the First Folio.

Gibson's 1985 application showed a similar creative pragmatism with regard to the contemporary contests over "theory":

The project's view of theory is relaxed and undogmatic. It will pay attention to the theory that exists (both about literature and about learning, education and schooling). It will be concerned to explore (even "test") theory where possible and sensible. But it is only fair to declare at this point the Project Director's concern to acknowledge teachers and pupils as capable, knowledgeable "individuals", whose human competence acts to reduce the possibility of prediction in social life.

Gibson's "relaxed" and eclectic approach to theory dissipated the intensity (and perhaps the intellectual rigor) of the contest over Shakespeare and at the same time was a fundamental requirement for the new methods of teaching Shakespeare. Gibson's Shakespeare in Schools project, established in 1986, sought to demystify "Shakespeare," to render his works accessible and available. The factors that were felt to have made the work inaccessible or unavailable were never made explicit. They were identified instead as a generalized mix of "middle-class" prejudice, examinations, and academic criticism: the whole panoply of discursive activity that stood between "Shakespeare" and the immediate experience of his plays. The thinking had to end so that the dancing could begin again. "Shakespeare" had been rescued from conservative educational ideology, and with his customary protean capacity morphed into the place of creativity and progressive child-centered education.

In order to retrieve the desired immediacy of experience, children transformed "Shakespeare" by retelling his stories in their own words, with endings changed according to their view of the characters' choices, and modern instances drawn from an abstraction of their themes. These pedagogic methods aroused enormous enthusiasm from teachers and have now become naturalized in much school teaching of Shakespeare. Their success and acceptability, however, depended both on the prior intellectual work that had been undertaken by theoretical debates and on a dissipation of its intellectual radicalism.

In particular, Terence Hawkes's complex account of the role of Shakespeare in the structuring of contemporary ideology had been reduced to the slogan: "we mean by Shakespeare" (Hawkes 1992: 3). It was read as an endorsement of individual judgments about the activities of particular characters freed from the constraints of the narratives or historical circumstances in which they appear. The eloquent struggle of characters to come to terms with the ineluctable reality of their circumstances could be easily resolved by the fun technique of "hot seating" in which the pupils interrogated characters about the options that the narrative seemed to offer them: Richard II's agonized question on the walls of Flint castle, "What must the king do now, must he submit?" can be easily answered by engaged and enthusiastic eight year olds.

It would be churlish to gainsay the achievement of projects such as Rex Gibson's that are now used in pedagogic practice all over the world.[4] All of them speak of the huge enthusiasm that this version of "Shakespeare" has generated in classrooms as diverse as those in rural primary schools or in a "racially mixed group in a Massachusetts women's correctional facility" (McManus 1994). Equally impressive are the examples of international cooperation through Shakespeare, such as the event that brought together a young people's theatre group, Nos do Morro, from the Brazilian favelas, with disadvantaged youngsters from ethnic groups in Birmingham,[5] or the activities of the London Shakespeare Workout that educates and, in some cases, transforms the lives of young prisoners through performing Shakespeare.[6] The stories they tell almost always speak of "the delight on the children's faces as they left the room." No one ever describes a bad class.

At the heart of this movement is a belief in education as a process for child development. In his discussion of the importance of creativity for child development, the educator Jonothan Neelands quotes a curriculum document for "English for ages 5–16" which asserts that drama "is one of the key ways in which children gain an understanding of themselves and of others" (Neelands 1992: 6). As a statement about child development, this seems plausible, but the drama referred to here is only tangentially related to drama as a script for performed theatre and is different again from the plays of Shakespeare. The curriculum documents prepared for teachers by Her Majesty's Inspectorate in the 1990s, however, saw these differences as part of an easily elided continuum: "Drama in schools is a practical artistic subject. It ranges from children's structured play, through classroom improvisation to performances of Shakespeare" (quoted in Neelands 1992: 8).

As part of children's education, the production of knowledge or even the products of earlier analysis have become merely grist to the mill of a child's self-development. The plays in this form of pedagogy are released from their texts to become opportunities for the children's creative imagination, the sources of imaginative empathy, a framework for exploring their relationships to one another and to their surroundings.

In the hands of engaged teachers and cooperative students, Gibson's techniques could produce exciting educational experiences. The cultural authority of Shakespeare endorsed the activity with particular value and the experience of playing with Shakespeare released the plays into an arena where the students could take ownership of that cultural value without having to go through the difficult and alienating process of negotiating unfamiliar language or complex questions of historical difference. The process reversed the traditional hierarchy of text to performance: texts, reduced to their narratives or to key scenes, became the raw material of performativity, evidence of a character's feelings that could be debated by children or translated directly into their physical experience by vocalizing rhythm and meter or by opening up their implied potential for different kinds of sound effects as the lines were whispered or shouted, chanted or sung. Questions of aesthetic effect or ethical value or historical authenticity were laid aside as the clowns spoke far more than was set down for them and Herod was out-Heroded in classrooms across the land. If the ensuing knowledge of Shakespeare was invoked at all, it was as the author of humanist values, the source of truth about "love" or "jealousy" or "power." Equally, though, it was assumed that the same work could be accessible via the children's' own experience, realized into action through play: I'd rather he dance, it'd be more fun!

Throughout the 1990s and into the new century this pedagogic practice has been endorsed by curricula and funding bodies all over the UK and the US. Yet every time a new project on "teaching Shakespeare" is announced, old oppositions between "academic" and "theatrical" Shakespeare, Shakespeare-read and Shakespeare-performed, accessible and inaccessible Shakespeare, are reasserted. Two decades after the success of Rex Gibson's project, the RSC's "Time for Change" project was reported in a national newspaper with the rhetorical question: "How is it that Shakespeare has become a byword for boredom among school children?" The report continued: "Teachers blame a curriculum that, in many cases, allows pupils simply to learn, by rote, a few isolated scenes without appreciating context, the play as a whole or the dramatic power of the Bard's work" (Walker, 2006).

The familiar opposition between learning as process and learning as an examined product lies behind that discussion, but even the much maligned Qualifications and Curriculum Authority (QCA) that recommends curricula for teaching English in schools insisted that "Students stress the importance of live experience of Shakespeare in particular – dry and irrelevant if simply read through – wanting at least to have the opportunity for seeing plays performed as films or on television, if not in the theatre" (QCA 2005: 23). This evidence that performed Shakespeare has been assimilated even into the QCA's thinking, and their document's emphasis on children's creativity as a necessary preliminary to learning, might suggest that the old oppositions between tedious textual Shakespeare and exciting performance are beginning to decline in significance. Nevertheless, behind the liberal consensus about the needs of the child and the importance of "fun" in education, lie a set of knotty contradictions between the value of knowledge and the development of the individual student, that are played out in every discussion of Shakespeare pedagogy. Shakespeare is valued as the highest artistic achievement of the human mind but a significant part of that value is felt to reside in his availability "to him that can but spell." The Works, it is asserted, embody the finest and most complex poetry ever written but the stories are also assumed to speak directly to the human condition. His work is "not of an age but for all time," yet it must speak particularly to the preoccupations of the twenty-first century. The work is transcendent and sublime, but it can also provide key skills for the post-industrial workforce.

Proponents of the new pedagogy insist that these contradictions can be resolved and their enthusiastic accounts of individual projects, together with their ambitious plans for teacher training, suggest that this may be the case. In the school curriculum, where the visit of a theatre-in-education company or the rare treat of a practice event is a welcome relief from the day-to-day tedium of lessons, the contrast between reading and performance can have pedagogic value. Nevertheless, at more advanced levels, the question of how this work relates to the knowledge of Shakespeare plays as objects of cultural production in history or the development of that knowledge through research remains at issue.

Back in the Ivory Tower

The implications of these developments for Shakespeare teaching in universities are complex. In the public debates that set tradition against innovation and knowledge against experience, academic work is almost universally assigned to the negative pole. Academic emphasis on historical knowledge, theoretical analysis, and discursive assessment allows it to be categorized as the antithesis of "fun," not least because the innovations of academic research produce findings that are necessarily counterintuitive and resistant to essentialist ideas of the transhistorical human that can be directly intuited from students' personal experience.

Since teachers in universities have traditionally been more committed to the findings of research than to the personal development of their students, they often face a conflict between their students' expectations of creative engagement and the need to develop the disciplines of higher learning based on skepticism, analysis, and argued evidence. Even when the curriculum content of a Shakespeare course includes performance, its relationship to theorized knowledge has been called into question by persuasive critiques of the assumptions behind what W. B. Worthen (1997) has called "the authority of performance"[7] and clear differences are discernible between the "Shakespeare" experienced in English departments and the role of Shakespeare in the training of actors or the serious study of theatre practice.

This skepticism about the relationship between performance, knowledge, and the advanced Shakespeare curriculum is seldom acknowledged in many accounts of "teaching Shakespeare" in universities. Instead these issues are often subsumed into a set of more or less effective "tips for teachers," building on anecdotes about pedagogic strategies that "work" in their classrooms. Discussions of contemporary classroom practice provide fascinating accounts of the role of "performance" in teaching that have developed conservatoire methods of actor training, revealed unexpected potential performance choices, or created a long-term engagement with a play through a whole summer of performance experiment (Loehlin 2005; see especially Loehlin's discussion of the "Shakespeare at Winedale" program, pp. 638–42).

The elision of performance pedagogy and discursive meaning seemed simpler two decades ago in the aftermath of the movement that J. L. Styan called, in 1977, the Shakespeare Revolution. As Cary Mazer has demonstrated (1996), the discursive gap between the real-time of performance and the problem of access to a historical event, long past, was resolved in the twentieth century by the semiotics generated by the abstract stage of avant-garde theatre. From William Poel's pared down "Elizabethan" theatre to Peter Brook's "Empty Space," the theatre of the early modern period was recreated in the twentieth century as a space of meaning in which performers and directors sought to present Shakespeare in ways that would provide access to the discursive significance of his plays as well as the experience of the embodiment of their narratives. This process involved collusion between practitioners and literary critics in which, as Alan Dessen proposed, "The modern director can learn from the scholar or critic a different, perhaps neo-Elizabethan, habit of mind, a way of seeing the personae and events of a Shakespearean play . . . as the unfolding of a larger pattern that can be enhanced and driven home by action, staging and gesture" (Dessen 1977: 29). Dessen acknowledges that the pattern is perhaps "not apparent to the casual reader or to many an actor or director bound by his own sense of theatre." The discursive meaning is not yielded up by the experience of theatre itself; it has to be created by a critical predisposition to identify (or impose) an essential unity in (or onto) the play, a unity that will gesture beyond performance to its larger significance.

The real-time experience of performance, however, can only yield those meanings with a good deal of discursive help. The thinking of the theatre practitioner may elide with the thinking of the critic or performance historian but the performance itself disappears as if it had never happened. Like Lucky, the performer "could dance first and think afterwards," as often happens in the process of interviewing and recording practitioners' views of their performances. The thinking involved, however, though it may claim to inform performance, is quite distinct from performance itself. Its articulation in the literature that now routinely surrounds performances, in the form of programs, interviews, and spin-off books, short-circuits performance by communicating meaning directly from director or critic to audience.

There is, of course, no necessary connection between the semiotics of performance and the readings that result from them. In the hands of skilled performance critics fascinating readings can be produced, but theorists are increasingly acknowledging that those readings depend on the predisposition to "read" performance and at best refer only to the results of particular codes of reading that can be made to apply to the particular performance seen by the critic in question.

Those critical maneuvers are often reproduced in teaching but it is hard to distinguish between a theoretically informed sense of the contingency of meaning and a consumerist free-for-all in which students feel both entitled to their "own interpretation" and an anxiety that the resulting account of the play's significance will not carry the authority required to achieve the necessary and desired high grade.

This consumerist version of "Shakespeare" is all the more difficult to resist because of its pervasive ability to assimilate resistances to it. The radical feminist and New Historicist work of the last two decades, that called into question the common-sense valuation of Shakespeare as humanist sage and generated a more robust critical methodology, has been easily absorbed into the dominant model of interpretative criticism. Feminist alternatives to that model are reduced to the sympathetic interpretation of women characters, but they are assimilated into the interpretative process in which the assumed emotional lives of the women characters are accounted for via personal motivation, and their narrative position defined as being constrained by a generalized account of a transhistorical "patriarchy." New Historicism has also been reduced to historical anecdote or historical fantasy in which a Shakespeare *de nos jours* flouts banned religion or state censorship in order to speak liberal truth to power. Shakespeare, like the characters of his plays, is essentially a man like us, feeling grief, tasting pain, beset with worries about an unattractive wife and a recalcitrant daughter. Very occasionally, and with an air of defiant transgression, he is presented as an enclosing landlord or an instrumentally commercial entrepreneur.[8]

The knowledges that can arise from such accounts of Shakespeare are always driven by analogy. The student's emerging ethical sensitivity to the pain of others, or conflict within the family, or even the impact of contemporary events such as war or social and racial conflict is always able to find a ready echo in preselected lines from the plays. The educational function is to find eloquent articulations of humanist commonplaces which may be deeply felt and appreciated but are essentially an exercise in solipsism, endorsing simple ideas with grand and historically resonant statements that close off rather than providing a route into the intellectual developments of modern times.

The apparent innovation of new performance experiences is equally grist to this mill of circulating commonplaces. Writing of the audience response to the all-male performance of *Antony and Cleopatra* at the Globe in 1999, James Bulman suggests that "By 1999, the idea that gender is performative rather than innate had circulated widely, and audiences were proving receptive to the argument that gender might be a cultural construct, and sexual desire dependent on forces other than biological difference" (Bulman 2005: 565). That view was certainly endorsed by many of the critics, though it would be equally possible to read their approval in terms of a more generalized appreciation of the performers' skill in impersonation, together with a more generalized sense of the metatheatricality of Shakespeare's work. The distinction between acting, performance, and pretence allows students to leave the performance firmly on the stage without any implications for the distinction between performance in a narrative and performance in the life-world of drag games or queer behavior. The emergence of gay stars on television (Graham Norton is the best example in the UK) and programs such as *A Queer Eye for the Straight Guy* (www.bravotv.com/Queer_Eye/) has normalized the adoption of gay styles without in any way shifting the essentialist notion of character as the inherent source of gesture and behavior and has left the generalized tolerance of liberal individualism firmly in place.

As Bulman points out, the critical responses to all-male performances benchmark their reading of the performance in terms of a prior reading of the narrative. Given the long tradition of subsuming sexual relations within a narrative of "love," and given the liberal assimilation of homosexual relations within the dominant romantic model, it is hardly surprising to find newspaper critics writing of "the transforming potency of love,"[9] regardless of the play in which this "love" supposedly takes place.

Teaching Shakespeare

The assimilation of quite distinct theoretical positions and critical practices into a generalized humanist interpretation of "Shakespeare" is one of the casualties of the management of higher education in the twenty-first century. Changes to the funding system in the UK have put pressure on universities to maximize their student-based income by overrecruiting in areas of high student demand and transferring the funds to expensive student facilities or high prestige research areas. The resulting large classes in English departments with high ratios of students to staff have imposed instruction-based pedagogy that leaves less scope for a creative challenge to students' assumptions. The department "Shakespeare" course – whether compulsory or not – is often one of the largest and the one least likely to demand prerequisites.[10] Delivery of a Shakespeare program that builds on expectations of an intuitive engagement with easily assimilated and universally available humanist narratives, together with the added attractions of a theatre trip, is a cheap, easy, and popular option.

These material constraints have been further facilitated by the generalization of the "Shakespeare" that is the object of pedagogic attention. One of the innovations of the new regulation of teaching in British universities has been the requirement that all courses identify their "learning outcomes." The learning outcomes of Shakespeare courses usually refer to the students knowing and understanding "Shakespeare" without acknowledging the extent to which academic work in Shakespeare studies covers a locus that includes the history of performance in mainstream and alternative venues from 1580 to the present; the adaptation of plays worldwide; the theories of representation, performance, and cultural production; together with multiple, culturally determined interpretative perspectives across 400 years of the history and practice of criticism. Mastery of any one of these topics would be difficult in the time usually allotted to a Shakespeare course and to create a curriculum that explicitly focuses on more than a few of these would significantly skew a crowded literature program.[11] Work on the text that does not scurry immediately towards interpretation and character often proves a challenging task for students. To read speeches and pay attention to their surfaces of linguistic play and poetic device goes against the grain of understanding a "Shakespeare" who is speaking directly to all time. Even more difficult, in my experience, is communicating the concept of language that is not the "expression" of a coherent subjectivity and may not even or always be in the service of constructing unique and individual characters.

Similarly the time required for serious performance work seldom allows for the kind of physical training that is commonplace in professional companies. Although it often produces intriguing flashes of insight about the physical relationships implied in particular moments in Shakespeare plays, the added value of creative work is more to do with the student's intuitive interpretation of the plays' narratives than effective training in the disciplines of performance or an understanding of the physical and cultural work undertaken by directors, performers, and film makers.

The recent UK survey of teaching Shakespeare in higher education (Thew 2006) reveals the contradictory responses of practicing teachers to these challenges. The survey's methodology took for granted the significance of Shakespeare's place in the curriculum and invited respondents to make eclectic choices among quite different intellectual traditions in the study of Shakespeare. The discussion of curriculum centered only on the number of plays chosen or on the place of "literary or non-literary Renaissance/Early Modern texts . . . useful for teaching Shakespeare" (Thew 2006: 22). The use of theatre visits, videos and DVDs, or other "electronic resources," presentist analogies between the plays' treatment of ethical issues and contemporary liberal commonplaces, or historicist approaches that require students to "read widely" in the historical literature, were all grist to the common cause of "teaching Shakespeare."

Each of these pedagogic strategies will, of course, produce quite distinct Shakespeares in the different kinds of knowledge that students will acquire. Each of them, moreover, requires the students to turn away from the task of reading and making sense of the Shakespeare text in search of other kinds of knowledge about particular past performances, history, or social and political concerns. "Shakespeare" was presented as the route into, or as a substitute for, other knowledges that are felt to be a desirable part of students' education.

Respondents to the English Subject Centre survey, only 11 percent of whom found their students "well prepared" for Shakespeare studies at university level, speak of "unpicking bad habits, in particular naive character criticism or flat-footed context" (Thew 2006: 10). It is commonplace to blame the students' prior education for these failings (just as creative teachers blame the examination system). The articulation of a Shakespeare curriculum that was explicit about the different disciplines and distinct practices that could be applied to Shakespeare's plays and was clear about the "knowledge" required for its fulfillment, might resolve some of the clashes of expectation that are implicit in current Shakespeare pedagogy. It might also release both students and teachers from the familiar binary opposition between "difficult/boring texts" and the unexamined pleasures of "performance," allowing them to explore, rather than assume, the connection between text, performance, and meaning in more explicit ways.

We should not, of course, underestimate the difficulty of doing so. It would require us to turn our back on the ready-made and familiar contests over "interpretation"; it would demand that we put on hold the immediate pleasures of empathy or its opposite, and it would impose the challenging task of separating out the analysis from the experience of Shakespeare. *Pace* Gibson and all the other gifted educators of children who have made the experience of "doing Shakespeare" such a pleasure, working on Shakespeare at advanced levels requires that the dancing stalls while the thinking goes on. It would be as well to be frank about the process and to be clear, as Beckett was, how much work is involved:

Vladimir: (*to Pozzo*) Tell him to think.
Pozzo: Give him his hat.
Vladimir: His hat?
Pozzo: He can't think without his hat. . . . [*With drawn-out business the hat is put on Lucky's head.*]
Estragon: What's he waiting for?
Pozzo: Stand back! (*Vladimir and Estragon move away from Lucky. Pozzo jerks the rope. Lucky looks at Pozzo.*) Think, pig! (*Pause. Lucky begins to dance.*) Stop! (*Lucky stops.*) Forward! (*Lucky advances.*) Stop! (*Lucky stops.*) Think!
Silence.

Notes

1 Full details of this correspondence are given in Hawkes (1992: 154).
2 This research informed Rex Gibson's influential book, *Teaching Shakespeare* (1998) and established his enormous influence on school pedagogy.
3 The end of the passage from F1 is, of course, an injunction to buy a copy of the Folio text.
4 See passim the English journal, begun by Rex Gibson, *Shakespeare and Schools* and the parallel journal from Ohio Northern University, *Shakespeare in the Classroom*, together with the education section of the websites of the Folger Library and the major theatre companies.
5 See RSC press release at <http://www.rsc.org.uk/press/420_2883.aspx>.
6 See <www.londonshakespeare.org.uk>.
7 See also Bulman (1996).
8 The most powerful articulation of this version of Shakespeare is to be found in Greenblatt's biography (2005).
9 Michael Billington, *The Times* October 14, 1991, quoted in Bulman (1996: 567).
10 For some indicative figures, see Thew (2006: 13).
11 Though see the admirable example in the English Subject Centre Survey which offers a "Shakespeare pathway" across all three years of the degree that "allows students to specialise . . . progressively, building their critical and textual knowledge incrementally" (Thew 2006: 11).

References and Further Reading

Beckett, Samuel (1956). *Waiting for Godot*. London: Faber and Faber.
Bulman, James C. (Ed.) (1996). *Shakespeare, Theory, and Performance*. London: Routledge.
Bulman, James C. (2005). "Queering the Audience: All-Male Casts in Recent Productions of Shakespeare." In Barbara Hodgdon and W. B. Worthen (Eds). *A Companion to Shakespeare and Performance* (pp. 564–87). Oxford: Blackwell.
Dessen, Alan (1977). *Elizabethan Drama and the Viewer's Eye*. Chapel Hill: University of North Carolina Press.
Erne, Lucas (2003). *Shakespeare as Literary Dramatist*. Cambridge, UK: Cambridge University Press.
Gibson, Rex (1998). *Teaching Shakespeare*. Cambridge, UK: Cambridge University Press.
Greenblatt, Stephen (2005). *Will in the World: How Shakespeare Became Shakespeare*. London: Pimlico.

Hawkes, Terence (1990). "Bardbiz." *London Review of Books* 11–13; reprinted, slightly emended, in Hawkes (1992: 141–53).

Hawkes, Terence (1992). *Meaning by Shakespeare*. London: Routledge.

King, Rosalind (1993). "Teaching and Examining Shakespeare in the National Curriculum at Key Stage 3," Report from the Theatres, Universities and Schools Conference on Shakespeare. *Times Educational Supplement*: September 3.

Loehlin, James N. (2005). "Teaching Through Performance." In Barbara Hodgdon and W. B. Worthen (Eds). *A Companion to Shakespeare and Performance* (pp. 627–43). Oxford: Blackwell.

Mazer, Cary M. (1996). "Historicising Alan Dessen." In James C. Bulman (Ed.). *Shakespeare, Theory and Performance* (pp. 149–67). London and New York: Routledge.

McManus, Eva B. (1994). "Untraditional Shakespeare Becoming Traditional." *Shakespeare in the Classroom* 2: 9–10.

Neelands, Jonothan (1992). *Learning through Imagined Experience: The Role of Drama in the National Curriculum*. London: Hodder and Stoughton.

Pogson, Rex (2006). Interview in *Warwickshire View* 12: 8.

Qualifications and Curriculum Authority (2005). *English 21 Playback*. London: QCA. Available at <http://www.qca.org.uk/qca_9930.aspx>.

Styan, J. L. (1977). *The Shakespeare Revolution: Criticism and Performance in the 20th Century*. Cambridge, UK: Cambridge University Press.

Thew, Neill (2006). *Teaching Shakespeare: A Survey of the Undergraduate Level in Higher Education*. English Subject Centre. Available at <www.english. heacademy.ac.uk/archive/publications/reports/shakespeare.pdf>.

Thompson, Ann and Neil Taylor (Eds). *Hamlet*. London: Thompson Learning.

Walker, Tim (2006). "RSC/Warwick Diploma in Teaching: Shakespeare Without Tears." *Independent* October 12. Available at <www.independent.co.uk/student/ postgraduate/rscwarwick-diploma-in-teaching-shakespeare-without-tears-419600.html>.

Worthen, W. B. (1997). *Shakespeare and the Authority of Performance*. Cambridge, UK: Cambridge University Press.

9

Communicating Differences: Gender, Feminism, and Queer Studies in the Changing Shakespeare Curriculum

Ramona Wray

In the context of a newly foregrounded sense of difference in the classroom, and in a situation where one may still come across fixities of cultural attitude, the teaching of Shakespeare plays a valuable and evaluative role. When teaching, I am passionate about ensuring that gender, feminism, and queer studies feature as crucial components in student encounters with Shakespeare and, at the same time, that a theorized appreciation of Renaissance texts and contexts emerges from, and is integrally related to, the provision of English at Queen's University, Belfast, my own institution. This essay maps some of the ways in which Shakespeare might be enjoyed in terms of developments in approaches to gender and theory, and pays particular attention to the potential embodied in interrelations among course offerings, to media and film as means of instruction, and to the specifics of the pedagogical experience. Ultimately, I will suggest, an integrated and incremental approach to Shakespeare which utilizes theory and film can result in a newly energized understanding of the text and a reinvigorated interest in the play as a representational medium deeply rooted in early modern practices and preoccupations.

I

The three-year English degree program at Queen's is divided into an Introduction to English Studies course (Stage 1), a number of historically based survey courses (Stage 2), and a series of research-led courses that concentrate on particular themes, writers, or periods (Stage 3). In practice, this means that the students, if they so choose, can concentrate on a discrete period, taking, for instance, a Renaissance survey module at Stage 2 and then a spread of early modern/Shakespeare-related specialist modules in the final year. The teaching ideal is that such a structure operates incrementally, with each stage testing new skills, expanding the knowledge base, and refining areas of intellectual interest. In addition, a mixed diet of teaching methods has the effect of exposing students to a range of pedagogical models which, as a whole, function to instill a greater responsibility for the acquisition and application of knowledge across the degree continuum. This, then, is a relational system in which a successfully running whole is intimately dependent upon the smooth unfolding of its multiple parts.

For the research-led offerings at Stage 3 to work effectively, a forward-looking Stage 1 is essential. A compulsory introduction which both un-teaches the student, disabusing him or her of assumptions culled from high school, and tutors in the skills required to read texts at undergraduate level, is the building-block upon which all subsequent explorations are erected. A principle at Stage 1 is that the core texts should reflect generic reach, modes of writing, gendered complexion/position, and national/historical traditions. Accordingly, *Othello* sits alongside "literature" as diverse as *Beowulf*, *Castle Rackrent*, *Mansfield Park*, *My Beautiful Laundrette* (the screenplay), *Slaughterhouse Five*, and *The Turn of the Screw*. A poetry anthology is also recommended, and there is always one "film," which is seen, of course, as a legitimate "text" with its own codes and conventions. Such a selection is key to an initial effort to dislodge and reassemble literary and/or canonical expectations, with the range of theories taught also assisting in the process. Thus, accompanying this textual grouping, students are also expected to read a theory primer and anthology. Each week, a text or group of texts is discovered in terms of a discrete method, whether that is psychoanalysis, historicism, intertextuality, formalism, deconstruction, or postcolonialism, with the same texts returned to in the context of later explanations: *Othello*, for example, is demonstrated to be open to more than one theory. Inevitably, only so much of the complexity of feminism can be investigated in the space of a couple of weeks, but a priority is to sensitize students to the meanings attached to the "representation of women in literature," to the "mechanisms of patriarchy," and to "reconstructing the lost or suppressed records of female experience" (Barry 2002: 122). Inside that unfolding, matters of "conditioning," "power," and "socialization" are introduced through a consideration of one of the early issues of feminism, that is, "whether or not there exists a form of language which is inherently feminine" (Barry 2002: 126, 133, 134).

A productive method of pursuing the question is through the stereotypical notion of the disorderly and/or temperamental woman. Students are sometimes surprised to discover that types such as Beatrice or Desdemona are integral to the binaries exploded by such critics as Luce Irigaray and, once informed, are ready to accept and debate a further dimension of French theory, namely, Hélène Cixous's discussion of a "common logic of difference" organized according to "male privilege" into a series of "dual, hierarchical oppositions" (Rivkin and Ryan 2000: 578, 579, 581). Initially, it can appear contradictory to go on to propose, as does Judith Butler, that "gender" may in fact be only a matter of "performativity, masquerade and imitation . . . cultural processes that generate . . . identities that [do not] . . . possess a pre-existing natural . . . substance" (Rivkin and Ryan 2000: 530); however, a modern analogue is often the solution to this impasse, and a current example of sexual indeterminacy or celebrity drag from popular culture can be used to illuminate a thesis of gendered immateriality. It is then a relatively easy step to the suggestion that, in the words of the anthology we use, "sexuality and gender . . . can take multiple, highly differentiated forms" (Rivkin and Ryan 2000: 677).

To stimulate students to think about the argument that sexuality and gender are variables is also to bring queer studies into play and to endorse some of its main concerns. Kate Chedgzoy observes that "the impact of feminism on queer politics and theory . . . demand[s] that we suspend what we thought we knew about the relation of sex to gender and think again" (Chedgzoy 2001: 8), and it is through invitations to embrace a corresponding readiness to revise that I incorporate gay and lesbian theoretical paradigms into my pedagogy. Once again, the immediate emphasis here is upon representational considerations, although I also attempt to alert students to a generous and mobile construction of gay and/or lesbian identities. Teachers can usefully set up "an extended, metaphorical sense of 'lesbian/gay' so that it connotes a moment of crossing a boundary, or blurring a set of categories" (Barry 2000: 148). It is important to ensure that students do not fall into the trap of branding alternative forms of gendered identity or sexuality as resistant; rather, I try to devolve attention to the range of meanings and effects attached to a gay or lesbian character or episode. When we consider, later in the degree program, Shakespearean representations encompassing a complexity of gay and/or lesbian identifications, these early discussions are well remembered. And, by teaching the differences that inhere even in expressions of difference, it is generally possible to arrive at the shared acknowledgement that gendered attitudes and positions are not universal but local, changing, and historically particular.

Lessons gleaned at Stage 1 can be productively applied to period-based encounters at Stage 2, including an introduction to Renaissance Literature. At its best, the degree program here enables both the exercise of cross-reference and the accumulation of theoretical expertise, with students importing prior experiences both theoretical and Shakespearean into more particularized modes of understanding. Thus, when students arrive to take my Stage 3 module on Shakespeare on Film, they are equipped and attuned, at ease in the task of talking about film, already schooled in early modern literary and cultural production, and generally accepting, if not excited about, the deployment of theory as a vital part of their interpretive toolkit. Frequently I will invite students to work on shared tasks in a spirit of what has been termed "cooperative learning" (Ramsden 1992: 101). In this connection, group presentations are favored, a strategy which matches my own use of small group work in the seminars themselves and which is pitched towards "encouraging active confrontation between students . . . within a clear and supportive structure" (Ramsden 1992: 165). For me, that structure has three components: a weekly end-of-class rehearsal of points of discussion and preparation for the next meeting, praise and encouragement in equal measure, and a dedicated session on writing skills in response to formative essay work and in anticipation of summative assessment improvement. And throughout, reminders of and conversations with feminist and queer theoretical approaches constitute additional means whereby the Shakespeare film and the Shakespeare student are brought into a productive intellectual partnership.

II

Empowering students in advance is integral to the formulation of a mindset within which feminism, gender, and queer studies can be pedagogically aligned. Thus, in my teaching, I regularly recommend to students filmic sequences that can be concentrated on, asking questions about the nature of the representation and the relevant theoretical questions that might be brought into play. This can be quickly appreciated as a procedure: inculcated with broad feminist trajectories, students are generally keen to read film – and Shakespearean ideas – in the light of an acquired gendered logic. For instance, my experience is that a class will seize upon the figuration of Shakespearean women as answering to a system that subordinates even as it may paradoxically emancipate. With Branagh's *Hamlet* (1996), a frequent source of interest is the way in which Ophelia (Kate Winslett) is repeatedly seen in terms of confinement. The grilles and bars against which she is pressed are read as the signs of incarceration; the straitjacket in which she is encased becomes a literal instance of her repression; and the tiled cell in which she is subjected to hydrotherapy is judged a potent symbol of an effort to quell a seemingly disturbed sensibility. Moving laterally to equivalent Victorian courses, the more informed interpreters will, in addition, recognize the context-specific nature of the representation, the implication that Ophelia, in common with her "mad" nineteenth-century counterparts, is being treated for hysteria or a "wandering womb": Polonius's daughter should not "wander," the film wants to argue, and must accordingly be located in a fixed material and ideological mold. Carol Chillington Rutter notes that Ophelia's "memories . . . seem to simulate a first-person viewpoint" (2001: 47) but, in the aftermath of the discussion about Shakespeare's heroine and representation, students more often than not suggest an alternative construction, one that contests and queries the ownership and circulation of *Hamlet*'s numerous flashbacks. Hence, the line, "I do not know, my lord, what I should think" (1.3.104), one class noticed, coincides with a flashback, suggesting that Ophelia is not wholly in command of her own remembered subjectivity. Because other flashbacks of Ophelia and Hamlet (Kenneth Branagh) making love accompany lines delivered by Polonius (Richard Briers), students in that class remarked on a powerful impression of a disputed terrain of sexuality, a policed arena in which "real" events and imagined projections jostle for prominence. Implicitly, Ophelia emerges as "not her own person," as in thrall to the physical and the fantastic policies of her regime. And, building upon its knowledge of secondary commentary on the film, the same class was accordingly fired to take confidence in the original findings that informed discussion had precipitated.

If Ophelia can be made to serve as a test-case for some of feminism's major preoccupations, then so, too, can related Shakespearean heroines. The idea that women are not in control of the social and cultural spaces they inhabit is usefully developed in focused discussion of other recent Shakespeare films. For example, in a film such as Oliver Parker's *Othello* (1995), which, students remind me, was billed as an "erotic thriller" at its release, the containment of eroticism at the level of gender is quickly apparent. Here, the representation of Desdemona (Irène Jacob) is revealing, particularly in the scene in which she is imagined seated and stationary beneath a summer marquee as her father (Pierre Vaneck) and Othello (Laurence Fishburne) walk and speak apart. The sequence is wordless, yet it still conveys separateness and even ostracism to some of its student spectators who are prepared to translate a film's visual grammar into a theoretical vocabulary. Even in filmic sequences that might appear to rise above gendered concerns and to endorse a universalizing essentialism, all-important questions, centered upon women, power, and representation, can still be aired via the classroom encounter. Branagh's *Much Ado About Nothing* (1993) is a case in point, and nowhere more so than in the final scene, the occasion of a choric rendition of the "Hey Nonny Nonny" refrain that extends to the entire cast. On the one hand, students tend to respond to the uplifting tone, lushly orchestrated score, and the spectacle of couples twirling happily in dance, arguing for a celebratory impetus; on the other hand, students are simultaneously prompted to reflect upon the prevailing point of view and to recognize that this is a moment that potentially denies women agency, organized as it is according to a scheme that downplays and makes indistinguishable the female voice. At the level of sound, and to a lesser extent appearance, the conclusion to *Much Ado About Nothing* can function resonantly to introduce gender issues if only by their apparent absence and exclusion.

In part the *Much Ado About Nothing* sequence works so well in teaching feminism and gender because of the ways in which the film inaugurates itself. Several weeks of our Stage 1 classes are devoted to the concept of "*écriture féminine*," which, as Peter Barry states, is by nature "rule-transcending" and "transgressive" (2002: 128). More specifically, as Hélène Cixous writes, such "writing" can feature as one of a number of "sorties" or exits through which women might "undo . . . cultural repression," "reclaim . . . their sex," and "affirm difference" (Belsey and Moore 1989: 229). Obviously, interweaving lessons learned incrementally, the endeavor is not to produce a one-dimensional critic or theorist; rather, in using Shakespeare film as a revealing instance, the purpose is both to canvass particular points of feminist intervention and to open students to the more general – and pervasive – ways in which gender can operate. Noting the juxtaposition of Leonato's (Richard Briers) painting and Beatrice's (Emma Thompson) book in the opening *mise-en-scène*, Douglas Lanier, for example, writes of *Much Ado About Nothing* that the sequence works to signal "the subordination of a static artifact . . . to its living enactment" (Lanier 1996: 192). The learning curve undertaken means that the stronger students will deploy such commentary as a starting-point and direct debate to the gendered nature of the "subordination" process. In such instances, it is soon observed that Beatrice's solitary voiceover at the start – she speaks but does not sing the "Hey Nonny Nonny" theme – is significant because it is a woman's perspective that is prioritized. Similarly, students may point out, the suggestion is that a canonical Shakespearean script is here experienced in a moment of revision; or, to adopt one of the concepts of the song, a woman authorizes a process of textual and ideological "conversion." "The woman vies for textual and representational space," and "Beatrice commands individual and then communal domains," are some of the additional observations generated from the discussion's lively exchanges. Jean Howard locates Beatrice's "iconoclastic voice" in the social contests of the early modern playhouse (Howard 1994: 68), yet a virtue of film is that it situates and translates those conflicts via an alternative visual and aural register: for students, the particular organizational modes of the screen can provide an enriched and an enlivening confrontation with central Shakespearean considerations.

Textual conversion may also facilitate sexual expression. That, at least, is the conclusion to which a class might be steered when *Much Ado About Nothing* is felicitously aligned with *Othello*. If Beatrice is distinctive, it is noted, for speaking and symbolically writing, Desdemona stands out as a woman who looks and acts. In the film's consummation scene, students remark, Desdemona is played, as Lisa S. Starks reminds us, as a "desiring subject": hers is the point of view that is privileged; the specular economy of the encounter belongs with her constructed experience (Starks 1997: 72). The realization is resonant, for it can entail the corresponding discovery that where, in the play, Desdemona is marked by "hear[ing]" (1.3.144) – she is, as Karen Newman writes, "represented in terms of an aural . . . libidinal economy" (Newman 1991: 86) – in the film, she has "observing" (1.3.149) as her chief characteristic. Arguably, the shift from one sensory mode to another is indicative both of an alternative (filmic) mechanism for the articulation of subjectivity and of a female type who is more actively conceived. The thesis is powerfully borne out when students watch the opening sequence: here, Desdemona is imaged running through a darkened colonnade. Flight is stressed, but so too are agency, movement, and a personality in purposeful transit. The veil concealing Desdemona's face is then removed in a gesture which, because it is accompanied by a look to camera or to some unspecified off-screen presence, takes on semidefiant associations. In retrospect, of course, the divestiture, or figurative unrobing, is constitutive of the film's representation of the sexualized Desdemona and, launched upon this theme, students display alacrity in spotting the parallel. Once again, the play is illuminated through sections of the film being pinpointed: hence, the notion of a "maiden . . . / Of spirit so still and quiet that her motion / Blushed at herself" (1.3.94–6) appears at odds with its filmic equivalent, to the extent that constructions emanating from a male hegemony appear by comparison idealized and untenable. A species of psychic misreading is pointed up in the screen's translation operations.

Both *Much Ado About Nothing* and *Othello* in their film manifestations are at points premised upon questions about female power that lie at the heart of feminist criticism and practice. Film, in these respects, is communicative and instructive, and particularly so when its visual appurtenances – colors, palette, composition, and connotation – are instrumental in promoting a reading responsive to the workings of gendered authority. Samuel Crowl notes that the "world" of Julie Taymor's *Titus* (2000) is "sexually decadent" (Crowl 2003: 208), and, in my gender-oriented classroom, it is the precise forms that "decadence" assumes that tend to generate interest. Having been encouraged to reflect upon the complexion of the rivalry between mothers and fathers in the play, students will usually point out that Tamora's relationship with Saturninus (Jessica Lange and Alan Cumming) is predicated upon maternal dominance and infantilized disempowerment. An early shot reveals Saturninus sprawling in a throne beneath a huge metallic head of a she-wolf. The spatial dynamics of the scene, students remark, reflect the character's diminution at the hands of a matriarchal regime: the animal represented is, of course, the adoptive mothers of the founders of Rome itself. A later sequence reveals Saturninus sporting gold eye make-up, a figurative expression, the class suggests, of his intimacy with and proximity to Tamora, whose golden breastplate conjures a militaristic and eroticized ethos. More arrestingly, when arrows pierce the confines of the palace, puncturing the huge-breasted blow-up goddess that floats in the pool, and when Saturninus is glimpsed naked nuzzling at Tamora's breast, the classroom is confronted with a complex of sexual substitution, maternal sublimation, childlike dependency, and adult sustenance. In the light of previous debates, and through the appropriate line of questioning, students are all too keen to adjudicate between pejorative and affirmative constructions of women's power and to recognize filmic decisions that variously play upon stereotypes and move beyond inherited representational molds. Such discussion is invariably aided, in the case of *Titus*, by the figuration of Saturninus, since the emperor is simultaneously discovered as affected and effeminized, as a type who, adorned in baubles and medals, is increasingly elaborated as sexually ambiguous. If only in a vulgarized fashion, the representation of Saturninus introduces the prospect of homoerotic impulses rather than heterosexual alliances and thus the possibility of queer interpretations. Moreover, if gay and lesbian identities have already been appreciated through teaching as encompassing the "crossing [of] a boundary, or [the] blurring [of] a set of categories" (Barry 2000: 148), then Saturninus, in his stereotypically camp aspects, constitutes both a place of departure and an imagining of a sexual persona to interrogate pedagogically.

Interestingly, in Shakespeare films, it is not so much the obvious and flamboyant type such as Saturninus that suggests a queer reading as the less strident, even invisible, male consorts and companions who throng the *dramatis personae* of the plays. Building upon Julie Rivkin and Michael Ryan's argument that "sexuality and gender . . . can take multiple, highly differentiated forms" (Rivkin and Ryan 2000: 677), I discuss with my students the range of gay and lesbian connections and relations in Shakespeare as they are envisaged in film, focusing initially upon issues of marginality and exclusion as they are played out in a type such as the chaperon, Boyet (Richard Clifford), in Branagh's *Love's Labour's Lost* (2000). Michael D. Friedman writes of *Love's Labour's Lost*, "there is hardly a moment . . . that does not . . . contribute to the viewer's awareness of . . . gender dichotomy and the ultimate pairing of male and female" (Friedman 2004: 137), and, in this connection, it is striking for students that, at the end of the film, Boyet is visibly taken out before the final montage of the D-Day celebrations. The solitary death that occurs in the previous sequence – a breakneck run-through of World War II composed of fictive interpolations and stock footage – is that of Boyet, significant for most students as the film's only sexually unattached individual. It is as if *Love's Labour's Lost* wishes to withdraw

from Boyet once the male-female matches have been made and, with the
ideological implications of his French resistance demise in mind, politically
aware students will make a connection between the sanitized appearance of
the war in the film (the sequence involves suggestive Nazi regalia suitable
for a family film) and the comparable sexual sanitizing of the *dénouement*.
Because single, Boyet is cosmetically removed, wiped out of the frame and
the film's aesthetic in a move which, classroom discussion suggests, is akin
to an acknowledgement of a gay or queer subtext. With the separate and
solicitous Boyet, it seems, excision becomes a means of accommodation.

Gay and lesbian readings take on an added force in filmic representations of same-sex relations. An intriguing manifestation of sublimated
homoerotic attraction is discovered in Branagh's *Henry V* (1989) in which
the traitors are met by the king on the eve of the French departure. What
strikes students here is an escalating tension that reveals itself in sexualized gestures, not least the swoop of hands reaching aggressively for
phallic swords, the balletic choreography of physically proximate bodies,
and the touch of Henry's (Kenneth Branagh) finger upon Scroop's
(Stephen Simms) cheek. Yet students in my experience are quick to
remark that this is no "queer utopia" (Burt 1997: 240): the highlighting
of the accompanying language suggests a connection between eroticism
and betrayal, political intrigue, and ideals of chastity and purity. Formalist
reading practices developed in earlier parts of the curriculum are essential
at moments such as these as a class, via the filmic decision, addresses
terms such as "bedfellow" (2.2.8) and "constant" (2.2.130) and reflects upon
their implications. *Henry V* conjures with homoeroticism as an episode or
as a moment to be transcended; by contrast, Michael Radford's *William
Shakespeare's The Merchant of Venice* (2004) takes the same-sex relationship of Antonio and Bassanio (Jeremy Irons and Joseph Fiennes) and extends
it into a constituent part of the narrative. A cluster of filmic emphases can
steer students to this interpretation – the visual/verbal juxtaposition of the
first glimpse of Bassanio and the taunt about "love" (1.1.46), the infamous
kiss in a sumptuously appointed interior red boudoir, the longing look that
Antonio throws back to Venice through the window of the Belmont
palazzo. Like Jessica and Shylock (Zuleikha Robinson and Al Pacino),
Antonio is figured in terms of loss, although, in his case, it is a personal/sexual
intimacy that has to be left behind. Underscoring the complexion of
Antonio's situation is the conclusion's paired arrangements: as Bassanio and
Gratiano (Kris Marshall) lament the relinquishment of their rings, Portia
and Nerissa (Lynn Collins and Heather Goldenhersh) kiss, giggle, and pop

pieces of fruit in each other's mouths. Via an approximation of lesbian desire, usually characterized by a class as "lipstick lesbianism," a fiction of supposed heterosexual treachery is entertained. The consumption/consummation equation evoked by the scene of feeding carries a powerful sexual charge, with lesbianism being seen, astute students will suggest, as a threat to the articulation of a coherent masculinity. In addition, because students will have already been introduced to contextual readings of Renaissance drama, including commentaries upon the same-sex functions of early modern playhouse practices, they are quick to note the ironies involved in the filmic spectacle of women playing roles that, in the sixteenth and seventeenth centuries, would have been taken by boys (themselves the selective impersonators of cross-gender identifications). The twinning of gay and lesbian connections in this instance functions to stimulate awareness not only of the cultural work performed by nonnormative sexualities, but also the contingencies and arbitrariness of gender itself.

It is in these respects that Shakespeare film can once again underwrite salient Shakespearean themes. If, in the plays, gender is a matter of negotiation, contest, interrogation, and transformation, then such a scenario is retold only in order to be amplified on screen. Gender can appear, in fact, as a floating signifier in film, a property that merges and fluctuates according to discrete locations and circumstances. On the one hand, students, excited by visual triggers and clues, tend to see the process resulting in a lack of distinction, a state of amorphousness or collapse. In Michael Almereyda's *Hamlet* (2000), for example, an immediate topic of discussion is the way in which the color-coded look of Ophelia (Julia Stiles) and Hamlet (Ethan Hawke) – both are represented as favoring red and black clothes and living spaces – has a deindividuating effect: the characters are difficult to disentangle, they appear biologically the same. Or, to adopt a formulation from Catherine Belsey, as did one class, Shakespeare film accentuates the ideological operations of the drama, which can be "read as disrupting sexual difference, calling in question that set of relations between terms which proposes as inevitable an antithesis between masculine and feminine, men and women" (Belsey 1985: 166). On the other hand, gender can be communicated in film as inherently unstable, subject to flux, mutability, unpredictability, and upset. Such is the reading an appropriately theorized class will produce when confronted with the opening of a film such as Nunn's *Twelfth Night* (1996), in which Viola and Sebastian (Imogen Stubbs and Steven Mackintosh) are figured as entertainers in a ship's concert party. Initially, the twins appear in oriental attire as women from a harem, yet, in the wake of the voices separating into soprano and baritone, and after the veils have been torn aside to reveal mutually worn moustaches, precise gendered affiliations are thrown into disarray. For students, the sequence raises key questions. Where are the dividing lines of gender drawn, and what categories can be invoked in its organization? To what extent is gender defined by appearance, or are there – can there ever be – intrinsic and/or essentialist determinants? Thus stimulated, students invariably go on to recognize that the accompanying song – a version of the "O mistress mine, where are you roaming?" (2.3.35) ditty – has been transposed to illuminate the predicament of gender and its "roaming" status. In addition, the fact that the film begins with a masquerade recalls, to some, previous discussions about "performativity": if male and female roles are only matters of enactment, students suggest, then, as Judith Butler makes clear, there is no "cultural process" that generates identity in terms of an inherent or "pre-existing natural . . . substance" (in Rivkin and Ryan 2000: 530). Gender, as expressed here, is accessible only through a register of theatre and play.

The notion of gender as performance is often the destination to which I aspire in my teaching, in part because Butler's conceptualizations of her subject facilitate a number of points of critical intervention. Hers is a plural and mobile sense of gender and its operations, one that emphasizes in an affirmative sense possibilities and opportunities. Working best for me, in this connection, is Baz Lurhmann's *William Shakespeare's Romeo and Juliet* (1996) and the performance, in drag, by Mercutio (Harold Perrineau) of the "Young Hearts, Run Free" number at the Capulet ball. What is typically arresting in the sequence is not so much the idea of a cross-gendered act that throws gender into confusion as the phenomenon of various identities being simultaneously held in play. This is most stridently articulated, the keenest members of my class invariably inform me, not in the film proper but in a DVD extra, which features the number in its entirety and furnishes a more precise fit between the screen imaginary and the verbal contents of the performance. Admittedly, at least at first sight, the song's words do not appear to offer a coherent narrative:

> Young hearts, run free,
> Never be hung up, hung up like my man and me
> . . . to yourself be true,
> Don't be no fool with
> When loving is all there is, say that I don't love you.

The thrill of the played occasion in class, however, can excite rationalized responses, as when students remark that the lyrics communicate a construction of roles negotiated and rejected, of restriction abandoned in the interests of an unfettered subjectivity. The message is that of emancipation, we generally conclude, of a bypassing of an already indeterminate part in order to privilege another position as yet not properly defined. "Young Hearts, Run Free," according to this logic, becomes a hymn to the leaving behind of gendered stereotypes, a celebration of the potential of finding new means of expression in materials inevitably compromised or adversely affected. Even if apparently set at an unbridgeable distance from a construction of "Shakespeare," moreover, the sequence can still lead us back, and particularly so in discussions of the ways in which both Romeo and Juliet are represented at the level of a coming to terms with, if not a transcendence of, normative barriers and cultural exclusion zones.

III

By way of a conclusion, I would like to stress again that the Shakespeare film functions pedagogically to return us to the text and also to critical perspectives that might be either embraced or interrogated. In this process, film is not an instrument of reification; rather, its deployment permits a range of versions of the dramatist, from early modern to postmodern, to be accessed in relation to feminism, gender, and queer studies and in the context of ongoing ideological debates. Films in and of themselves can draw attention to particularized textual questions and, in their translations of gendered performances, open windows onto the conventions whereby sixteenth- and seventeenth-century desires were staged and ventilated. Often it is what film misses out that brings the play back into the fold. Hence, in Alan Sinfield's words, the "amatory sacrifice" that, in *The Merchant of Venice*, is linked to "homoerotic excess" (Sinfield 1996: 125) is drawn attention to in the film via the omission of Antonio's famous "I am a tainted wether of the flock" (4.1.113) speech, with its castration-invoking associations. But the relation can also operate in the opposite direction, for, in the place of the play's downplaying of a linguistic presence (Antonio's silence at the end), the film substitutes a visual reminder (the merchant's traversing before the camera at the *dénouement*). Working forwards and backwards, the filmic/dramatic connection is mutually illuminating. Omissions, then, facilitate rereadings of character and situation:

Almereyda's *Hamlet* is pertinent here, since the spectacle of a genderless romantic couple recalls the highly charged expressions of anxious masculinity, and bouts of misogyny, that belong with the play's incarnation of the protagonist. Filmic amputation skews but does not eradicate a dramatic original's ideological unpalatability.

Often, that reencounter with the play necessitates a confrontation with drama's defining features and dimensions. For instance, the filmic construction of Ophelia's "wandering womb" in Branagh's *Hamlet* plots a route back to Shakespeare's elaboration of a woman whose only access to a sexualized self is through language, the "mad scenes" being a particularly resonant case in point. Few moments of private reflection are permitted Ophelia in the play, since dramatic conventions do not trade so obviously upon the periodically inserted flashback; instead, the focus falls upon words that convey, or chart the collapse of, the character's status as subject. A class reminded of dramatic language and its spheres of operation may, at such a point, instance *Much Ado About Nothing* and the ways in which, in that comedy, Beatrice is defined by her militaristic "skirmish of wit" (1.1.51) with Benedick, and Hero is both maligned and reconstructed through men's verbal agency. By the same token, a class prompted to recall earlier instruction in feminist theory may build upon this discussion to note that, as Cora Kaplan writes, the "field of language," although erected around a "male-centred . . . tradition," is still susceptible "to invasion and subversion by female speakers" (Kaplan 1986: 92). A film evokes a drama cut across by the possibilities attached to, and the limitations inherent in, gendered modalities of linguistic resistance.

If *Much Ado About Nothing*, some students note, might be seen as concerned with women's efforts to rewrite or reverse the narratives that have insisted upon either silence or subordination, other plays in the canon flag up the relations between men necessary for maintaining the (sometimes fragile) edifice of male authority. In the context of such relations, the exclusionist policies in operation at the end of the filmic *Love's Labour's Lost* take on an added force, with the celebrations surrounding the reunited heterosexual couples being read as response to the generic anomalousness of the play. The drama's conclusion is identified by its unconventional deferral of sexual consummation – its continuing privileging of male-male alliances – and it is towards a more acceptable redefinition of that situation, a particularly illuminating class discussion suggested, that the film is geared. Via engagement with the play's avoidance of the anticipated *dénouement* all classes can be invited to consider the frames of reference within which sexuality was historically articulated. Crucially, when students address Branagh's film version of *Henry V*, they are primed to assess not only the variety of male-male ties of fealty in the play (as expressed in, for instance, notions of fraternity and *communitas*) but also the particularized forms that these points of connection assumed in the sixteenth- and seventeenth-century discursive formation. The scene in the film devoted to the revelation of treachery in Henry's camp is useful in these respects, for, by investing in signifiers of sublimated homoeroticism, it causes students to think about the equivalent rhetoric of approximation familiar to Shakespeare's audience. Alan Bray's argument that a "deep . . . physical intimacy" could be enacted in ideals of male "friendship" (Bray 1994: 44) comes as no surprise to students when they are led on a trajectory that commences with the film, progresses to the play, and ends with a consideration of the complementary devices that both mediums deploy in their respective representations of gendered experience.

Even in Shakespeare films in which gender is expressed at the level of interpolation, as in *Twelfth Night*, a confrontation with some of the play's perennially intractable questions can be facilitated. Valerie Traub writes that *Twelfth Night*, the play, "explores a diversity of desire, proceeding with erotic plurality as far as it can; then, in the face of anxiety generated by this exploration, it fixes the homoerotic interest onto . . . Antonio," closing down "the possibility of . . . play" (Traub 1992: 123). Yet my classroom experience suggests that, delighted by the obvious "play" of the film's inauguration, the dramatic "original" is judged a far more slippery and inchoate affair, with students homing in variously on the figuration of a count who appears still attracted to the spectacle of the cross-dressed Viola, of a "desire" that continues to be male-male in orientation, of a heroine who remains suspended between genders, existing in a limbo of indecision and indeterminacy, and of a semantic nexus that, invoking euphemisms for sexual parts and trade – "habits" (5.1.374), "mistress" (5.1.375), and "queen" (5.1.375) – insists upon a system of identification that has not yet resolved itself into clarity. In the wake of the filmic encounter with Shakespeare, the play can assume these and related depths and mysteries, inconsistencies and intractabilities.

How far these sorts of encounter enable a politicized classroom is a matter for conjecture. We must, of course, guard against the illusive fiction that, as Dympna Callaghan states, "transvestite destabilizations . . . offer . . . liberating possibilities for feminism" (Callaghan 2000: 32), yet it is also salutary, surely, to agree with Catherine Belsey when she suggests that one of the virtues of Shakespeare's plays is that they make available "definitions and redefinitions which make it possible to reinterpret a world we have taken for granted" (Belsey 1985: 190). By scrutinizing such "definitions," and arriving at "redefinitions," in a classroom in Northern Ireland, students, I like to think, are enabled to arrive not only at a fresh sense of their agency but also at a consciousness about their own positions in a society that has historically traded upon fixed roles and that has often elected to judge on the basis of predetermined affiliations. It is here that gender-aware pedagogy might have an effect, even a transformative function, one that invests in local policies and practices in order to fashion more constructive modes of understanding and ultimately political engagement. The context of the place of learning is, in this arguably idealized prognosis, a facilitative one for the emergence of new forms of interpretation that can boast a significant cultural purchase. "To expose and question that complex of ideas about women and men which . . . are confirmed in our literature," states Judith Fetterley, "is to make the system of power . . . open not only to discussion but eventually to change" (Rivkin and Ryan 2000: 566). The Shakespeare classroom, film, and play can contribute to such change if the appropriate methods and aspirations are enlisted; the balance of power will shift again; and the world may yet appear, in the words of *Twelfth Night*, in "other habits" (5.1.374) and different colors.

References and Further Reading

Barry, Peter (2002). *Beginning Theory: An Introduction to Literary and Cultural Theory.* Manchester and New York: Manchester University Press.

Belsey, Catherine (1985). "Disrupting Sexual Difference: Meaning and Gender in the Comedies." In John Drakakis (Ed.). *Alternative Shakespeares* (pp. 166–90). New York: Methuen.

Belsey, Catherine and Jane Moore (Eds) (1989). *The Feminist Reader: Essays in Gender and the Politics of Literary Criticism.* Basingstoke, UK: Macmillan.

Bray, Alan (1994). "Homosexuality and the Signs of Male Friendship." In Jonathan Goldberg (Ed.). *Queering the Renaissance* (pp. 40–65). Durham, NC: Duke University Press.

Burt, Richard (1997). "The Love That Dare Not Speak Shakespeare's Name: New Shakesqueer Cinema." In Lynda E. Boose and Richard Burt (Eds). *Shakespeare, the Movie: Popularizing the Plays on Film, TV, and Video* (pp. 240–68). London and New York: Routledge.

Callaghan, Dympna (2000). *Shakespeare Without Women: Representing Gender and Race on the Renaissance Stage.* London and New York: Routledge.

Chedgzoy, Kate (Ed.) (2001). *Shakespeare, Feminism and Gender.* Basingstoke, UK: Palgrave.

Crowl, Samuel (2003). *Shakespeare at the Cineplex: The Kenneth Branagh Era.* Athens: Ohio University Press.

Friedman, Michael D. (2004). " 'I Won't Dance, Don't Ask Me': Branagh's *Love's Labour's Lost* and the American Film Musical." *Literature/Film Quarterly* 32: 134–43.

Greenblatt, Stephen, Walter Cohen, Jean E. Howard and Katharine Eisaman Maus (Eds) (1997). *The Norton Shakespeare.* New York: W. W. Norton.

Howard, Jean (1994). *The Stage and Social Struggle in Early Modern England.* London and New York: Routledge.

Kaplan, Cora (1986). *Sea Changes: Essays in Culture and Feminism.* London: Verso.

Lanier, Douglas (1996). "Drowning the Book: *Prospero's Books* and the Textual Shakespeare." In James C. Bulman (Ed.). *Shakespeare, Theory, and Performance* (pp. 187–209). London and New York: Routledge.

Newman, Karen (1991). *Fashioning Femininity and English Renaissance Drama.* Chicago and London: University of Chicago Press.

Ramsden, Paul (1992). *Learning to Teach in Higher Education.* London and New York: Routledge.

Rivkin, Julie and Michael Ryan (Eds) (2000). *Literary Theory: An Anthology.* Oxford: Blackwell.

Rutter, Carol Chillington (2001). *Enter the Body: Women and Representation on Shakespeare's Stage.* London and New York: Routledge.

Sinfield, Alan (1996). "How to Read *The Merchant of Venice* Without Being Heterosexist." In Terence Hawkes (Ed.). *Alternative Shakespeares, Vol. 2* (pp. 122–39). London and New York: Routledge.

Starks, Lisa S. (1997). "The Veiled (Hot)bed of Race and Desire: Parker's *Othello* and the Stereotype as Screen Fetish." *PostScript* 17.1: 64–78.

Traub, Valerie (1992). *Desire and Anxiety: Circulations of Sexuality in Shakespearean Drama.* London and New York: Routledge.

Filmography

Hamlet (1996). Directed by Kenneth Branagh. Castle Rock, videocassette.

Hamlet (2000). Directed by Michael Almereyda. Miramax Films, DVD.

Henry V (1989). Directed by Kenneth Branagh. Samuel Goldwyn Company, DVD.

Love's Labour's Lost (2000). Directed by Kenneth Branagh. Miramax Films, DVD.

Much Ado About Nothing (1993). Directed by Kenneth Branagh. Samuel Goldwyn Company, DVD.

Othello (1995). Directed by Oliver Parker. Castle Rock, DVD.

Titus (2000). Directed by Julie Taymor. Fox Searchlight and Clear Blue Sky Productions, DVD.

Twelfth Night (1996). Directed by Trevor Nunn. Fine Line Features, videocassette.

William Shakespeare's The Merchant of Venice (2004). Directed by Michael Radford. Sony Pictures Classics, DVD.

William Shakespeare's Romeo + Juliet (1996). Directed by Baz Luhrmann. Twentieth-Century Fox, DVD.

10

Teaching Shakespeare and Race in the New Empire

Ania Loomba

You can't be president of the United States unless you have read Shakespeare. (Thorndike, 1927: 15)

Why teach issues of race and colonialism in relation to Shakespeare? What can we achieve through such a pedagogy – a deeper understanding of Shakespeare and his world, or a greater engagement with our own? One answer is that we don't really have a choice – Shakespeare has *already* been, and continues to be, taught, performed, and written about in highly racialized ways, and for highly racialized purposes. We must necessarily either challenge these histories, or rehearse them. There is no middle ground.

Anthony Appiah (1992: 48) writes that the terms "Race, nation, litera-ture . . . are bound together in the recent intellectual history of the West . . . Nation is the key middle term in understanding the relations between the concept of *race* and the idea of literature." Since Shakespeare's own day, the concepts of "race" and "nation" have developed as interlinked "imagined communities," and, since at least the late eighteenth century, literature has been seen as their "natural" expression. The English canon, with Shakespeare at its apex, was formed as the expression of an Anglo-Saxon sensibility, which, like the institutionalization of English literary studies, was itself partly the product of colonial governance.[1] In the colonies Shakespeare was taught as the simultaneous epitome of a *particular* (spe-cial and unique) "Western" and "English" culture, and of *universal* human values, an approach that is still widely recycled (see, for example, Bloom

1998: 9). Thus Shakespeare, race, and colonialism have been connected by the very approaches that claim to be "above" or not interested in these issues.

It is a measure of how racialized scholarship on early modern culture has been that in the 1970s the novelist Michelle Cliff completed a dissertation on Italian Renaissance art without "dealing with the fact that the slave trade began in the Renaissance. . . . We were studying – now you'd have thought the slave trade would have come into this – the explorations of the Renaissance into the New World and how they influenced art" (Raiskin 1993: 62). Such pedagogy is not an act of oversight; as Kim F. Hall observed, "in most Renaissance classrooms" students are *"taught not to see* issues of white privilege and power" (K. F. Hall 1996: 461; emphasis added). Despite the scholarship and pedagogy that has made it increasingly possible for a teacher to provide alternative perspectives, this is still largely the case. But I want to add something to Hall's formulation: most students of the Renaissance, especially in the US, are also *taught not to see* issues of colonial and neo-imperial privilege and power. If racial ideologies shaped, and were themselves reshaped by, European expansion and the formation of the colonial world system, today, in the age of yet another globalization, they continue to be complexly intertwined with global asymmetries. Today, issues of race relations and cross-culture contact are often discussed as if they are entirely a matter of individual identities and personal choices; both in public culture and in certain parts of the academy, they are separated from questions of history, class, and global relations. And I want to argue in this essay that it is a necessary pedagogic task to make visible these intersections, especially at this time when global relations are so obviously reshaping racial and national identities everywhere, and when the United States stands at the apex of a new global empire.

The assumption that "Shakespeare," "Western Culture," and "America" are seamlessly connected hinges on the presumed whiteness and Anglo-Saxon heritage of all three terms, and has long been harnessed to a racialized vision of the United States (Bristol 1990: 142). In the post-9/11 context, the idea of a Shakespeare who unites "Western civilization" has been widely reiterated. To take but one example, the American Council of Trustees and Alumni (ACTA), in a report called *The Shakespeare File* (1996), suggested that reading Shakespeare "properly" would inculcate the right "American" and "Western" values. Lamenting that Shakespeare had lost ground to topics such as "AIDS activism," "people of color," "insurgent nationalism," "homophobia," "third world liberation struggles," "urban poor,"

and "vagrancy," it concluded that "This country cannot expect a generation raised on gangster films and sex studies to maintain its leadership in
the world. Or even its unity as a nation . . . Shakespeare's works provide a
common frame of reference that helps unite us into a single community
of discourse." While there may be nothing new in this, it is worth noting
that the "culture wars" and questions of US race relations are now increasingly linked to American global supremacy, and to the so-called "clash of
civilizations." Thus, after the events of September 11, 2001, ACTA published
another report called *Defending Civilization: How Our Universities Are
Failing America and What Can Be Done About It* (February 2002), which
claimed that "academe is the only sector of American society that is distinctly divided in response" to the war in Afghanistan; it suggested that
this division was the direct result of "an educational system that has
increasingly suggested that Western civilization is the primary source of
the world's ills even though it gave us the ideals of democracy, human rights,
individual liberty, and mutual tolerance." More recently, race and colonialism
are explicitly named by ACTA (2006) as issues that are detracting from the
real mission of education, and especially from the real task of humanities
and literature classes.

Unfortunately, ACTA does not represent a loony fringe – ever since the
invasion of Iraq, policy makers, politicians, public figures, and scholars
have exhorted the United States to don an imperialist mantle by learning
actively from the history of the British empire. If the British empire spread
"Western Civilization" across the globe, the American empire will save such
a civilization now. Advocates of a new US empire regard institutions of higher
education as crucial to the task of global supremacy: Niall Ferguson (2003)
urges the United States to send out its "best and the brightest" students
(instead of its new immigrants) on the imperial mission, while other writers suggest that postcolonial critiques are detrimental to US national and
international interests. If Shakespeare was used as the literary lynchpin of
that empire, what is his place in the new one? *Henry V* has been widely
invoked by the media to draw comparisons between Hal and George Bush,
both "wastrels" turned decisive imperialists, and the play has been handed
out in a new "Armed Services Edition" to troops overseas (see Newstok
2003). Even *Othello* has been used to make an argument for invading Iraq.
Political, military, as well as business elites now conduct training sessions
via Shakespeare.[2]

While it is productive to introduce these contemporary debates into
our classrooms, what do they contribute to our understanding of early

modern culture? Francesca Royster rightly warns us that if, at one time, early modern race studies needed to "bridge once separate critical traditions like Shakespeare studies and African American studies," now "we may be at risk of losing a complex view of historical contexts as we, Shakespeare scholars and cultural critics, seek to make contact with the present" (Royster 1998: 69). But, on the other hand, can we really make contact with the past by unmooring ourselves from the present? In seeking too strenuously to maintain a critical distance between our contemporary concerns and the past, there is the danger that, as Kim Hall puts it, race might become just another "new frontier for literary criticism, yet another way to reanimate Renaissance studies rather than to produce antiracist criticism and potentially forceful pedagogy" (Hall 1995: 225).

In this essay, I want to explore the possibilities of bringing both historical complexity and antiracist and anti-imperialist pedagogy into simultaneous focus. I will suggest that the complexities of difference in our contemporary world *help* us attend to the nuances of early modern ideologies of difference, and to their expression in literature. Ironically, even as it is often suggested that racial ideologies and colonialism in the modern sense did not exist during the early modern period, we also hear that the world has now moved on "beyond race," and that we have left the legacies of colonialism behind. At the juncture at which we stand, it is particularly fruitful to bring these two worlds into conversation, not with a view to establishing neat convergences, but to look at differences as well. Because it is my experience of teaching Shakespeare in a variety of situations that has constantly led me to rethink race and its connections with colonialism, it is to some of these that I want to briefly turn.

I

I started teaching in an undergraduate college in New Delhi, India. After nearly 13 years, including three and a half years in Britain as a PhD student, I moved to a largely postgraduate university in Delhi, and then on to several very different campuses in the United States. And as I write this essay I am teaching a Shakespeare class in London. Moving around like this, I have become acutely aware that there is no single way to be an "effective" teacher: just as the meanings of Shakespeare change across the globe, so do the specific implications of racial difference, colonialism, and empire. I do not mean that these terms can never be defined, understood, or challenged, but rather that the diverse histories and implications of racial and colonial experiences are precisely what have shaped any general meaning we may assign to them.

My first entry into these subjects was via the question of colonial education, rather than race. Shakespeare was a compulsory part of virtually all undergraduates' curricula at the University of Delhi, whether or not they had the necessary linguistic competence, and whether they came from humble provincial schools or elite Westernized ones. Sometimes I would find myself desperately translating for students who had little investment in Shakespeare beyond the necessity of passing their exams; at other times, I would marvel at the breathless enthusiasm of the more elite students who seemed to have no distance from the truisms trundled out by mainstream criticism about the value of Shakespeare. This experience prompted me to think about how we got there in the first place, or the colonial history of Shakespearean education.

Shakespeare's empire in the colonies extended well into the postcolonial era. The patriarchal aspects of this pedagogy were especially obvious in 1970s and 1980s India, but it is an index of middle-class life in metropolitan India that I didn't reflect much about race as such – for the most part, urban middle-class Indians like me thought of themselves as racially unmarked, much as white subjects are in the West. Till today, "race" is a subject that is undertheorized and discussed in India, even by scholarship on the Indian empire. After I went to Britain to do my doctoral work, I found myself, for the first time, as part of a racialized group, and was deeply influenced by attempts to forge common ground among Asian, African, and Caribbean immigrants, and especially among women. At that time, the term "Black" was adopted as a political term that would unify those fighting against racism, as in the "Southhall Black Sisters," a mixed-race antiracist and feminist group. As Stuart Hall described it, "the term 'black' was coined as a way of referencing the common experience of racism and marginalization in Britain and came to provide the organizing category of a new politics of resistance, among groups and communities with, in fact, very different histories, traditions and ethnic identities" (S. Hall 1996: 441).

I focused on the intersection of race and gender in my work on early modern culture and literature, on the making of racial identities during colonialism, and the ways in which diverse subjects were constituted as "black." Like others who were arguing for the very validity of studying race in the Renaissance and of connecting these texts to our own lives, I tended to underplay the heterogeneity of racialized subjects, the diverse histories of contact in the early modern world, as well as the differences between early modern and modern worlds. But Asia, Africa, and America are not all one "non-European" world and not all were colonized in the same way or at the same time. Skin color, religious difference, and class intersect in the making of race. These issues were brought to the fore by my teaching experiences in India as well as in the US, and by the heterogeneity of my classrooms in both contexts.

First India. During the 1990s, discussions about the colonial heritage of English literary education took on a distinctly chauvinistic flavor; many critics and teachers suggested that all Western texts were irrelevant, as were supposedly "Western" ways of analysis (which included, not surprisingly, feminism and Marxism). Indian "authenticity" is often a barely disguised upper-class Hindu patriarchal perspective which completely distorts the reality of the Indian cultural landscape as well as the potential of all literary texts to speak to varied audiences. In this situation, I found myself arguing (along with some of my students), that there was nothing *necessarily* retrograde about studying Shakespeare, just as there was nothing necessarily *radical* about simply shifting the object of critical inquiry from Western to Indian texts (Loomba 1991). One of the problems with this ultranationalist literary critique was that it glossed over internal hierarchies in India, which have meant that lower castes, religious minorities, and people from India's own underdeveloped borders are viewed and treated in ways that can be understood as racial. As one critic points out, from the point of view of historically oppressed castes, Shakespeare or Milton are not necessarily more alien than a Sanskrit text that advocates caste hierarchies (Ilaiah 1996: 15).

Since the 1990s, moreover, the racialization of religious difference in India has become increasingly evident. Hindu fundamentalism has been aggressively consolidating itself both rhetorically and through organized pogroms against Muslims that have been inspired by, and can be compared to, fascist "ethnic cleansing." As I watched my students getting divided into religious and caste factions on an unprecedented scale, I became more sensitive to the question of religion in early modern Europe, and its central place in the consolidation of the very idea of race. Conversely, as I read about that history, I was alerted to the many ways in which religion and culture are becoming pathologized in our own world. I remember a Muslim student coming up to me with a copy of a book I had written, open to the page where I discussed early modern English views of Islam and the Qur'an. This student argued that I was wrong in writing that the faithful would be rewarded with young boys in paradise; I found it hard to convince him that my quotations from the stereotypes circulated by early writers were critiques and not endorsements of their views. His obduracy was, I think, at least partly shaped by his experience of being a Muslim – the misrepresentations of and attacks on Islam that I had cited were close to those he heard around him.

The overlaps between race, religion, and caste were the focus of intense debate at the 2001 World Conference Against Racism, Racial Discrimination, Xenophobia, and Related Intolerance in Durban. Those who wanted caste and religious discrimination (including Zionism) discussed at the conference insisted that these supposedly "social" categories have been just as pernicious as the ones that were understood as "biological," and that both religious minorities and lower castes are oppressed and even pathologized along similar lines. Some of those who wanted them excluded insisted that the society/biology distinction is crucial (Beteille 2001). These debates are not entirely new – their earlier versions have centered around whether anti-Semitism is a form of racial discrimination – but they are still absolutely crucial for all pedagogy on race, and, as I discuss below, especially important for early modernists.

It is still common to hear the view that because there was no developed "biological" vocabulary for difference, "race" was not a "fully developed" discourse in the early modern period. Such views take at face value, instead of interrogating, the vocabularies of racist pseudo-science that were developed during colonialism (Loomba 2002; see also Loomba and Burton 2007: "Introduction"). A growing number of scholars have queried the division between "social" and "biological" categories of difference, both theoretically and in relation to premodern Europe (see especially Heng 2003). Historically, "social" differences have neither been neatly distinct from, nor necessarily more pliable than, differences cast as "natural": indeed both categories are relational and historically mutable. "Biological" explanations for all kinds of social and somatic difference emerged alongside the growth of modern science; earlier the same differences were explained in religious terms, but that did not mean that they were understood as more flexible, or transient. Thus, for example, the conversion of Jews to Christianity was portrayed as a fraught and impossible process. Indeed, religious and physical differences shaded into one another, as for example, when blackness was simultaneously described, by the same author and in the same piece of writing, as an "infection" *and* as the result of Noah's curse upon his son Ham (Best 1578: 24–6). In medieval and early modern writings, blackness is often a metaphor for, or a literal manifestation of, a lack of true faith: thus, in the commonplace that it is impossible to wash an Ethiope/a man of Ind/a blackamoor white, the subject is not really blackness but the impossibility of changing the heart of unbelievers or heretics.[3]

Of course, these commonplaces simultaneously entrench views about the indelibility of, or inferiority of, blackness, but the point is precisely that both frames of reference work in tandem. The theoretical possibility of religious conversions is the instance most frequently cited to demarcate a biological discourse of race from a supposedly permeable theological boundary. But it was in and through the controversies and anxieties around religious conversion that what we recognize as a modern vocabulary of race developed. Even after they converted, Jews and Muslims were regarded as carrying intrinsic traits of difference, which were all the more dangerous *because not always visible*. Thus it was that the Spanish "blood-laws" – often understood to be the first modern codification of "race" – sought to pinpoint the difference between Old Christians and various types of convert, both within Spain and abroad. Older notions that Jews and Muslims are visibly distinct from Christians (darker, more effeminate, stinking) provide a reassurance of their safe distance, and the fact that early modern literature reverts to such stereotypes is an index of the crisis provoked by the possibility of crossovers, mingling, and the dissolution of difference.

Indeed, both skin color and religion are further enmeshed with notions of class, which is also understood by us today as a social and permeable category, but which, in the early modern period, is the basis for the idea of lineage or a bloodline. Thus the dark-skinned man who cannot be washed white is, in the original version of the story in one of Aesop's Fables, a *servant*, and some of the key features of racial discourse had emerged out of a vocabulary of class. Noah's curse upon Ham was used to explain the servitude of peasants long before it became an "explanation" for blackness.

Both positions – (1) that an inferior inner essence corresponds with an easily identifiable exterior, and (2) that it does not always do so – as well as the contradictions between the two, can be explored in a number of early modern writings, including many of Shakespeare's plays. Where the physical body and moral characteristics do not easily intersect, there is a crisis, as in *Othello*, where, initially, the hero's physical appearance is understood not to mirror his mental or moral qualities. By the end of the play, many readers feel, Othello's physical being and his moral being have been brought into alignment. The intersection of religion, color and body, class, culture and language, empire and power in this play and other early modern writings allows us to discuss the complexities of race as an idea. So the double meaning of the word "Moor" – black *and* Muslim – points, not to two distinct histories confused by a fuzzy term, but to multiple and intersecting histories that are impossible to separate.

The histories of racism remind us that far from a division between nature and culture, "culture" can function "like a nature" as Etienne Balibar puts it (Balibar 1991: 22), which is to say that it is often invoked as an impermeable boundary between human groups. In fact, in the early modern period, so much did the vocabularies of nature and culture overlap that some writers even suggested that social practices would result in permanent biological mutations (Bulwer 1650: 30, 260–62, 311–12, 398–402, 533–4). *The Tempest* illustrates the way in which a discourse of race is forged through multiple vocabularies and practices spanning different periods – Caliban's monstrosity is shaped by an amalgam of older ideas about natural slavery, serfdom, and class, and newer views about servitude and difference engendered by the colonial dream. The combination produces something new and irreducible, which Miranda now names as "race": "thy vile race . . . had that in't which good natures / Could not abide to be with" (1.2.360–2). This difference is expressed in a quasi-biological vocabulary that nevertheless still harks back to older theological categories: Caliban is, Prospero says, "a born devil, on whose nature / Nurture can never stick" (4.1.188–9).

Thus Judith A. López is right that "a discussion of race that begins by establishing a dichotomy between black and white . . . obscures the prominent intersection between race and religion" and contributes to "our inability to see the complexity and importance of a developing discourse of race in the pre- and early modern periods" (López 1998: 49, 51). But, as I have been suggesting, religion is only one of the many categories that complicate early modern ideas of difference. Early modern vocabularies which feed into a discourse of race also include geography, class, language, the humors, diet, ways of governance, gender, and lineage.[4] All of these can be invoked to reshape, consolidate, or manage relations of power, and none of them can be understood by simply counterposing the biological and social. I am equally concerned that any simple binary also obscures the complexity of *contemporary* identities and power relations. We often hear the argument that scientific racism has now morphed into a "'new racism' that focuses on cultural difference instead of phenotypical differences" and that "cultural difference is the latest boundary of difference" (Pieterse 2002: 22). But early modern literature and history show us that culture and religion are one of the earliest and constant boundaries of difference, often visible precisely when they are supposedly excluded.

It is important that Balibar offers his reading of early modern anti-Semitism out of his need to understand contemporary neo-racism. In the years since Balibar wrote his essay, religion and culture have become more important than ever in the discourse of difference in Europe, in the United States, in India, and elsewhere. Samuel Huntington's infamous proclamation of a "clash of civilizations" (1993) is now echoed by Christian and other conservatives who suggest that Muslims and Asians can never assimilate into Western societies, but also by Islamic and Hindu fundamentalists who suggest that there is an unbridgeable gap between different "cultures." While I am not suggesting that the early modern and contemporary discourses are identical, it is worth noticing that in both cases "race" and "religion" are yoked together in the context of an anxiety about national identity as well as the international movement of peoples. It is also striking that neo-racism can often advance precisely the same conclusions as the old racism, while claiming that it is not racist because it does not believe in the older ideologies of biological difference.

A notorious instance is Richard J. Herrnstein's and Charles Murray's *The Bell Curve* (1994) which endorsed older racial hierarchies of human intelligence while claiming that they were not racist because they were based on social observation rather than biological research. Endorsing these conclusions, Dinesh D'Souza writes:

> Racism is what it always was: an opinion that recognizes real civilizational differences and attributes them to biology. Liberal relativism has been based on the denial of differences. Liberals should henceforth admit the differences but deny their biological foundation. . . . The racist fallacy, as Anthony Appiah contends, is the act of "biologizing what is culture." (D'Souza 1995: 537–8)

This is, in fact, a misappropriation of Appiah, who discusses how the opposition between nature and culture "has been understood in radically different ways in different periods" (Appiah 1992: 80). D'Souza argues that the success of Asians proves that "race" is a nonissue in the US: "Why can't an African American be more like an Asian?" (D'Souza 1995: 436). Racial hierarchies can be reinscribed while parading as *antiracist* because based on "culture" rather than "nature," as in *The Bell Curve*. Moreover, even as "cultural" differences are invoked as if they indicate permanent and unchanging human essences, we are also witnessing a new rise of a pseudobiological discourse which invokes genetics to "explain" all facets of human behavior; again it is notable that many of the conclusions of sociobiology simply rehearse age-old ideas about gender and race.[5]

D'Souza's book is also a reminder that while black/white binaries do not express the complex realities of discrimination, such binaries are constantly reiterated by racist discourse, and widely internalized even by minorities. Thus various immigrant communities in the US have secured their own footing by trying to become "honorary whites." Such a process is not just a matter of color, for even black immigrants are often seen to have participated in what Toni Morrison has called "this most enduring and efficient rite of passage into American culture: negative appraisals of the native-born black population" (quoted in Prashad 2000: 163). It would be a mistake to ignore the continuously fluctuating nature of these alignments; after the events of 9/11, many South Asians were eager to demonstrate that they were not Muslim, because Muslims were now widely perceived as threats to an American *national* culture, and to a Western civilizational ethos (Prashad 2005). The fact that a large percentage of US Muslims are also African-American only complicates a scenario where the official sorting of groups into races and ethnicities often "resembles a tale from Lewis Carroll" (Vigilant 1997: 59). These changing contours of difference and their attendant tensions inform our society and classrooms. It is my belief that literature in general, and early modern literature in particular, offers us a remarkable opportunity to discuss them in a sane yet engaged way.

II

Teachers routinely find that race is a subject which students are uncomfortable dealing with or talking about in the classroom (see Andreas 2001). Like many others, I find that student papers tend to focus on gender differences in *Othello*, often going out of their way to avoid discussing race. One of my students said that she had a professor who had proclaimed himself to be "color-blind" and had announced that he simply did not see any difference at all. By discussing race in detail, she asked, were we not simply reinscribing it? As we know, conservative scholarship also continues to make this point, and so do opponents of affirmative action (Thompson 2006).

In this situation, I have found it helpful to encourage an open discussion in the classroom about these hesitations, and what frameworks are useful for discussing race. It is crucial to steer students towards making connections between racial divisions and other social structures – in short to encourage a perspective that is not simply identity-driven. I agree with Peter Erickson that "it is imperative to preserve the intellectual distinction between reductive and subtle versions of identity politics against critics who insist on collapsing all discussion into the former category" (Erickson 1998: 35). Students' own identities can sensitize them to particular aspects of race relations in Shakespeare's plays and times, as discussed by Rebecca Ann Bach (2002). Such investments are powerful and necessary starting points into dismantling racial prejudices. At the same time, there is a value in reaching beyond one's own particular identities when analyzing racial histories and politics.

If in India it was possible to imagine that racism was not immediately relevant to us, in the US students tend to collapse it entirely into individual attitudes, something that can be erased if they proclaim their "respect" for "other cultures." It is also significant that the word "culture" widely replaces terms like "race" and "society," often serving to place social customs above critique (Bartolovich 2000). Timothy Brennan argues that during the period between the end of the Vietnam War and the presidency of Ronald Reagan, political belonging was "ejected from the idea of identity" which now came to center solely on "forms of being" or identities based on inheritance and circumstances of birth (Brennan 2006, especially pp. 1–64). Brennan makes an eloquent plea for the importance of "forms of belief" as a crucial part of our identities. And indeed, the point of any pedagogy of race would be not to simply confirm the importance of cultural, racial, national, and other categories of belonging (even though they can serve as platforms of radical critique and have historically done so), but also to explore alternative possibilities, both individual and collective.

Early modern histories can help our students understand the differences between Shakespeare's times and our own in a way that will productively challenge some of their own senses of self. I begin many of my early modern courses with *The Merchant of Venice*, whose racial politics, most students assume, hinge upon the Jewish question. But this is a play that also offers intersections and differences between "Moors" and "Jews" that students are not aware of. We might explore the fact that both Muslims and Jews were expelled during the Spanish *Reconquista*, and read accounts that show how both were not only racialized in analogous and overlapping ways by Christians, but were seen to be working in alliance.[6] Given the contemporary tensions between Jews and Muslims, students are surprised to learn that, after being expelled from various Christian territories, Jews were widely welcomed in Muslim lands, where they rose to hold economic and even political power.[7] Why then does early modern English literature sometimes pit Moors against Jews and sometimes show them working in tandem? By placing *The Merchant of Venice* with *The Jew of Malta* and passages from contemporary travelogues, my classes discover that if early modern literature speaks to our own complex cultural and political landscapes, it is not always in the ways that we expect.

It is something of a critical commonplace that one way to question racism is to show that it has a history. But although this approach has intellectual currency, often it does not inform pedagogy on race. For example, at the University of Pennsylvania where I teach, student groups have been rightly concerned that it is entirely possible to graduate without having taken a single course on the question of race. They consulted with me while compiling a list of classes that could serve to remedy this situation, and were surprised at the suggestion that a course on Shakespeare and race could be very useful, because it would discuss the long histories of race, as well as making the point that there are *no* scholarly areas which can be sealed off from questions of race and cultural difference. They were even more resistant to my suggestion that the teaching of race needed to include an international dimension, and confessed that they had been repeatedly told that US race relations were unique. While there is a legitimate concern that in the name of internationalism, the concerns of racialized groups within the US can be marginalized, at this moment a polarization of the local and the global does not help us understand or challenge racism.[8] Early modern texts and contexts can allow us to trace the connected histories of Africa, America, and Asia, and to discuss how international travel, trade, and colonialism are manifestly connected with the formation of racial ideologies *within* particular societies. Thus we can raise the question of longer histories and wider geographies in a productive fashion, connecting them to contemporary debates on these questions.

I design my undergraduate early modern classes according to two broad patterns – in the first, the syllabus includes only early modern writings, but I create space for discussions in which students comment on the relevance (or otherwise) of such writings to their own context, or comment on existing adaptations. The second kind of class has twentieth-century adaptations as an explicit part of the syllabus. In both cases, however, I insist that we engage with early modern texts historically before we draw any analogies with the present. Thus, even in a class of the second kind, called

"Shakespeare and Empire," students first engage with early modern texts and contexts, before moving on to questions of colonial pedagogy, or post-colonial and antiracist adaptations, or indeed producing their own versions of early modern texts. In both classes, I encourage students to consider the weblike relations between skin color and other somatic differences, faith and religion, and empire, trade, and colonialism. I tell them that they cannot use the word "culture" in the first half of the semester, but must find other terms when they want to use it. Do they mean society? Do they mean religion or language? Do they mean custom? How are "cultures" internally contested and fragmented? Even a quick session devoted to these questions (and this can be combined with the larger questions of race discussed earlier) becomes energizing and useful. By the second half of the semester, I find that their use of the word culture is accompanied by self-reflection, and it stops becoming a catch-all phrase.

In the past four years, I have found that in both classes, students have connected questions of race and identity with those of social structure, empire, and globalization in a range of ways. Thus, in an introductory class on Renaissance literature which I taught in the spring of 2006 at the University of Pennsylvania (this is a class where we study no modern texts, but students can comment on them in class seminars which take place thrice in the semester), one group of students meditated on the connections between Edmund Spenser's *A View of the Present State of Ireland* and contemporary US immigration. They reflected on the ways in which language, religion, sexuality, skin color, empire, and migration were similar or different in the two periods. In another class on "Shakespeare and Empire," students offered their own adaptations of Shakespeare's plays, showing how these amplify a crucial aspect of the original play. It was striking how many chose to place their adaptations in the context of contemporary globalization and its intersection with local politics. One group depicted Prospero as the CEO of a multinational company that was taking over construction sites in the historically disadvantaged neighborhood of West Philadelphia, where the University of Pennsylvania is situated. Caliban was a black union worker, and Miranda a girl who ultimately helps break the union, marrying the son of another CEO. Another group adapted *Antony and Cleopatra* by making Antony the CEO of an international oil company. Strikingly, both Antony and Prospero were portrayed as graduates of Penn's prestigious Wharton Business School, and the University was seen to be collaborating in their ventures. This last touch prompted a rich debate on Prospero's books, and the relationship between learning and power in the play. I am sure these critiques express the contradictions in my students' own lives, since many of them are themselves Wharton students. But, as they explain the choices they made, and in what way these choices departed from, or amplified, the original contexts, I like to believe that they are that much closer to understanding both Shakespeare and their own complex world. In some classes, I organize a seminar on Shakespeare and America, in which students critique educational and institutional history, the history of performance, the media, and the invocation of Shakespeare in politics. I find that combining these questions with those of race helps to interrelate structures and identities, attitudes and politics.

Finally, as the US expands its global hegemony, it is more important than ever for us to challenge the insularity which can inform American students of every shade. The ideology of a multicultural melting pot in the US puts a not-so-subtle pressure on non-Americans to change their language, dress, style, and behavior. A "foreign" accent and clothing can be distinct disadvantages, especially in a Shakespeare class, which, most students assume, has a direct link with a Western high-cultural heritage. Thus I often begin my early modern classes by drawing attention to the fact that my own accent and vocabulary are different from those of most students in the class, but that none of us uses what many other parts of the world think of as "standard" English. If I speak an "Indian English," they speak various "American Englishes," and both are different from contemporary British Englishes and also from Shakespeare's English. I invite a discussion on these variants, but instead of simply sending students to the *OED* to see how Shakespeare's English might have been different from ours, I also discuss how the English language expanded in Shakespeare's own time, and swelled with words added not only from Portuguese, Spanish, and French but also from (among others) Arabic, Persian, Malay, and Malayalam. I ask the class to search for such imported words in Henry Yule and A. C. Burnell's wonderful compilation *Hobson-Jobson* (1903), a glossary of English words imported from Asian languages, which is now readily available online. Among the ones that turn up are bazaar, barbican, beryl, boutique, cashmere, calico, caste, caravan, catamaran, carpet, chintz, coffee, dinghy, dungaree, jungle, khaki, magazine, pariah, pajamas, punch, shampoo, shawl, tank, toddy, and verandah. Which of these words came in during Shakespeare's times? Did he use any of them? What about those that came in from the New World? Going to the *OED* to find an early modern meaning of a word becomes a radically different exercise when it is coupled with a reflection on the cosmopolitanism of language.

These discussions not only illuminate early modern cosmopolitanism, which provides an often surprising angle on questions of race and colonialism, but help enable nonwhite and bilingual students to contribute to discussions about language and meaning. They also allow the class to think about the very making of "the Renaissance," the place of Arab and Jewish scholarship in the "rediscovery" of classical learning, and the exchanges of information, art, and learning during the period.[9] *The Tempest* is often read as a play about linguistic colonialism, the silencing of non-Europeans, and subaltern self-representation, for which Caliban's curse has become shorthand. My hope is that by the time students come to read this play, they will be aware that global contact did not simply entail the European silencing of "others," but also the appropriation of foreign languages; not merely the imperial *export* of language but also the import of words and practices that have contributed to the making of English itself.[10]

My students in India were always quick to express impatience with the kind of criticism that continuously emphasizes how the "others" of European colonialism were silenced. In teaching Shakespeare's plays, it is not easy to amplify the voices of non-Europeans, but we can adopt the following strategies. Firstly, we can foreground representation as a complex and layered issue. What is at stake when Prospero says that Caliban has no language? What kind of "voice" is allowed to characters such as Aaron, Othello, Cleopatra, Caliban, and Shylock? What are the differences between them? What difference does it make that these plays were being staged to an all-white audience? What are the differences between cross-gender and cross-racial performance? Secondly, we can approach the question of non-European self-representation by juxtaposing Shakespeare's plays with the work of those who amplified issues of race and colonialism in the plays so as to speak to their own situations (such as George Lamming's *Water with Berries* or Aimé Césaire's *A Tempest*), or with contemporary books that resonate with these plays (such as Toni Morrison's *Tar Baby*). We can encourage a discussion of the way in which racialized figures within Shakespeare's plays appropriate or question dominant discourses with strategies employed by writers, actors, and activists in relation to Shakespeare. Thirdly, we can offer a nuanced view of early modern travel and contact, showing how non-Europeans were not only brutalized, silenced, and colonized, but, during the early modern period, also provided the European world with images of learning and civilization, sophistication and urbanity. Complicating the histories of contact can help qualify the notion of an endless history of Western hegemony.

During the early 1990s, I designed a graduate class called "Renaissance Colonialisms" which brought together plays, travelogues, and other writings which would explore the differences and connections between Turkey, India, Moluccas, Persia, Barbary, Morocco, Egypt, Ethiopia, and other places. Juxtaposing (for example) *Othello*, Massinger's *The Renegado*, *The Tempest*, Fletcher's *The Island Princess*, and Heywood's *Fair Maid of the West*, we can explore the fact that early modern Europeans were not just confident and successful imperialists but often supplicants for Eastern trade. Examining how Barbary might be viewed differently from Morocco helps students acknowledge that even today they do not know the varied geography of Africa. I first tried out "Renaissance Colonialisms" (the name was to change subsequently to "Re-Orienting the Renaissance") at the graduate level, but in subsequent years it shaped my pedagogy at every level. In recent years, I have found early modern histories and literature invaluable in exploring the long and complex histories of globalization, a phenomenon which is neither as new nor as "flattening" of global asymmetries as its advocates suggest. Indeed, early modernists can help qualify the often narrow presentism of postcolonial studies and globalization studies. The overlap between trade and conquest in the early modern period helps us demystify the ideologies of trade in our own world. And in turn, a focus on early modern relations of power allows us to understand better all aspects (including formal and linguistic) of Shakespeare's work.

To conclude, then, courses on Shakespeare (and early modern literature and culture), race, and colonialism can provide both a historical distance that facilitates discussion on race, a historical depth that illuminates our own times, as well as an affective dimension that is necessary for discussing questions of racial and colonial domination. Conversely, these questions provide a vital and necessary perspective on the plays themselves, allowing students to both connect with and critique them. Such classes can be doubly useful in an undergraduate curriculum, and allow Shakespeareans to make an intervention in the larger university curriculum. Such a pedagogy will not change the world, but it may help our students to engage with it in a more meaningful way.[11]

Notes

1   See, for example, Viswanathan (1989). For Shakespeare in the colonies, see
    Orkin (1987), Johnson (1996), Loomba (1998).

2 See for example the website of the group "Movers and Shakespeares," <www.moversandshakespeares.com/>.

3 See for example Palmer (1988: 56), Whitney (1586: 57), and Jeremiah 13: 23–5 in *The Geneva Bible* (1560), *The Bishop's Bible* (1568), and *The King James Bible* (1611).

4 Examples of all these can be found in Loomba and Burton (2007).

5 I make this argument in Loomba (2006).

6 See for example *The Jew of Malta* 2.3.176–8, 184–99 (Marlowe 1994: 22–3), Heylyn (1621: 319), de Nicholay (1585: 130–1); Calvert (1649).

7 On a campus like Penn, where Jewish students vastly outnumber Arab and Muslim students, I do find some resistance to these ideas: it is much easier to read *The Merchant* as a play that solely addresses the place of Jews.

8 Malini Johar Schueller (2004) argues that postcolonial intellectuals in the US have marginalized the question of race; conversely, Josie Saldaña-Portillo (2007) calls for ethnic studies to move beyond the framework of the nation state to encompass a critique of US imperialism.

9 Jardine and Brotton (2003) is very useful for students.

10 Hulme (1986) remains the best account of this subject. Such a discussion also helps establish overlaps between different early modern contexts – having thought about Caliban's "gabardine" (2.2.37) in relation to the Irish mantle, my students never fail to spot the reference to Shylock's "gabardine" in *The Merchant of Venice* (1.3.111) which leads to a comparison between the two contexts.

11 My students at various institutions have generously given me feedback and ideas; at the University of Pennsylvania members of my "Shakespeare and Empire" seminar (Spring 2005) and "Renaissance Literature and Culture" class (Spring 2006) were especially generous, particularly Julija Zubac, Daniel P. McIntosh, Andrine Wilson, and Laura Murray. Skip Shand's comments were crucial in shaping the essay.

References and Further Reading

ACTA (American Council of Trustees and Alumni) (1996). *The Shakespeare File: What English Majors Are Really Studying.* Available at <www.goacta.org/ publications/Reports/shakespeare.pdf>.

ACTA (2002). *Defending Civilization: How Our Universities Are Failing America and What Can Be Done About It.* Available at <www.goacta.org/publications/ Reports/defciv.pdf>.

ACTA (2006). *How Many Ward Churchills?* Available at <www.goacta.org/ publications/Reports/Churchill%20Final.pdf>.

Andreas, James R. (2001). "Rewriting Race Through Literature: Teaching Shakespeare's African Plays." In Sharon A. Beehler and Holger Klein (Eds). *Shakespeare in Higher Education: A Global Perspective. Shakespeare Yearbook 12* (pp. 215–36). Lewiston, NY: Edwin Mellen.

Appiah, Anthony (1992). *In My Father's House.* London: Methuen.

Bach, Rebecca Ann (2002). "Teaching the Details of Race and Religious Difference in Renaissance Drama." In Karen Bamford and Alexander Leggatt (Eds). *Approaches to Teaching English Renaissance Drama* (pp. 127–33). New York: Modern Language Association.

Balibar, Etienne (1991). "Is There a Neo-racism?" In Etienne Balibar and Immanuel Wallerstein (Eds). *Race, Nation, Class: Ambiguous Identities* (pp. 17–28). New York: Verso.

Bartolovich, Crystal (2000). "Shakespeare's Globe?" In Jean E. Howard and Scott Cutler Shershow (Eds). *Marxist Shakespeares* (pp. 178–205). London and New York: Routledge.

Best, George (1578). *A True Discourse of the Late Voyages of Discovery, for the Finding of a Passage to Cathay by the Northwest.* London: Henry Bynnyman.

Beteille, Andre (2001). "Race and Caste." *The Hindu* 10 March. Available at <http://wcar.alrc.net/mainfile2.php/For+the+negative/14/>.

Bloom, Harold (1998). *Shakespeare: The Invention of the Human.* New York: Riverhead Books.

Brennan, Timothy (2006). *Wars of Position: The Cultural Politics of Left and Right.* New York: Columbia University Press.

Bristol, Michael D. (1990). *Shakespeare's America, America's Shakespeare.* London and New York: Routledge.

Bulwer, John (1650). *Anthropometamorphosis: Man Transform'd: or, The Artificial Changeling.* London: J. Hardesty.

Calvert, Thomas (1649). *The Blessed Jew of Marocco or a Blackamoor Made White.* York.

D'Souza, Dinesh (1995). *The End of Racism: Principles for a Multiracial Society.* New York: Free Press.

de Nicholay, Nicholas (1585). *The Navigations, Peregrinations and Voyages Made into Turkey.* T. Washington, Trans. London.

Erickson, Peter (1998). "The Moment of Race in Renaissance Studies." *Shakespeare Studies* 26: 27–36.

Ferguson, Niall (2003). "The Empire Slinks Back." *The New York Times Magazine* April 27: 52.

Hall, Kim F. (1995). *Things of Darkness: Economies of Race and Gender in Early Modern England.* Ithaca, NY: Cornell University Press.

Hall, Kim F. (1996). "Beauty and the Beast of Whiteness: Teaching Race and Gender." *Shakespeare Quarterly* 47: 461–76.

Hall, Stuart (1996). "New Ethnicities." In David Morley and Kuan-Hsing Chen (Eds). *Stuart Hall: Critical Dialogues in Cultural Studies* (pp. 441–9). London: Routledge.

Heng, Geraldine (2003). *Empire of Magic: Medieval Romance and the Politics of Cultural Fantasy.* New York: Columbia University Press.

Herrnstein, Richard J. and Charles Murray (1994). *The Bell Curve: Intelligence and Class Structure in American Life.* New York: Free Press.

Heylyn, Peter (1621). *Microcosmus.* Oxford.

Hulme, Peter (1986). *Colonial Encounters, Europe and the Native Caribbean 1492–1797.* London: Routledge.

Huntington, Samuel P. (1993). "The Clash of Civilizations?" *Foreign Affairs* 72(3): 22–49.

Ilaiah, Kancha (1996). *Why I Am Not a Hindu: A Sudra Critique of Hindutva Philosophy, Culture and Political Economy.* Calcutta: Samya.

Jardine, Lisa and Jerry Brotton (2003). *Global Interests: Renaissance Art Between East and West.* London: Reaktion Books.

Johnson, David (1996). *Shakespeare and South Africa.* Oxford: Clarendon Press.

Loomba, Ania (1991). "Teaching the Bard in India." *JEFL* 7/8: 147–70.

Loomba, Ania (1998). *Gender, Race, Renaissance Drama.* Manchester: Manchester University Press.

Loomba, Ania (2002). *Shakespeare, Race and Colonialism.* Oxford: Oxford University Press.

Loomba, Ania (2006). "Human Nature or Human Difference." In Robin Headlam Wells and Johnjoe McFadden (Eds). *Human Nature: Fact and Fiction* (pp. 147–66). London: Continuum.

Loomba, Ania and Jonathan Burton (Eds) (2007). *Race in Early Modern England: A Documentary Companion.* New York: Palgrave.

López, Judith A. (1998). "Black and White and 'Read' All Over." *Shakespeare Studies* 26: 49–58.

Marlowe, Christopher (1994). *The Jew of Malta.* James R. Siemon (Ed.). London: Norton.

Newstok [aka Newstrom], Scott (2003). "'Step Aside, I'll Show Thee a President': George W as Henry V?" Available at <www.poppolitics.com/articles/2003/05/01/George_W_as_Henry_V?>.

Orkin, Martin (1987). *Shakespeare Against Apartheid.* Craighall, South Africa: Ad. Donker.

Palmer, Thomas (1988). *The Emblems of Thomas Palmer: Two Hundred Poosees.* "Impossible Things." John Manning (Ed.). New York: AMS Press.

Pieterse, Jan Nederveen (2002). "Europe and its Others." In David Theo Goldberg and John Solomos (Eds). *A Companion to Racial and Ethnic Studies* (pp. 17–25). Malden, MA and Oxford: Blackwell.

Prashad, Vijay (2000). *The Karma of Brown Folk.* Minneapolis and London: University of Minnesota Press.

Prashad, Vijay (2005). "How the Hindus Became Jews: American Racism After 9/11." *South Atlantic Quarterly* 104: 583–606.

Raiskin, Judith (1993). "The Art of History: An Interview With Michelle Cliff." *Kenyon Review* 15: 57–71.

Royster, Francesca T. (1998). "The 'End' of Race." *Shakespeare Studies* 26: 59–69.

Saldaña-Portillo, Josie (2007). "From the Borderlands to the Transnational? Critiquing Empire in the 21st Century." In Renato Rosaldo and Juan Flores (Eds). *Blackwell Companion to Latino Studies* (pp. 502–13). Oxford: Blackwell.

Schueller, Malini Johar (2004). "Postcolonial American Studies." *American Literary History* 16: 162–75.

Thompson, Ayanna (Ed.) (2006). *Color-blind Shakespeare: New Perspectives on Race and Performance.* New York: Routledge.

Thorndike, Ashley (1927). "Shakespeare in America," Annual Shakespeare lecture of the British Academy. London: Oxford University Press.

Vigilant, Linda (1997). "Race and Biology." In Winston A. van Horne (Ed.). *Global Convulsions, Race, Ethnicity and Nationalism at the End of the Twentieth Century* (pp. 49–62). Albany: SUNY Press.

Viswanathan, Gauri (1989). *Masks of Conquest, Literary Study and British Rule in India.* New York: Columbia University Press.

Whitney, Geffrey (1586). *A Choice of Emblemes.* Leyden: Francis Raphelengius.

Yule, Henry and A. C. Burnell (1903). *Hobson-Jobson: A Glossary of Colloquial Anglo-Indian Words and Phrases, and of Kindred Terms, Etymological, Historical, Geographical and Discursive.* William Crooke, Ed. London: J. Murray. Available at <http://dsal.uchicago.edu/dictionaries/hobsonjobson/>.

11

Learning to Listen: Shakespeare and Contexts

Frances E. Dolan

I think, worry, and talk about teaching constantly. Yet I feel at a loss when called upon to write about teaching because I do not possess what is too often required of those seeking jobs or promotions in US colleges and universities: a coherent "philosophy of teaching." I could produce one if required to do so for institutional reasons, but my heart would not be in it. Nor would it bear much relation to what I actually do. When I speak or write about teaching I usually resort to anecdotes because they are the only way I can convey the ad hoc, seat-of-the-pants nature of teaching as I experience it. I often feel that I get through a class "on a smile and a shoeshine."[1] To the extent that I have a philosophy it is that the anecdotes that substitute for that philosophy should convey not what is charmingly or at least laughably inept about students (too often the function of teaching anecdotes) or what is admirable about me (although if I could think of an anecdote that would show that I would probably tell it) but what is chaotic and unpredictable and rewarding about the collective enterprise that is teaching undergraduates. I always have a carefully worked out plan for each class; I usually abandon it midstream. For me, a dull class is one in which no student was able to throw me off my charted course. Teaching is a dynamic interaction with a particular group of students; it is so immediate that it is hard to know what to say about it afterwards.

Dear reader, I have wracked my brain for some advice I can offer you. I have come up with the following: (1) get a good night's sleep and do not sacrifice sleep to preparation; (2) eat breakfast; (3) once in the classroom, look around expectantly, take a deep breath, and ask a big, open-ended question; (4) attempt to listen to what students say in response and then run with it, wherever it takes you. Well, that's it. I feel most confident about the first two suggestions.

Having absolved myself of my felt obligation to offer concrete advice, I want to turn to the messier business of reflecting on a challenge that currently engages me, which is how to braid together three aims: valuing and working with students' first responses to their reading; trying to engage them in producing historical knowledge; and challenging, perhaps even confiscating, some of their assumptions. These concerns can seem irreconcilable but I am experimenting with attending to them all at once.

I solicit and value students' first responses because I feel that we have already accomplished something if they have read and responded. When I ask my students what reading a Shakespeare play is like they say that it's like starting to watch a hit sitcom after it has been on the air for several seasons; like going to a party where everyone else knows one another and there are a lot of "in" jokes. When you read Shakespeare, they say, you know it's worth it but you're not sure why. There are so many reasons for our students not to read. Plays require readers to do more of the work. I find that some students do not really attend to who is speaking in a play; they just read top to bottom and have a hard time visualizing bodies moving in space, different people speaking. While some like the challenge of making their own imaginary movies, others would much rather watch someone else's movie instead – although one of my students recently said that if she sees the film version before she reads a play she feels that her imagination has been "incarcerated." On top of the challenge that all plays seem to pose, early modern plays, with their huge, unfamiliar vocabularies, Latin phrases, bewildering sentence structures, and layers of allusion often work to exclude and discourage students. Many students attempt to squeak by on the SparkNotes or CliffsNotes summaries. They're used to multitasking and multimedia, and sitting down to read a difficult play is so oppressively focused, so inward and quiet. Such disincentives are the reason that I think the most basic thing we do has become countercultural – everyone in the class reads one play and then we sit in one room and try to talk about it. My students long to surf as they sit there, I suspect. It's a small triumph that they can't. So it's already a pedagogical victory if students have read a play and want to raise their hands and say something about it. For that reason, I *try* to work with what they want to talk about rather than censuring their opening remarks.

What my students want to talk about first is usually characters. Especially when I read their papers I want to remind them that characters are not real people and that they should try to refrain from harsh moral judgments, praise and blame. For instance, the thesis statement in a paper on *Measure for Measure* that I received, "Isabella is one judgmental lady," is not very compelling and the paper that follows from it is predictably grim and itself very judgmental. But I don't want to shut down this mode of engagement because it is where many of my students begin and where I often reside as a reader. One of the pleasures of reading is identifying with and evaluating characters. Why, a student asks with a pained expression, doesn't France stay with Cordelia when she battles for her father's cause? After we discuss that for a little while, I ask her why she thinks that would matter or would help. "Well," she says, "when I first met France, I loved him. He says 'She is herself a dowry' and I was like 'Yeah, France.' I kind of wanted to see France again." I have to like a reading response that is this passionate and especially the way that this student grounded her response in the text, weaving Shakespeare's language and her own together.

For good reason, many teachers think that it is a bad idea to ask students how they feel about what they read. I cannot resist doing so, in part because I really want to know. If students have a vivid response and are willing to try to articulate it then all kinds of unpredictable paths open up for exploration. Why have they responded this way? What in the text triggered that emotion? Do other students agree or disagree? What were they expecting from the text or hoping/fearing that they would feel? When a discussion begins with untutored and unedited responses, students will often set the terms for ensuing discussions. If I say "Let's talk about the depiction of women in this play," they might balk. Few identify themselves as feminists. But they tend to attack and defend characters in ways that provoke debates about women, gender, and feminism in which they will engage if they can speak, at first, in their own terms. In one class, a male student derided Ophelia as a "wimp." A female student, seldom roused to response, jumped to her defense. "I mean think about how she stands up to what's-his-name, you know, the brother? Hanging around in that castle with all of those men and no friends. Those guys *drove* her crazy. I like the way she started out." In a discussion of *Measure for Measure*, one student said of Angelo: "Anyone who tries to nail an almost-nun is looking for trouble." When another student persisted in claiming that Isabella was "asking for it," a line-up of four women pointed at their books and yelled in unison, "Show me the evidence!" Students are disappointed that in *The Tempest* Miranda doesn't get to leave the island and date a little before settling down to marry Ferdinand. In *Taming of the Shrew*, some want to know why Kate can't get a studio apartment and a job instead of marrying Petruchio. They want to know why the women who stick up for themselves are "dressed as boys or about to be dead." In the course of a class, students can learn new vocabularies for such discussions. When they articulate their responses first in their own terms, they sometimes seize on more precise categories and words as a gift rather than an imposition. Furthermore, we cannot begin to answer the questions they raise without attending to both historical and generic possibilities and limits. As this suggests, they aren't simplistic responses at all.

Most students readily perceive that as one put it, Shakespearean tragedy is no picnic for men either. True, the women all end up dead. But most of the men are dead, too. The issues regarding gender equity are subtle. The question is not just who lives and who dies, but who has more lines and more options, who is put in the position to engage us most deeply, whose suffering and death are taken most seriously.

Similarly, if I announce "masculinity" as a topic, nobody wants to talk about it. But we spend a lot of time talking about the obligations that go with the status and power of men in the tragedies. When I taught on a campus with a vigorous fraternity culture, I found that my students were pretty smart about why, for instance, Othello believes Iago rather than his wife. In the midst of analyzing the first speech in *Twelfth Night* one student burst out that "Orsino is not a serious dude." I was a little taken aback by this comment, in part because I find that my students busily police masculinity and femininity, and they have the capacity to wound one another in that process (as in others). So I asked what isn't serious about Orsino and the student said "Well, he says he's so into, um, Olivia but he's never even with her and he just lies around listening to music and talking to his friends." Suddenly, I realized that the question is "Who or what is a serious dude"? Some thought and discussion followed. Finally, "Antonio," he tells me. "He rescues Sebastian, they're together nonstop for three months, he gives him his purse, and he's willing to fight for him. Antonio is a serious dude. If he loves you he means it and he doesn't stop. You can count on Antonio." Interesting, I say. Moments like these make me glad I bit my tongue and didn't jump in too soon – as I so often do.

While my own research interests tend to run toward disorder and transgression, I've learned that in the classroom it works best to begin with or at least include some discussion of what constitutes order in the world of a play. In *Measure for Measure*, for instance, where is the acceptable, nontransgressive sexuality? Or in this particular discussion of *Twelfth Night*, who is a serious dude? Before students employ a standard, I want them to tell me where they can locate it in the text under discussion. It's also important that they articulate their own standards for me because a lot of the time the standards they apply are not what I expect or not ones I share or are not even coherent. How do you know what is normal or acceptable or approved or even possible? Sometimes this question rebounds on me because I think I know what a plausible answer is for the early modern period. My students are usually guessing, scrambling to piece together information from the text. Their desperate inventiveness forces me to think about why I think I know what I know. I recently interrupted students who were blithely repeating that there is a love triangle in *Twelfth Night* – which many had got from a study guide – by asking them who is in it. Who are Orsino and Olivia, for instance, in love with? I thought this was a very good question but no one else did. "Well," says one student, "it's not about seeing or knowing one another, exactly. It's like that 'reduce, reuse, recycle' triangle. It's about seeing something you already have in a new way, so that you don't have to get rid of it and replace it. Orsino repurposes Cesario as his bride." Beginning with a sly reference to the triangles stamped on the bottoms of recyclable plastic containers, this student offered us a set of terms we could then ourselves "reuse" in our discussions of other plays. Shakespeare does a lot of recycling, as we started to discover when we looked through the lens this student (a chemical engineer) offered us.

My students are also deeply interested in the plot. While I am often a ruthless and eager reader for the plot, that just isn't my experience of Shakespeare anymore. My students routinely get me on the ropes with very specific questions about plot. Their questions humiliatingly remind me that I skip over some things in the interests of focusing on others. I'm like Desdemona trying to remember the willow song: "Nay, that's not next." I often don't notice just what puzzles them – the exact sequence of events, the placement of a scene I skim over as "minor," or the trajectory and relevance of a plot I think of as "subordinate" and they assume to be equally important. Many of my students see everything as potentially important so they latch on to things I ignore. I take some comfort in Northrop Frye's claim that "in the direct experience of fiction, continuity is the center of our attention; our later memory, or what I call the possession of it, tends to become discontinuous . . . and regrouped in a new way" (Frye 1963: 23). What I would add to this is that maybe a professor who has thought about a play a lot might actually sound confused, unprepared, and unhelpful if you asked her about the basic sequence of events precisely because she's already rearranged it in her head in some really meaningful way. At least I like to think so. Every reader has his or her own map of a play, with different peaks and valleys. If first readers operate on the assumption that everything has an equal claim on their attention this might be why the least experienced readers are sometimes the most open to offbeat scenes and minor characters, problem plays and late plays. Such readers are also sometimes more open to texts such as homilies, ballads, pamphlets, or legal treatises than their teachers are. Unschooled in the text/context division and unaware of a hierarchy that denigrates such materials as extraliterary, nonliterary, or subliterary, the least experienced students just try to read what they've been assigned. No expectations to disappoint, no investment in what we might call literature, no hierarchies to overturn. Whatever.

However I might try to rationalize the gap between what I emphasize and what my students do, it is certainly true that they want to talk about the plot a lot more than I do. In a midterm evaluation one year many students asked that I begin class by reviewing the plot. I attempted this and then quickly tired of it: they have access to so many plot summaries; I don't want to spend class time on it, and anyway it's very hard to do. In a time-honored teaching trick I turned the tables and asked them to do it. We were on *Othello*. We got off to a very turgid start so I tried to urge them to think like storytellers or screenwriters. "So this guy is denied a promotion . . . ," "So this man and woman run away to get married . . . ." They made some interesting attempts. Sometimes they started with what was represented in the first scene. Sometimes they started in the backstory. Sometimes they started in another location at the same time – such as with Desdemona and Othello. It was fascinating to talk about the story as a continuum that was reordered in the telling; that you could make the same story more exciting or disturbing or confusing by thinking about what to show and what to describe and when. Of all the ways that this story could begin why start like this? Then one student who had been paging through his book says "So this Egyptian gives a woman a handkerchief." I can't help but intervene: "Or did a man give his wife a handkerchief?" Some muttering. This is just the kind of thing that will screw you up on the final. "No wait, wait," another student says. "If you're gonna go with this how about 'Some maidens die and their hearts get cooked into mummy?'"

In what became a collaborative game, these students revealed that they understood that objects can be characters, and can have stories of their own. Focusing attention on objects and places often helps struggling students get some traction in or control over the plays. Students uncertain about many details have ready answers to questions like "What props couldn't you do without?" and "Where do you first see that purse or that handkerchief" and "Where does it go from there? Whose hands does it pass through and why does it move?" As a student recently noticed in tracking gifts in *Twelfth Night*: "Everyone wants to give stuff to the twins."

My point is not that students intuit all of the insights of recent criticism about Renaissance material life but instead that their observations and questions help me recapitulate how and why scholars turned their attention to things. Listening to students talk about their experiences of reading reminds me that critics are all readers and that it is often most effective to introduce critical insights and discussions of method in response to students' observations and questions. It is inevitably also more ad hoc. Rather than planning in advance that they will read a particular body of critical essays in order to learn a vocabulary or set of questions, I tap dance in the moment to think up what they should read given the interests they express. Many of these suggestions are not pursued but I think it's still worth it. I try to remind my students that a famous critic asks just that question, or has written a whole essay about the word or phrase or object on which they are focusing. The untutored or unedited question has the most in common with the best criticism because eye-opening essays begin when a critic asks a great question or takes a fresh look or notices something strange. In my own experience as a reader, for instance, I remember seeing things differently as a result of Louis Montrose's attention to the beginning of *As You Like It* (Montrose 1981) and Valerie Traub's discussion of the play's homoerotics (Traub 1992); Mary Beth Rose's inquiry into where the mothers are in Shakespeare (Rose 1991); Margaret Ferguson's unpacking of the meanings of "incorpsing" in *Hamlet* (Ferguson 1985); or Dympna Callaghan's observation that Othello and Desdemona were both played by white men (Callaghan 2000). Essays such as these – and, of course, the list is a long and growing one – have changed the way I understand and teach certain plays. They have also helped me understand how an argument begins with a question, an observation, or a problem. Befuddlement is generative. I want students to trust their own instincts. If they think something is interesting or important or simply weird they are, I think, inevitably right. What they need to work on is explaining why! In *Hamlet*, what does it mean that the Ghost doesn't appear and isn't mentioned after the closet scene? In *As You Like It*, why is there a wrestler and why does the word "wrestle" appear so many times?

I don't require that my students "appreciate" Shakespeare. I sometimes do and sometimes don't and what interests me is often what I find disturbing rather than beautiful. I want them to read it and be willing to engage with it. Period. If students actually *wrestle* with these plays, then they can see that, in my view, nobody ever ruined anything by looking at it more carefully. Critique *is* pleasure.

In part because study guides instruct students to keep track of the fates of characters – Who marries whom? Who dies and how? – their interests in character and plot conjoin in an acute attention to the plays' endings. What happens to each person, what sense does that make, and what satisfactions (or dissatisfactions) does that outcome offer the viewer or reader? How are we to assess the absences, exclusions, and loose ends? For instance, what happens to Antonio, that most serious dude, at the end of *Twelfth Night*? I certainly have students who are uncritically homophobic, who seem bewildered at the idea that happy endings might have many shapes, who roll their eyes at all of these intimate friendships and cross-dressed girls and ambiguities. In Act 4, scene 1 of *As You Like It*, when Celia presides over a marriage between Ganymede and Orlando, we see a stage picture that remains a shock to many students and their parents, the kind of thing you might go to the polls just to discourage. The classroom discussion of this scenario can provide an opportunity for conversations about issues that are very much unresolved and that desperately matter.

It's important to talk about the exclusions and subordinations that are part of the operations of Shakespearean comic form without seeming to naturalize them. I don't want to make it too easy for students to conclude that "Oh, Rosalind and Phebe or Antonio and Sebastian could obviously never be together" in Arden or Illyria or anywhere. Sometimes students who haven't mastered the rules of literary engagement are especially open to experiencing plots as unpredictable and in play – maybe it will turn out differently this time. Anything could happen.

A few years ago, a student asked "What do you think next Christmas will be like for the characters in *Twelfth Night*? It'll be like 'Hey, remember how you used to work for me but I thought you were a guy, and I thought I loved my sister-in-law here, and I said I was going to kill you, and you seemed to go along with that, and . . .'." "People," I said, "is it just my family? I can picture that Christmas. But for my family imagine a Christmas, Hanukkah, Kwanzaa, Solstice sort of event." One student in this class had shaved his head and wore only black for several weeks because, he said, "I like Hamlet." He comes to my rescue. "No," he says, "I don't think it's only you. I for sure had that Thanksgiving." Another student is very disgusted with both of us and our weird families. "Yeah, like what?" he says, very cranky. "A shipwreck? A lost twin? Falling in love with a man who turns out to actually be a woman – or, you know, whatever?" "OK," says my goth Hamlet, "Don't go there. It's just like – strange . . . histories. But . . . we're a family as much as anyone; and . . . we eat dinner." It's really not that hard to envision these people in Act 6. I like to imagine that Orsino sometimes says, "Much as I love your maiden's weeds and everything, why don't you wear the Cesario outfit tonight?"

I often reach for the historical to help me in the project of grounding standards of evaluation – knowing that historical knowledge complicates more than it ever clarifies. For instance, looking at the vocabularies for monitoring sexual infractions in the plays and in defamation suits helps us to speak more precisely about which behaviors were monitored and which weren't. But the result is a pretty messy picture of changing, contested standards of sexual conduct. Students hope that history can resolve all mysteries but it's important to disabuse them of this hope. Trying to talk to students about what we know about early modern culture constantly reminds me of my own status as student. I depend on my reading to help me in the ongoing process of identifying the assumptions that blind me, the generalizations I make a little too easily or to which I've become attached because they are so familiar. To describe this experience of abandoning outmoded knowledge I rely on a line from Act III of Shaw's *Major Barbara*: "You have learnt something. That always feels at first as if you had lost something." Just as one of the most important things I do in the classroom is take things away from my students, so I have to give up my own tired generalizations and treasured assumptions. Teachers and students only have to give things up and change our minds if we are paying attention. This is one of the ways in which teaching and research are and must be related. Our knowledge changes constantly. We don't just transmit a stable body of knowledge, because it doesn't exist. We constantly remake it and we do so in a collaborative way.

Given that this is the case, students can participate in that collaboration. I am experimenting with making historical lectures as spontaneous and motivated as possible. For instance, in one class about *The Winter's Tale*, some of my students wanted to know what Hermione and Paulina, who seems to have kept her secreted away, were doing for all of those years. One wondered whether they could be considered to have had a "Boston Marriage." (This is a term for the "romantic friendships" or "marriage-like" relationships between cohabiting women in nineteenth-century America.) As she said: "Sixteen years and I'm supposed to believe Hermione is in suspended animation? I don't think so." These kinds of responses are wonderful opportunities. A minilecture on the possibilities for and spaces of female attachments finds a more interested audience when it responds to student questions. Or students who asked these questions can be engaged in a research project that enables them to find some of their own answers. The challenge is to remain flexible and responsive. The next time I teach *The Winter's Tale*, I'll be all pumped up to discuss female community and that group will probably say, "Yeah, yeah, back to the bear. Do you think it's a real bear or some guy in a bear suit?"

To enable students to pursue their own inquiries, it is helpful to make other kinds of materials available, by teaching them how to use the Early English Books Online database, if your school subscribes to it, and/or by using textbooks that make a range of texts available and accessible. Such textbooks depend on canonical texts for their market and therefore their existence, and they use a variety of terms to describe what they offer in addition to those headliner titles: contexts (Bedford), backgrounds (Norton), and perspectives (Longman). I suspect that no one is happy with these terms. Nor is there a perfect place to locate these materials in a book or on a syllabus. Unsure what to call them, where to put them, or what to do with them, we are still struggling to implement a basic theoretical insight. As Louis A. Montrose explained:

> The newer historical criticism is *new* in its refusal of unproblematized distinctions between "literature" and "history," between "text" and "context"; new in resisting a prevalent tendency to posit and privilege a unified and autonomous individual – whether an Author or a Work – to be set against a social or literary background. Briefly and too simply characterized, its collective project is to resituate canonical literary texts among the multiple forms of writing, and in relation to the non-discursive practices and institutions of the social formation in which those texts have been produced . . . (Montrose 1986: 6)

According to Jean Howard (1986: 25), "Literature is *part* of history, the literary text as much a context for other aspects of cultural and material life as they are for it." The challenge, of course, is how we live this insight in a curriculum that remains organized around "authors" and "works." If the goal is to cover as much Shakespeare as possible then there is no room for anything else. This is the same principle behind the "more is better" approach to editing that produced conflated texts of plays like *King Lear*. But if we're trying to help students read critically, think deeply, conduct research, and develop historical awareness, then enabling them to explore the relationships among different texts, and pursue their own questions across a diverse terrain, can prove invaluable.

In a review of Barbara Hodgdon's "texts and contexts" edition of *The First Part of King Henry the Fourth*, David L. Kranz (2000) worries that it will take time "to bring out the virtues of the contextual matter for undergraduates . . . time that should not be stolen from a close reading of Shakespeare's play itself." He recognizes that, "in a traditional Shakespeare course, use of Hodgdon's edition would probably require that students read fewer plays, unless one assigned the documents as optional resources not reviewed in class." Kranz, whose author's note says that he "teaches Shakespeare through performance," concludes: "For most undergraduates, especially freshmen and sophomores, an approach through performance (live and on film) rather than historical contexts will probably be a more effective way to teach Shakespeare." Kranz assumes that we all know and agree what we are teaching when we teach Shakespeare and that we know and agree how to do so "effectively." But this is not at all obvious. Furthermore, why are performance and "contextual" or "historical" approaches incompatible? Asking students to act out a trial account or sing a ballad helps them find the drama – and often the unexpected humor – in those texts, too. Asking a group to cut a sermon, as they might cut a scene for performance, helps them identify its structure, rhetorical strategies, and use of evidence. Students might also act as dramaturges, designing a program or a lobby installation that could prepare audiences to think about a play's relationship to other texts. Understanding and explaining the relationships among texts is a fundamental theoretical and methodological challenge. By experimenting with how to do that, students engage in the debates that animate study of the early modern period.

Kranz's assumption that a contextual or historical approach is unfruitful stems from his assumption about how it might work. If we treat "contexts" as those texts that are not required nor discussed, those that don't demand or reward "close reading," then we should not be surprised if students find them uninteresting. Yet students often do not share their teachers' investments and hierarchies. They are open to finding anything assigned to them equally boring or interesting. Reading very different kinds of texts makes them more self-conscious about how and why they read. One cannot really evaluate such a method until one tries to teach the contexts: assign them, give a reading guide for them, discuss them, and ask students to write on them – place them at the center and not the margins. Doing so then requires teachers, like students, to interrogate what is actually being taught and why. What is a Shakespeare course about and for? This can be uncomfortable. It also means that teachers inevitably find themselves outside of their comfort zones and their expertise, scrambling to keep up.

It is much more interesting to let go of the map and the compass. This is why it is important to avoid short excerpts of early modern texts. If you want to use a quotation to support a point, do so but admit that is what you're doing. Students usually resist an excerpt that is presented to them as evidence in support of your (or an editor's) thesis. The best texts are those in which students can get lost, that is, in which they might come up with something you can't predict. This is why I love the *Book of Homilies* (Cranmer 1562, Jewell 1570); or long weird trials in their early modern printed accounts or in crazy-quilt later versions such as those in *Cobbett's Complete State Trials* (Cobbett and Howell 1809–28), the provenance of which students can dissect and assess; and pamphlets in their entirety. It is also important, I think, to provide as much information as possible about the production, dissemination, transmission, and reception of a text under discussion. Just as most Shakespeare teachers will talk about quartos and the First Folio, it is worth doing what we can to explain that there is a history of the production and consumption of every text and that history might shape how we understand it. So, for instance, if I want to talk about how Anne Boleyn's history haunts Hermione's trial in *The Winter's Tale* I also want to talk about how we have access to that history: the rumors, the missing evidence, the warring interpretations. Of course, I know more about some contexts than I do about others. But I try to gesture toward depth, mess, and instability whenever I know enough to do so.

Much as I value getting lost and wallowing in uncertainty, I recognize that one sometimes needs some traction. One of the simplest ways to engage students in creating historical meaning while remaining focused is to start with a word. In my own experience, editing forces me to slow down, to move down a page word by word. Slowing students down works too. What I like about exercises in which they have to edit a short passage or look up a word in the *Oxford English Dictionary*, a Shakespeare concordance, and in the British Library's *English Short Title Catalogue*,[2] is that it requires a bifocal operation: close and broad, near and far. Many students fasten on words that shift from class insults to terms to describe general moral turpitude: knave, carlot, villain. Or they find the words that shift from class insults to gender insults. Lynda Boose tracks changing meanings of terms such as "harlot," "shrew," "hoyden," "scold," and "bawd," as they move from "contemptuous expressions for lower-class males into terms that gendered such hostility, displacing it away from the threat of male class revolt which remained real throughout the era and redirecting it at women" (Boose 1994: 222). Students working with the *OED* can recapitulate her process. A concordance can help them do some of what Patricia Parker does in her influential book *Shakespeare from the Margins*: pressing on words so that they spring open and flower out. Just as performance and history can be compatible, so careful attention to language provides a way into rather than an escape from history. As Parker puts this, "reading historically, with the resources not just of literary or dramatic texts but of a full range of early modern discourses, is . . . a way of avoiding taking the iteration of a particular orthodoxy at face value rather than interrogating what might be motivating its insistent repetition" (Parker 1996: 11). Students cannot consider repetition unless they are allowed to read across an evidentiary field (in however limited a way). Only then can they consider, for instance, why there are so many versions of shrew-taming stories, why Shakespeare chooses to tell one, and why he tells it in just the way that he does. And if certain stories are reiterated, whose stories or what stories do not seem to be told in the period? What can we make of that?

It is another kind of bifocal operation to look at the present and the past simultaneously. When talking about the meaning of a word, this works particularly well. What are the connotations of this word now? How do you use it? Is there an equivalent insult in your own vocabulary? How can we assess the similarities and differences? Some people assume a sharp opposition between "presentism" and "historicism," insisting that presentists project their own concerns on the past and ignore or erase crucial differences between then and now whereas historicists attend carefully to difference over time. Like other critics who posit more complicated relations between past and present (Charnes 2006, Freccero 2006, Hawkes 2002), I do not experience this as a productive opposition, especially in the classroom. Students always oscillate between then and now and they need to get some traction in the present to motivate and ground their inquiry into the past. For instance, by bringing me clippings about recent crimes and scandals, my students taught me something that has reshaped my own work on marriage and domestic violence: it is not required that one move in chronological order, and attending to historical continuity is just as "historical" as considering historical change (Dolan 2008). While we lament our culture's historical amnesia, and students' sense that "medieval" and "Victorian" are pretty much interchangeable words for "back in the day" or "the olden days," we can miss other kinds of insight students have into the conditions under which history might seem to matter to them. By constantly asking themselves how the past bears or lands on them today, students inject urgency into their engagement with the past in ways that I find inspiring. Other teachers have sometimes shared with me their concern that allowing students to make connections to the present encourages relativism, a cavalier disregard for the otherness of the past, sloppiness. This is not an anxiety I've ever shared. I prefer chaos to silence any day and those often seem as if they're pretty much the alternatives. Furthermore, as soon as a group is discussing connections it is also, inevitably, discussing ruptures. I do not think that we have to choose between a focus on students and a focus on magisterial expertise and authority, between performance and historical context, or between present and past, continuity and change. I think that it's possible, even inescapable, and exhilarating to attempt to keep all of those balls in the air at once. The result can be a clownish, undignified series of dropped balls and pratfalls. But, to me, that feels like life.

Notes

1 This line occurs in a requiem for Willy Loman at the end of Arthur Miller's *Death of a Salesman*.
2 The *English Short Title Catalogue* catalogue is available online at <http://estc.bl.uk/F/?func=file&file_name=login-bl-list>. There is an online Shakespeare concordance at <www.opensourceshakespeare.com/concordance/>.

References and Further Reading

Boose, Lynda E. (1994). "*The Taming of the Shrew*, Good Husbandry, and Enclosure." In Russ McDonald (Ed.). *Shakespeare Reread: The Texts in New Contexts* (pp. 193–225). Ithaca, NY: Cornell University Press.
Callaghan, Dympna C. (2000). "'Othello Was a White Man': Properties of Race on Shakespeare's Stage." In *Shakespeare Without Women: Representing Gender and Race on the Renaissance Stage* (pp. 75–96). London and New York: Routledge.

Charnes, Linda (2006). *Hamlet's Heirs: Shakespeare and the Politics of a New Millennium*. New York and London: Routledge.

Cobbett, William and Thomas B. Howell (Eds) (1809–28). *Cobbett's Complete Collection of State Trials and Proceedings for High Treason and Other Crimes and Misdemeanours from the Earliest Period to the Present Time . . . from the Ninth Year of the Reign of King Henry the Second, A.D. 1163 to . . . George IV, A.D. 1820*, 33 vols. London: R. Bagshaw.

Cranmer, Thomas, et al. (1562). *Certaine Sermons Appoynted by the Quenes Maiestie, to be Declared and Read, by All Persons, Vicars, and Curates, Euery Sundaye, Holy Daye, in Theyr Churches*. London.

Dolan, Frances E. (2008). *Marriage and Violence: The Early Modern Legacy*. Philadelphia: University of Pennsylvania Press.

Ferguson, Margaret W. (1985). "*Hamlet*: Letters and Spirits." In Patricia Parker and Geoffrey Hartman (Eds). *Shakespeare and the Question of Theory* (pp. 292–309). New York and London: Methuen.

Freccero, Carla (2006). *Queer/Early/Modern*. Durham, NC: Duke University Press.

Frye, Northrop (1963). *Fables of Identity: Studies in Poetic Mythology*. New York: Harcourt Brace.

Hawkes, Terence (2002). *Shakespeare in the Present*. London and New York: Routledge.

Howard, Jean E. (1986). "The New Historicism in Renaissance Studies." *English Literary Renaissance* 16: 16–43.

Jewell, John, et al. (1570). *The Second Tome of Homilees of Suche Matters as Were Promysed, and Intituled in the Former Part of Homilees. Set Out by the Aucthoritie of the Queenes Maiestie*. London.

Kranz, David L. (2000). Review of Barbara Hodgdon's *The First Part of King Henry the Fourth: Texts and Contexts*. *Shakespeare Quarterly* 51: 239–40.

Montrose, Louis Adrian (1981). " 'The Place of a Brother' in *As You Like It*: Social Process and Comic Form." *Shakespeare Quarterly* 32: 28–54.

Montrose, Louis A. (1986). "Renaissance Literary Studies and the Subject of History." *English Literary Renaissance* 16: 5–12.

Parker, Patricia (1996). *Shakespeare from the Margins: Language, Culture, Context*. Chicago: University of Chicago Press.

Rose, Mary Beth (1991). "Where are the Mothers in Shakespeare? Options for Gender Representation in the English Renaissance." *Shakespeare Quarterly* 42: 291–314.

Traub, Valerie (1992). *Desire and Anxiety: Circulations of Sexuality in Shakespearean Drama*. London: Routledge.

12

Divided by a Common Bard? Learning and Teaching Shakespeare in the UK and USA

Richard Dutton

This is less about Shakespeare's plays, or the sheer joy of teaching them, than you may have hoped. My education and career in England coincided with a revolution in university education there – from an elite, meritocratic, fully state-funded education of less than 10 percent of the population (including me) in a small number of research-led universities, to a far-from-elite teaching of 40 percent or more of the population (who very substantially pay their own way, sooner or later) in a wide variety of higher education institutions. In short, I have seen English tertiary education transform into something more like that which has been embedded in the United States for many years. And as I review my experience of Shakespeare, as student and teacher, I realize that it is the pressure of those changes – and how they have affected the educational experience – that loom largest with me, larger than most of the individual events that have taken place in the classroom. So that is what I shall be talking about.

I say that the English system is now "something like" that of the USA (and they continue to converge) but it would be a mistake to think of them as the same.[1] English education, secondary and tertiary, remains far more narrowly focused than that in the States: students still study fewer subjects more intensively and (most critically) within strictly three-year undergraduate degree schemes, the shortest in the world, for all the similarities of semes- terized schedules, more varied curricula and, often enough, American-style classes. Successive governments have proclaimed the need not only for more graduates, but for more roundly educated ones, flexible enough to meet the global challenges of the twenty-first century. But the reality is that universities have only edged in that direction, not embraced it whole-heartedly. And within the apparent commitment to change there has been a lingering commitment to some older educational values, but without the resources to realize them, making the experience at the chalk face often more confusing and painful than it might have been.

The differences between teaching Shakespeare to undergraduates in England and in the USA are, I suggest, dictated almost entirely by the differences between the educational philosophies of the two countries. They have nothing to do with the innate ability of the students, or indeed with the general cultural standing of Shakespeare, which seems to me pretty similar in both places. Shakespeare is a bedrock figure in high school literature on both sides of the Atlantic, an iconic figure of English-language culture. In England, he is a required element in the National Curriculum taught in secondary schools; in Ohio, where I now teach, those who intend to be high school teachers are required by state law to study Shakespeare as undergraduates – and I believe that is fairly common in other states. England may have Stratford-upon-Avon, a Royal Shakespeare Company, and a Globe on the Bankside; but the US has the Folger Shakespeare Library, perched so symbolically between the Library of Congress and the Supreme Court, innumerable Shakespeare festivals, and several replica Globe and Blackfriars theatres. In both countries the increasingly transatlantic publishing industry is committed to milking a still-buoyant textbook market. Shakespeare remains institutionally central to both cultural heritages, even as both of those heritages are being reshaped by (rather different versions of) multiculturalism.

And those heritages have interestingly crossed and merged in our generation's filming of so many of the plays. Kenneth Branagh's *Henry V* and *Much Ado*, Oliver Parker's *Othello*, Trevor Nunn's *Twelfth Night*, Adrian Noble's *Dream*, Richard Loncraine's *Richard III*, Baz Luhrmann's *Romeo*, everybody's *Hamlet* (even – God help us – Zeffirelli's with Mel Gibson), among many others – these are, for modern students the common language of Shakespeare on both sides of the Atlantic. The differences in teaching Shakespeare, therefore, derive mainly from the different structures of education (and not just higher education) in the two countries, not from any greater or lesser attachment to Shakespeare himself and what he represents.

But who am I to be offering these grand and eminently suspect generalizations? My first teaching (1971–4) was in a US college, but hardly a
typical one. I taught at Wroxton College in Oxfordshire, the English arm
of Fairleigh Dickinson University in New Jersey. By an exquisite irony it
was housed in the ancestral home of Lord North, Prime Minister when
Britain lost its American colonies. Being barely 20 miles from Stratford we
all got to see a lot of Shakespeare, but I was never allowed to teach him
there, so Wroxton plays no further part in this narrative. My first taste of
true US teaching was an exchange semester at Notre Dame in 1994, too
brief to register all that much. And now things have come, as it were, full
circle. Since 2003 I have taught at Ohio State University (OSU), where to
date I have taught four undergraduate Shakespeare classes, all at 500 level
(juniors and seniors) and two graduate ones. This of course qualifies me
to pontificate grandly on all aspects of US Shakespeare teaching (and college football).

Between times I taught for 29 years at Lancaster University, just south
of the Lake District. It has never been very big – maybe 4,000 students when
I got there, 10,000 when I left – but its scholarly record was impressive,
especially given how remote it is from major libraries and other resources.
In the Research Assessment Exercises (RAE) which began to plague British
academics in the early 1990s, it has always rated nationally around 10th
or 12th: fighting above our weight was how we put it. This was hardly
"typical" (I doubt if any university is) but my experiences there were, I
suspect, symptomatic of wider changes.

These will be more intelligible if I tell you something of my own education. I was part of the postwar baby-boomer generation, where state-
schooled sheep were divided from goats by examinations at the age of 11:
those who passed went to academically slanted grammar schools, those who
failed went to vocationally orientated secondary modern schools (and left
school at 15). At my grammar school, at the age of 14 I had to choose between
a humanities and a science bias (no chemistry, biology, or geography
for me), and from 16 to 18 studied only three subjects for "A" level, the
university-qualifying exam: English literature, history, and Latin. These "A"
levels were assessed entirely on the basis of multiple three-hour written-
essay exams. I passed these well enough to progress to King's College,
Cambridge (the first in my family to attend any university), where I read
English literature – and nothing but English literature – for three years.
For the first two years I surveyed the high peaks of English literature from
1350 to the present day. One of those peaks, E. M. Forster, was still alive
and pottering around the college, so it was very tangibly a living tradition.

Salman Rushdie, a future peak, was a year ahead of me, reading history. Of course, I only appreciated being at this literary crossroads later and with much hindsight. At the time I never felt comfortable at a college heavily dominated by those like Rushdie from "public" (i.e., private) schools.

When I say I "read" English literature, that is fairly literal. There were no *courses* as such. We knew that, at the end of two years, we would have to sit yet more three-hour written-essay exams – on the whole of English literature, divided up into historical periods, plus one or two specialist papers – one on Shakespeare, another on Practical Criticism, Cambridge's own version of New Criticism, which was very much the dominant critical methodology on offer. (I, for one, was never really aware that any other was possible.) Shakespeare, of course, was the ideal New Critical subject: the plays were examined in ahistorical isolation for linguistic patterns, for ironies and ambiguities, in effect treated as long verse poems. And there was a general underpinning of E. M. W. Tillyard (who, of course, had been a Cambridge man), transmuting everything into a context of "natural" order. This was the era of the Vietnam War and student revolution in Paris, but Britain remained characteristically phlegmatic: the worst atrocity was an egg thrown at the Prime Minister (by, I can reveal, one of the dons at King's). But I have no memory of connecting any of this with the study of Shakespeare. To steer us towards the exams, the college offered us weekly tutorials – one hour per week (in a leisurely eight-week term), in which conversation largely focused on a 2,500 word essay we had written for it, based on our week's reading. (By "we" I normally mean two of us, occasionally just the one.) As students we very much set our own agenda – no one thought it their duty to force us to read anything in particular or to think in particular ways.[2] Lectures were handled by the university at large, rather than the individual colleges. They bore only an accidental relation to the final papers. Lecturers usually read from their current research – Raymond Williams read from *The Long Revolution*, for example, even though it was already in print. Lectures, moreover, were entirely optional and only in the mornings (nothing should interfere with sport). So they were much more commonly honored in the breach than in the observance. L. C. Knights had people sitting in the aisles of the largest lecture theatre when he lectured on Shakespeare – the patent sincerity of his reading of *Lear* was deeply moving. But he was very much the exception. After Part One, the final year was much more thematic – papers such as Tragedy, the Moral Philosophers, the Single Author option (Chaucer in my year) – but otherwise much the same, culminating in (yes) more three-hour written-essay exams.

American readers will probably recognize this syllabus as more akin to an MA than a BA, and we did receive an MA of sorts for it, three years after graduating.[3] It was, of course, only possible because of the intensively focused (i.e., narrow) secondary education we had received,[4] and it meant that at the end of it some of us were already prepared to take on a doctorate, which simply meant completing a dissertation: no coursework was involved. (I did mine at Nottingham in two years.) The differences from the American model could hardly be more pronounced: there the BA is commonly very general, with the major often accounting for less than a third of the total courses taken; General Education Curriculum (GEC) requirements send English majors off into courses on science, civics, languages, social sciences, anything and everything. And a course *is* a course, with a syllabus, aims and objectives, a reading schedule, and required attendance a couple of days a week. At the end *nobody* is solely assessed on the basis of three-hour written-essay exams, a methodology which was critical in a few cases I encountered at Lancaster, where very bright visiting American students stayed on to do a full degree – and finished up with quite poor results. Whatever their other skills and virtues, they never mastered the breadth of reference and sophisticated argument expected in unseen exam papers, which for so many years were (and often still are) central to the English assessment system.

People at Cambridge will doubtless tell you it isn't like the 1960s any more, and maybe in some ways it isn't, but the spirit lives on (alongside that of Oxford, with its distinctive differences but much deeper similarities) as a kind of gold standard against which all other education in England is implicitly measured.[5] The government still pays them extra fees to keep alive the 1:1 or 1:2 weekly tutorials, which no other universities can now afford to mount. And a wholly disproportionate number of Golden Triangle (Oxford, Cambridge, London) graduates – like me – become the lecturers at British universities, perpetuating the memory of such tuition even in contexts where it cannot be replicated. Other universities never went down quite the exclusively "single honors" model of Oxbridge – English majors would take a minor in, say, French or history, which might occupy a quarter of their degree time. And there would be recognizable taught courses, with a syllabus of hourly lectures followed up by smaller classes called tutorials or seminars. But this was still light years removed from the generalist BA normal in the US and (in different modes) throughout most of Europe.

This was what I brought to Lancaster in 1974. The university was only eight years old, one of a small wave of new universities created by the Labour

Government of the 1960s. Universities were still something of a rarity – I think there would have been fewer than 30 of them in 1960. After Oxford and Cambridge (rarest of the rare) most of the others were nineteenth-century foundations, led by London and followed by most of the major conurbations (such as Manchester, Birmingham, Leeds, Bristol, and Liverpool, one of whose buildings conferred the generic title of "redbrick" on them all). Few followed until the 1960s new wave, which also included York, Warwick, East Anglia, Essex, Sussex, and Kent. The names are right out of a Shakespeare history play, resonant of ancient shires and peerages. They were almost all built on picturesque greenfield sites, away from centers of population and industry, each a little dreaming spire. They represented an expansion of higher education, but they also recreated by other means a sense of universities as elite institutions. And that was something all universities were made to pay for in the years ahead.

Lancaster in 1974 did not feel like a privileged institution, but with hindsight certainly was. Its founders were bent on expanding the students' curriculum, a revolutionary cause repeatedly espoused in England over the years – and one repeatedly thwarted. You have to see that in relative terms. What they did at first was to insist that, whatever the students' declared major, they must take three subjects equally in their first year. Thereafter a degree was divided into nine units, six in a major, two in a minor, and one in a "removed minor," unconnected with either the major or the minor. To someone with an Oxbridge mindset this was utterly disconcerting: students could spend barely half their university time on their major. There was no way they could read their way through English literature, 1350 to the present day. Indeed, the issue was even more acute than that because the founding head of the English department was convinced that the future of "English" lay with the new language studies: linguistics, stylistics, and more "scientific" ways of reading. So half of all English courses were language courses, and English literature *per se* occupied barely a quarter of an English major's three years.

The history of the degree scheme at Lancaster has actually been one of slow retreat from the revolutionary ideals of its founders, under pressure both from what remains (despite tinkering) narrowly focused secondary education and the wishes of students themselves, many of whom resented being forced to work outside the subject of their choice. The "removed minor" became a course that could be added on to the major or the minor; eventually it was abolished altogether. And it became possible to minor in the same subject as the major. When I left, they were talking of reducing Year 1 from three subjects to two. Within English, language requirements were progressively reduced, and the linguisticians floated out of Humanities altogether and into their own department in Social Sciences. The pressure of the "single honors" model of an English degree remains extremely strong, despite the efforts of places like Lancaster to broaden the educational base.

What, then, were the implications of this sad, eventful history for the teaching of Shakespeare? First, of course, it meant defining what "Shakespeare" was in a context where no student could conceivably study the whole arc of English literature – even though, in the range of courses we offered, they still had the option of choosing among all the eras from *Beowulf* to Angela Carter. I will spare you all the wranglings in committees by which the initial position (Shakespeare divided between Elizabethan and Jacobean drama courses, which included survey lectures on the likes of Lyly, Greene, Beaumont and Fletcher for students who would never read their works) changed to one where by about 1980 Shakespeare was taught on a course all of his own. Or to be precise two courses all of his own – a literary course and one on "Shakespeare and the history of the language" (students could take either or both, though the latter was always a minority option, and people like myself who had absolutely no grounding in language study never taught on it). Henceforth "Shakespeare," the literary course, was always at the center of my teaching commitments. It was initially a second-year option, and later could be taken interchangeably by second-year and third-year students, but always as an option: it was never compulsory, though year on year it was the most popular course we taught.

Here, however, I need to define a course, since what we offered was very different from most US "courses" or classes. First, it ran for the whole year, across the three 10-week terms of the academic year, though classes gave way to revision sessions and exams in the final weeks. And for most of the time I was there, whichever year the students took a course, they were examined on it in their final year. We believed (and there is evidence to show this) that students matured critically over their degree span, and wrote exams with more sophistication in their final year. This outweighed the fact that they inevitably lost their immediate familiarity with individual texts.[6] All of this played into the traditional English obsession with the "honors" degree: all English students aspire to a final grading of first class or upper second class honors (the less fortunate have to settle for lower second class or third class honors), measures of overall achievement, not just a mechanical accumulation of marks. And those who teach them devote a ludicrous amount of time and effort on exam boards every summer to slotting them into these classifications, in a way that has no parallel in the US. The one-year Shakespeare course at Lancaster was effectively one ninth (later one eighth) of the students' entire degree assessment, since first-year courses were qualificatory only. It inevitably loomed *much* larger in their consciousness than any single course or class in a US degree.

It loomed much larger in the consciousness of the faculty too, because it was also taught differently. The course was not owned by an individual but taught collectively by as many of the specialists in the subject (usually three or four) as were available that year to work on it. This was not team-teaching as it is generally understood, but simply a division of labors: class time for the students amounted to an hour's lecture, in which anything from 100 to 160 students would listen to one of us spouting off each week; and an hour's seminar, for which they were divided into much smaller groups and allocated to one of us for the year. This implied, of course, a common and agreed syllabus, in which we all taught pretty much the same plays (somehow the nondramatic verse never squeezed on to the syllabus), and aimed to provide the students with an element of continuity through our lectures, however different our critical models and emphases might be. So whereas at Ohio State 520.01 Shakespeare is a blank space, on which I can write pretty much what I please – maybe do all histories this quarter, or look at illustrations of Shakespeare through the ages – Lancaster's 292 Shakespeare was a carefully negotiated, contractually defined entity, whose description, syllabus, and reading list were on the university's books, and varied little from year to year.[7] This was also critical to an important feature of those three-hour written-essay exams by which the students would one day be measured: they would all be double-marked. That is, two people from those who taught the course would assess each (anonymized) script independently, and then get together to agree a mark for it. This has long been a cornerstone of the British academic process, aimed to ensure impartiality and uniform standards (though it is strained to breaking point by the sheer number of scripts each person has to read these days).[8] Most Americans I have spoken to find it incomprehensible, if vaguely worthy. But in the States I admit to still feeling guilty when I act as judge and executioner for every script I read, and know exactly whom I'm condemning as I do so.

I suppose it is never easy to agree on a consensual syllabus of the kind I have described, but back in the 1980s – the height of the theory wars – it was particularly difficult, all the more so because I had a fair number of colleagues who (irrespective of their research interests) all figured they could "teach Shakespeare." At various times these included one whose critical horizons had never extended beyond Tillyard, a post-Marxist (who was also more or less openly gay), a devotee of Georges Battaille, a feminist skilled in theatrical practice, and one whose seminars were said to consist of reminiscences of his war experiences in Burma. And what was I? Well, I had it on the irreproachable testimony of no less than Stanley Fish that I was "a partly reconstructed New Critic."[9] I was also a wishy-washy liberal, who liked to settle for consensus over confrontation.

But I also became seriously confused about what I thought I *ought* to be teaching. Cambridge-style Practical Criticism, with its moralistic Leavisite overtones, came very easily to me – I had lots of exam results to prove it. My graduate work at Nottingham included no coursework and did nothing to challenge my fundamental methodologies. I had read nothing of Foucault or Althusser. Stephen Greenblatt's (1980) *Renaissance Self-Fashioning* was compelling, but I know I did not grasp its poststructuralist underpinnings at the time. Jonathan Goldberg's (1983) *James I and the Politics of Literature* I found incomprehensible until about the third time I read it (at which point I realized how profoundly I disagreed with it). Jonathan Dollimore's (1984) *Radical Tragedy* immediately struck me as simplistic, if engagingly iconoclastic. All of these (and, later, feminist equivalents) found their way on to the "agreed" syllabus, but what exactly I was supposed to be doing with any of this in my own classes was far from clear, at least to me.

It was about this time that the late, much-missed Raman Selden joined the department and defused many of the tensions over "theory" that wracked so many other English departments. Under his guidance we instituted a fairly impartial Literary Theory course, a survey from Saussure to (eventually) Kristeva, which became the only required course on the syllabus, in effect the defining point of "honors" English at Lancaster. Students took it in their second year, when they were just beginning to concentrate on literature. So, in effect, a course on the hows and wherefores of reading took the place of reading literature itself from 1350 to the present day. And students took it when their actual reading of the literary canon was extremely limited: many of those struggling with Derridean deconstruction had never read a Dickens novel; by the 1990s hardly any of those reading Lacan had read a word of Chaucer. The Shakespeare course, which most of them took in tandem with Literary Theory, thus unfolded with no grounding in medieval literature, or in the rest of the Renaissance, but was underpropped with occasional smatterings of Bakhtin, Greenblatt/ Foucault, Dollimore/cultural materialism, and various shades of feminism. Carnival, cross-dressing, and subversion reigned, until the Ash Wednesday of *Discipline and Punish* imposed containment.

In my own research, mainly on Jonson, this partially reconstructed New Critic had certainly run up against the limits of my education. I had instinctively moved beyond the limits of the text to see that Jonson was always implicitly playing on the expectations and responses of his audiences. This led me into censorship, which offered an incontrovertible moment of historic reading, something that could perhaps be reconstructed and interpreted . . . and thereby hangs a tale of 20 years' work, which still wags my career in a number of ways. At the level of teaching I had at least worked out that I was a historicist; I was interested in what texts meant in history, and I wanted students to be interested in that too. I wasn't quite sure what kind of a historicist I was – not a Marxist, not a cultural materialist. I am a depressingly empiricist Anglo-Saxon, averse to abstract formulae. It was several years before I discovered that the appropriate label was "revisionist," which I think was a term of abuse. But it fit the facts.

There were limits, however, to the usefulness of this in the classroom: students simply did not have time to learn early modern history *and* read the plays. Lectures tried increasingly to cover for the gaps in students' knowledge (be it history, other texts, or theoretical concepts). A course needed shaping, defining, contextualizing so that it could stand on its own – even, say, for a business major who just wanted a Shakespeare minor on the side. Without the framework of "literature 1350 to the present day," students needed setting on *some* rails as quickly as possible, and the lectures were those rails (even if, week by week, they sometimes spun off at different theoretical tangents). Seminars, meanwhile, were Lancaster's answer to the Oxbridge tutorial – the defining classy element in English higher education that separated us from the mass systems in Europe (lectures of 600+, nothing smaller) and even most US colleges. We couldn't afford to mount 1:1 or 1:2 tutorials, but in the early days we did contrive groups of six to eight, small enough to allow no hiding place. And they were *supposed* to be student-led. They were supposed to be the place where students could air their own responses to the week's reading, and indeed the week's lecture, and ask questions. The tutor was in theory a benign facilitator, helping the conversation to flow and grow productively, occasionally acting as a fount of useful knowledge. And we had the great luxury (envied in most other universities) of our own spacious offices where the seminars were held. It was as if, Oxbridge style, the students were just dropping in for a chat.

And sometimes it worked. But rather painfully often it didn't, for a number of reasons. One is that English state education has never been very strong on producing people willing to express themselves orally: put them in a three-hour written-essay exam and they are unbeatable, but face-to-face diffidence and an instinct to defer to others tend to predominate.[10] I used to pray for older students (women coming back to education after raising a family, for example), who *really* wanted to talk, and had something to say. Or American year-abroad students, who were almost invariably more forthcoming than their English counterparts. I wouldn't make a total cultural generalization about this. Although at OSU it is definitely easier to get (some) people to talk than it would be in England, it does not normally extend to a whole class of 40 students. Year-abroad students tend to be a self-selecting elite: the very fact that they have the initiative to study overseas (many of my current students have never left Ohio, never mind gone abroad) predisposes them to be keen in class as well. So they were always welcome in my classes.

There were other issues as well that militated against flowing conversation. Students had not written any kind of essay ahead of the class (assessment essays always came at the end of term), and so had not been required to bring their thoughts together, Oxbridge-style. Nor could they be expected to do so, since this class would be only one of four or five they would be taking that week – seminars in such numbers can hardly have the concentrated force of a tutorial, or be approached with the same enthusiasm. Where at Cambridge I had a full week to engage with each of *Hamlet*, *Othello*, *Macbeth*, and *Lear* (Shakespeare got a full term of tutorials – as much as any century of other authors), Lancaster students in reality would only be able to devote a day or so to each of these, and that probably chopped about by their schedule. Over time we took to taking two weeks over each of *Hamlet* and *Lear*, but even so that only meant two days or so actually devoted to each text (and the dubious bonus of two of our lectures). In reality they barely had time to absorb the text, never mind formulate thoughts and questions about it (much less begin to grapple with historicist perspectives of any substance).

So we had to think of ways of getting them talking. Sometimes I would assign a student a brief introductory paper, and they were often quite good – but they usually had the effect of killing conversation stone dead. Sometimes I would divide the class into smaller groups and get them to discuss particular issues, which they could later share with the others. This often worked well: they talked much better among themselves than they did with a tutor listening. But it was very time-consuming in what was effectively only 50 minutes, and covered only small aspects of the text. This became an urgent issue in itself: the Cambridge tutorial was never under any pressure to "cover" everything – the student was always expected to flesh it out himself (King's was still all-male in my day, more's the pity). But the Lancaster formula put pressure on the tutors to "cover" a good deal of the text, to point out features and issues which we suspected students would never reach by themselves. For me, it became increasingly tempting to expect that we would spend each class looking in detail at two or three key passages (so designated by me), which had the virtue of ensuring that they got some experience of close reading, while also getting some directed "coverage." (Just how competent they were to construe the texts on their own, for all their "A" level training, which probably included detailed study of two Shakespeare plays, was always a worrying question.) The detailed examination of two or three passages also had the advantage that I made this the bedrock of preparing them for their end-of-term essays, and indeed exams. I encouraged them similarly to find two or three passages of their own in each play, particularly highly charged with the themes and issues they wanted to explore, and to build essays or exam answers around detailed readings of those passages – ensuring specificity and engagement with the text. I developed a party-piece on "The Mousetrap," showing how it could be used to underpin any number of discussions on acting, identity, subjectivity, meta-theatre, revenge, gender roles, language, political theatre, and so on, in *Hamlet*. Of course, all of this might have been done more "efficiently" in lectures, since the seminars – we might well each have three to five every week (sometimes half our entire teaching load) – all began to cover the same material. But, as we have seen, lectures were already expected to carry a lot of other freight.

It was a good use of the students' time, in the circumstances, but it did amount to a tacit admission that the original rationale of the seminar had failed, that the tutor had taken over in terms of setting the agenda – and it was never too clear how, when, or even if the student would ever take it back. Happily, every now and again a genuine conversation would break out, and I would abandon the tacit ground plan. It could be exhilarating – I remember one discussion 20 years ago that really went to town on gender and cross-dressing in *Twelfth Night* (but I still managed to feel guilty at the end of it about all the other issues we had "missed"). And, somewhere in the 1980s, the students began to make links between Shakespeare and politics. The Falklands War of 1982 was a big turning point: the similarities with *Henry V* were just unavoidable, and after that power, hierarchy, and patriarchy came to seem the "natural" language of seminars – Practical Criticism was well and truly dead. For the most part, however, while lectures and seminars were "coaching" students in ways of reading Shakespeare, it was less clear that we were training them to read for themselves. They were always adept at imitating the models we offered, though only the really bright ones struggled through to use these models independently. And the less bright ones could get really confused between the different models on offer, between the various lecturers and their seminar tutors. At the same time, an inexorable rise in class size meant that seminars grew to 10, 12, 14, and beyond, doubling over the time I was there. And somewhere in that gradation the opportunity for individuals to hide increased enormously, and the chances of spontaneous conversation all but died. With apt symbolism, just as I was leaving in 2003, the university decided we could no longer hold on to our spacious offices – they all had to be subdivided, and seminars (which by then could, anyway, barely squeeze in without people sitting on desks and radiators) had to be moved to designated teaching spaces. The last vestiges of Oxbridge tutorial disappeared.

All of this was a direct consequence of government policy. The resolutely utilitarian Tory governments of Margaret Thatcher and John Major (1979 to 1997) had nothing but contempt for what greenfield universities like Lancaster represented. UK universities are still state-funded to a very large degree.[11] Autonomous agencies maintain a façade of academic independence, but doubt not that he who pays the piper calls the tune. Over that period universities were subjected to a range of efficiency incentives, which resulted in them teaching many more students (almost twice as many) – but the funding per student fell by 40 percent. In 1992 the country's polytechnics, which had no degree-awarding powers and traditionally focused on vocational training, became universities – a deliberate challenge to the elitism of the old guard. They had not normally taught humanities to degree level: but new funding models soon changed that. Implicitly this introduced into Britain for the first time a distinction between universities which were research-led and those which were primarily teaching institutions. But the RAE (Research Assessment Exercise), introduced at the same time, put the "old" universities on notice that their elite status and funding were not guaranteed. Over time it seems increasingly likely that a small core of universities (not all of those around before 1992) will be formally designated as research institutions, while others will not. Which will in effect also codify at least two levels of teaching, with markedly different faculty-student ratios. This has long been a fact of life in the publicly funded universities in the US, and faculty are employed knowing these differences. But it is still new to the UK, and working in institutions which have been struggling to come to terms with these implications has become more fraught.[12]

Of course, the government did not really want swarms of additional English majors in all of this, but grudgingly accepted that they were a cheap way of achieving the more widely educated population they were looking for. I have a sad little footnote – sad for me as a liberal and a child of the Welfare State – to the Thatcher revolution in higher education: the less cocooned students in these less privileged times work a darned sight harder. There are widespread mutterings that too many students graduate with upper second class degrees, that standards are falling: not in my experience. With loans to repay, students' eyes are firmly fixed on getting a job, and they work accordingly. The introduction of student fees – the Blair government brought them up to levels comparable with some at US state colleges – has all but completed the translation of students from elite, grant-aided pupils (like me) to loan-bearing, competitive customers.

My move to OSU – at the very moment my old office was being divided to house two – was thus, from my perspective, both timely and seamless. The conventional undergraduate class of 40 students was small by the lecture standards I was used to, large by the seminar ones. But most intimidating was the fact that it ran almost two hours: nothing in my training had prepared me for that at all – pacing it, keeping them (and me) involved. I quickly discovered that technology could be very useful here: video and DVD were readily available in OSU classrooms, and here I had the time to use them. They were more messily available in Lancaster, but the problem was always the 50-minute time-slot: even two sequences from a movie took a large slice of the available time, and had to be especially pertinent to warrant use. With two hours I could use as much or as little as I needed, and it always seems to make sense: film is the language all students have been brought up on, and even the less gifted ones have something to say about it. It is the perfect ice-breaker, especially given the wealth of Shakespearean film since Branagh's *Henry V*.

At the same time I was, for the first time ever, absolute master of my own classroom. I set my own syllabus, chose my own plays, the order in which to study them, and the perspective from which they would be studied; I chose and set my own forms of assessment – all freedoms which

US professors take for granted, but which are still rarities in England. Of course, the students' own culture sets tacit parameters beyond which I cannot stray, though this is not as different from what you would find in England as you might expect. When I started in England there were still a few students who had studied classics at school, but that had disappeared long before I left: at OSU some of them may actually have done, say, *The Aeneid* (in translation) as a GEC requirement. Again, when I started, most students had been drilled at school through the political history of the Tudor period (though, ironically, I did little to exploit the fact). But after the school shift to project-based history, somewhere around 1990, that became rarer to find: if you were lucky, they knew the ins and outs of Henry VIII's wives, but more often than not they had studied World War One two or three times over. So comparable ignorance in the US about the sixteenth century was no shock. I was told to expect that OSU students would be much more religious than their very secular counterparts in Lancaster. This is true in the sense that they wear their Christianity very conspicuously, but hardly at all in the sense that they actually know the Bible by which many of them set such store: I have yet to find an undergraduate student who recognizes a Christ-echo in Cordelia's "O dear father, / It is thy business that I go about." I was also told to expect them to be, on the whole, much more politically conservative, and this as a generality is true. But there are usually a few in every class who pick up my inadvertent liberal body language and respond to it. These days, rather than the Falklands, it is difficult to tiptoe through *Henry V* without being conscious of the Iraq war in some shape or form. Recently I was dealing with Canterbury's Salic Law speech and asked for a modern equivalent of what it amounted to: one student promptly offered Colin Powell's speech to the UN about Iraq, which I thought was pretty sharp. In these respects, though styles are superficially different (Midwestern students are unbelievably polite), I see no fundamental differences between my US students and my UK ones. The Honors students in my classes are as bright and eager as anyone I ever taught at Lancaster; those who cannot follow a syllabus, or whose alarm clocks do not go off, are a universal breed.

The real difference I have to negotiate is literary theory, which is a closed shop to virtually all my American students. They may be exposed to some of it in a 10-week writing course that is compulsory for all majors, but this is far too basic to make a real impact on their reading habits. They seem to pick up bits of feminism and ethnicity issues, but little that is class-based (Marxist) and nothing systematic. The fact that the Shakespeare course, too, is only 10 weeks long, and one of many, inevitably reduces its impact.

All of which means that, as with historical context, I have to draw in my horns: we can talk about festivity in *Twelfth Night* and maybe think a bit about how carnival works. But they know nothing about Bakhtin, and these classes do not seem to be the place to start telling them. In a *Henry V* class I mentioned Michel Foucault: for all they knew, he might as well have played goalkeeper for Senegal. (Americans do know a bit about soccer these days – and endlessly assume that I miss it and want to talk about it.) And, again, this didn't seem to be the place to start tampering with their ignorance.

By and large, this seems to be a situation my colleagues agree to live with. It is built into their understanding of the difference between under-graduate and graduate: everyone starting an MA takes a compulsory crash course in theory, similar to (though much shorter than) the course Lancaster students take as second-year undergraduates. The implication is that serious theory starts there, not earlier. And I confess that I am comfortable with that. On reflection, the Lancaster mode (which I know has many parallels throughout England) of building a syllabus around a literary theory course, as in some ways a substitute for trying to cover the whole canon of English literature, is a dubious expedient. It tries to give students skills for thinking about literature when they have encountered precious little literature to think about. They learn to deconstruct the canon before they have encountered most of the items on it.

The OSU undergraduate syllabus, partly driven by the 10-week quarter system (longer and fewer semester-length courses would make a big difference), implicitly keeps the pressure low. Try a bit of this; try a bit of that. One of those bits may be Shakespeare. (I recently helped my chair draft a response to an alumnus who complained that Shakespeare was not compulsory for our majors. Most of them take it, anyway – many because they want to be teachers – and there are always waiting lists on the course.) The real pressure is on graduate students, who have to step up a gear or three, and it is a real pleasure to be involved in their education – Lancaster was never able to generate a significant number of Renaissance graduate students (again, the Golden Triangle takes so many).

I am struck by the things my graduate students do not know – and few of these were OSU undergraduates, so this is not institution-specific. Theory apart, not one of them in my classes has known anything at the outset about the multiplicity of Shakespeare's original texts and the editorial practices to which this gives rise. They know that boys played the women's parts, but after that they tend to know very little about Elizabethan theatre practice. Their knowledge of Queen Elizabeth is unfortunately confused with the Cate Blanchett version (I am hoping they can be converted to Helen

Mirren, though I remain a Flora Robson man myself). Their acquaintance with Renaissance drama outside of Shakespeare (and a little Marlowe) is very thin and predictable, as is their grasp of the history of the era. Clearly an MA is where they expect to learn all of this. And they do: most of those I have taught have been whip-smart. I like the fact that their graduate education is part of a coherent training to be academics – most of them teach as they are taught. In England they are still primarily students. They may well be paid to do some teaching, but this is often casual and unpredictable, and there is not much institutional support for getting them into the academic profession.

"Profession" is actually a key subtext to these words, words, words. The old English universities are often still at heart gentlemen's clubs, elitist, clannish, and in some important respects amateur: breeding grounds of "natural" Elizabethan world pictures. Successive governments, increasingly concerned to account for the public money pouring into them, have tried to professionalize them. They have traumatized the careers of many academics in the process, as they have scrambled to keep up with institutional change, RAEs, TQAs, and evolving measurements of "value." The English cultural materialists of the 1980s and 1990s were fighting this as much as they were resisting other aspects of government policy, fighting on behalf of the coal miners and their own sense of what their profession should be, on the battlefields of Arden, Agincourt, and Dunsinane. Somehow I negotiated one and then the other. But it is, candidly, a relief to be out of the struggle. I know that I am singularly lucky to be at Ohio State, a massive public institution with a mission to be world class. I am lucky to be senior, tenured, and blessed with fine colleagues (as indeed I was at Lancaster). But I also think it is not just luck that I find myself within a stable, knowable, academic environment, where the Shakespeare I teach may be an ill-favored thing, but is mine own. It is a genuine professional environment, where the skills of our "mystery" are respected. Doubtless cynics will be muttering " 'Tis new to thee," but I think I am finally old enough to know a hawk from a handsaw.

Notes

1 Please note that I am carefully saying English, not British. Much of what I am saying applies to Wales and Northern Ireland, but not to Scotland, which retains a very different – many would say superior – educational structure.

2   When I was "doing" the seventeenth century I admitted a deep Leavisite aversion to Milton, so my tutor suggested I do Dryden instead; the tutor was John Broadbent, an eminent Miltonist.

3   Historically, the six-year MA was the true degree, the bachelor's only a staging post. Oxford and Cambridge have never seen the need to change that, but the final three years are education-free.

4   English students receive 13 years of precollege education, compared to the 12 in the USA, which partly accounts for the three-year degree pattern. My thanks to Carol Rutter for reminding me of this. Equally critical, however, is the way that general education in England ends at the age of 16, with a range of General Certificate of Secondary Education (GCSE, which replaced "O" level) qualifications that can be quite thorough, and even today "A" level concentrates for two years on very narrow curricula.

5   The current Cambridge syllabus may be viewed at <www.newn.cam.ac.uk/admissions/course info.shtml#english>.

6   Before I left, the university changed the rules on this: driven by science and social-science models, they insisted that all students be examined in the year in which they took the course.

7   As things got tighter, in the 1990s, the government played the double whammy of simultaneously reducing resources and insisting on tighter standards. Many Americans have heard of the RAE, but Teaching Quality Assessment (TQA) and its successor regimes are much less well known. Teams drawn from other universities would turn up every five years or so to review teaching procedures. Much of TQA was about ensuring that the paperwork for courses etc. had gone through all the right committees in the right order, and got all the necessary approvals. We also had to learn how to define a course's Aims and Objectives. (I could once have told you what the difference was between an Aim and an Objective, but since coming to the States I have forgotten.)

8   Unlike the Cambridge of my youth, Lancaster has always taken coursework into account, so that the outcome does not hang entirely upon the dreaded exams. But the examination element always has to predominate – something which has intensified rather than diminished as the Internet has increasingly called the integrity of coursework into question.

9   This came with his reading of an article of mine, submitted to *Studies in English Literature*.

10 When I say "state education" I am implicitly contrasting this with private education, in what the English laughably call "public schools." The latter set a premium on self-confidence and robust self-articulation, and since their products continue to have a wholly disproportionate representation at Oxbridge, this helps to perpetuate the somewhat overrated tutorial system. Public school types were a rarity at Lancaster.

11   There is an exception, the University of Buckingham.
12   See Note 7 on specific ways in which things became "fraught."

References and Further Reading

Baldick, Chris (1983). *The Social Mission of English Criticism, 1848–1932*. Oxford: Clarendon Press.

Cruttwell, Patrick (1954). *The Shakespearean Moment*. London: Chatto & Windus.

Dollimore, Jonathan (1984). *Radical Tragedy: Religion, Ideology and Power in the Drama of Shakespeare and his Contemporaries*. Brighton, UK: Harvester Press.

Goldberg, Jonathan (1983). *James I and the Politics of Literature*. Baltimore, MD: Johns Hopkins University Press.

Greenblatt, Stephen (1980). *Renaissance Self-Fashioning from More to Shakespeare*. Chicago: University of Chicago Press.

Richards, I. A. (1929, rev. 1930). *Practical Criticism*. London: Routledge and Kegan Paul.

Selden, Raman (1984). *A Reader's Guide to Contemporary Literary Theory*. London: Longman.

Selden, Raman (1989). *Practicing Theory and Reading Literature*. London: Longman.

Sinfield, Alan (1992). *Faultlines: Cultural Materialism and the Politics of Dissident Reading*. Oxford: Clarendon Press.

Tillyard, E. M. W. (1943). *The Elizabethan World Picture*. London: Chatto & Windus.

Tillyard, E. M. W. (1944). *Shakespeare's History Plays*. London: Chatto & Windus.

Traversi, Derek (1957). *An Approach to Shakespeare*. London: Sands.

Part V
And in Conclusion . . .

13

Playing Hercules or Laboring in My Vocation

Carol Chillington Rutter

Pondering the questions, "Why do I teach Shakespeare?", "Why do I *keep* teaching Shakespeare?", "Why do I teach Shakespeare through performance?", Mote and Mark Antony have been much on my mind – the "well educated infant" of *Love's Labour's Lost*; the "Mars of men" and "triple pillar of the world" of *Antony and Cleopatra*.[1] They aren't, perhaps, the most obvious roles to couple in thought. But their very incongruity helps me frame some responses to those questions about Shakespeare and teaching that have been occupying me. Mote and Antony turn out to be curiously alike – if I "crush" them a little, the way Malvolio crushes "M.O.A.I" to find "simulation" in a "fustian riddle." They connect the pupil, the pedagogue, and the performer; the midget and the mighty: apt role models for those who would teach the plays Shakespeare writes. Let me unpack my riddle.

Mote, Don Armado's "well educated" sidekick, doesn't appear to have done schoolboy duty at the vaguely Hogwarts-sounding "charge-house on the top of the mountain" (5.1.77) where Holofernes, the pedant, "teaches boys the horn-book" (5.1.45). Nevertheless, the "acute juvenal" has somewhere acquired the rhetorical equipment of a grammar school education. He's been taught. He's stuffed with quips and quiddities. He's "quick in answers" (1.2.29, where "quick" means not just "speedy" but "alive"). The child knows how to conduct a "demonstration" (1.2.9), to "prove" an ingenious argument (3.1.36), to turn a "most fine figure" (1.2.55), and to "Define, define" (1.2.90). He even turns the tables to stand pedagogue (literally, from Greek, "leader" + "boy") to his love-baffled master, schooling Armado in the basic rudiments of knowledge: "But have you forgot your love?

Negligent student, learn her by heart" (3.1.31, 33). More than a pert pupil, Mote is a forward performer, an impromptu rhymester (in the Iago school of sententious paradox, 1.2.94–101) who can also "Warble" a "Sweet air" (3.1.1, 4). So, it seems, it's not just enough to receive an education; you have to play it back, turn it into action, do something with it. When Mote is recruited to the "show" of "the Nine Worthies" that Holofernes (in a coproduction with Armado) stages for the royal entertainment, the kid is assigned, somewhat improbably as Armado objects, the part of Hercules. Mote is "not quantity enough for that Worthy's thumb," "not so big as the end of his club" (5.1.124–6). But Holofernes, wiser than he is aware (knowing instinctively, like teachers everywhere, who the true Hercules is in any classroom or academic demonstration), has devised an ingenious solution to the physical discrepancy of heroic scale. Mote will play "Hercules in minority," figuring the infant prodigy, who, yes, would grow up to kill "Cerberus, that three-headed *canus*," but even more amazingly, when yet "a babe, a child, a shrimp," "did strangle serpents in his *manus*" (5.2.584–6).

It's Mote playing Hercules that triggers the associative leap to Mark Antony. In Plutarch (and in Shakespeare) we learn that Antony adopted the hero as his ancestor, as "the god" he "loved" (4.3.13); that he affected his dress, his loose, rough tunic, the low sling of his belt; that he wanted to play Hercules's part, to be seen as his avatar (Spencer 1964: 177). We also learn in Plutarch (and in Shakespeare, *Julius Caesar* this time) that Antony loved performance: was a reveler, kept street musicians, dancers, and common players in his household; in *Caesar*, he "loves . . . plays," "hears . . . music," "is given / To sports, to wildness, and much company" (1.2.204, 205; 2.1.188–9). We don't know what kind of schoolboy Antony was (unlike, say, Casca, who was "quick mettle when he went to school," *Julius Caesar*, 1.2.296), but when he hits rock bottom, when he has lost at Actium and must sue to the "scarce-bearded Caesar" (*Antony and Cleopatra*, 1.1.22) for his life, he does something astonishing, something utterly, devastatingly poignant. He sends as his ambassador "his schoolmaster" (3.12.2), a man who, standing before Caesar, quietly introduces himself: "Such as I am, I come from Antony." Then observes:

> I was of late as petty to his ends
> As is the morn-dew on the myrtle leaf
> To his grand sea.
>
> (3.12.6–9)

Yet insignificant as this schoolmaster is to Antony's huge conquests, his extravagant feasts, his inordinate love, his world travels, his adulthood proxying Hercules, the Roman general has kept his tutor somewhere near at hand, knows where to find him in that "grand sea" when he needs him, submits himself a pupil once more, wants that master's voice to negotiate his future. A voice embodying a trace of childhood?

From out of this tangle of prompts and crossed-leads and glanced associations, Herculean Mote and Mark Antony tell me something about the teacher and the taught – and about why I teach. They offer two models of the pedagogue. On the one hand, the conceited and faintly ridiculous wisecracking smart aleck, too big for his breeches. (That's me! Lecturing – performing – in a packed lecture theatre to two hundred eager-to-be-impressed undergraduates, speaking Shakespeare's words, playing all his parts, I dazzle! I'm a diva of the lecture stage! But I'm aware that it's a risky business, this self-exposed playing, and that I'm always dancing on the verge of the pratfall.) On the other, the opposite number: the pedagogue as unassuming "petty" gravity. (That's me, too, knowing I am no more than the "morn-dew on the myrtle leaf" to Shakespeare's "grand sea" – or indeed, to that of my students. He, "Billy Big Boy" – as some Northern English actors call him – what can he possibly gain from my ambassadorship? And they, brave bright undergraduates, are the ones who are going to conquer the big world while I remain behind in the enclosed dusty grove of academe – right? But for some of them, at least a trace memory of the old *magister* may travel with them.)

So why do I teach? First, because I was well taught. Because I was left an inheritance that I must leave as a legacy; from, to begin with, my mother, who, at a small Texas college for women in the early 1940s wrote a master's dissertation on "Shakespeare's Four Great Tragedies" – without ever having seen any of the plays staged. Her leather-bound Shakespeare was the biggest volume on the bottom shelf of the bookcase in our living room, and fascinated me as a child as much for the binding and watermarked fore-edge as the impressively biblical double columns of text. How I wanted to own the gold lettering, the tantalizing mustiness of the leather skin the book was shedding.

But now, holding this *Complete Works* in my grown-up hands, I realize with a shock that I've mistaken not just the book's provenance but my inheritance. This 1873 reprint of the 1773 Steevens edition couldn't have been my mother's. Hers was most certainly the 1935 green-bound Tucker Brooke college edition shelved, at home, beside it – marked with her unmistakable neat handwriting in the margins: undergraduate line glosses like "play on words," "first tactical error," and "true love does not come through the intellect," to which, I observe, I've added my own commentary, written in high school, by which time the book had migrated to southern California, turning my mother's Shakespeare into a palimpsest of my own first serious play reading: "gives the feeling of wrenched intimacy," "this is another reversion to role-playing," " 'suburbs' = red light district." But the Steevens edition: that must have been my *father's* Shakespeare, or perhaps even my grandfather's (both of them were great readers), carried from the old world to the new when the family immigrated from Wales in the first decade of the new century, packed in a parcel of necessary books for the literate working class that included Dickens and Walter Scott (books I still have, too). Lo and behold, then, imagining all this time that I claimed Shakespeare "from the female," I discover a *double* patrimony. Though, alas, there's nothing of my father in the margins, I realize that Shakespeare has been "doing" in my family for generations.

Still, it was very definitely my mother who sat her fifth, sixth, and seventh-grade children down night after night in the family living room to read through *Macbeth* – before driving us up to Los Angeles to see the Old Vic on tour. Something about that opening – "When shall we three meet again?" – captured my mother's youngest child's future as inescapably as the Witches' naming captured the Scottish thane's: "Who to meet with?" I can still remember my mom's bare feet propped up on the coffee table. And business the Porter performed on the way to opening the door.

As an undergraduate I was taught by Moelwyn Merchant, who made students see Shakespeare through his hands; at graduate school in Ann Arbor, by Clifford Leech. ("Most people," he said, *so kindly*, having listened to me mangle the unfamiliar name in the astonishing new play he'd just exploded onto my consciousness, "pronounce it 'Thersites.'") And Russell Fraser (a Renaissance-style guru whose mantras we learned by heart: "gloss Shakespeare with Shakespeare," "the meaning of the play is the play," "nothing in Shakespeare precipitates out"). And Bill Ingram (more of a fisherman than a guru, casting bread upon the waters where the PhD trout fed; more interested in questions than answers; one who taught the nuts and bolts of early modern theatre research: how to read secretary hand, how to access archives, how to deal with the absent record, how to be patient with the past). And then, in the UK, when I'd crossed the ocean and burnt my bridges behind me, Reg Foakes (listening, indulgently, to the greenhorn from the US who, trying to present her *bona fides*, trying to impress on him that she knew *something* about her dissertation topic, was making a right mess of it; standing up, opening his filing cabinet, taking out a thick bulk of papers and handing them to me, saying, "You might find this useful": the only copy of a typescript of Henslowe's *Diary* arranged in chronological sequence. I still have it). Behind me, these giants. Behind them, more "petty" Herculean masters, connecting us all in genealogies of intellectual influence and indebtedness: Fraser was taught by R. P. Blackmur; Foakes by I. A. Shapiro and Allardyce Nicoll (Foakes 2005: 132–6).

But I had, too, a parallel Shakespeare education. In the theatre, I was tutored across two extraordinary seasons at the Royal Shakespeare Company by the formidably brilliant director (and equally brilliant pedagogue *in potentia*), Terry Hands, who allowed me in to his rehearsals for his 1977 *Henry VI* trilogy and 1978 *Coriolanus*. Permitting me a freedom as liberal as the theatre cat's to roam backstage, front-of-house, and in the actors' company, Hands gave me a crash course in *looking* at Shakespeare, in *hearing* Shakespeare, in thinking about Shakespeare in, and through, and on the body, a politicized, eroticized, culturally implicated Shakespeare making meanings that mean *now*. After the summer of 1977 it never occurred to me to think of Shakespeare without thinking of performance.

If I teach because I was well taught, I teach, too, because teaching, like theatre, is a way of talking (and listening) in public about things that matter. "Do you know this play, Tereus?" asks the Athenian King Pandion of his culturally challenged visitor from Thrace as they sit watching *Phaedra* in Timberlake Wertenbaker's *The Love of the Nightingale*. Then he observes: "I find plays help me think." Just so. And teaching helps me think, too, not least because like Phaedra disturbing Pandion, students constantly challenge thoughts that might be settling, ossifying in my mind. In the university where I teach, students listen to me or one of my colleagues twice a week for 20 weeks give one-hour lectures across the Shakespeare canon, some 25 plays, with four Marlowes, two Jonsons and a couple of Middletons thrown in for good measure. Then roles are reversed as they split into groups of a dozen to 15 to meet me once a week in an hour and a half no-holds-barred seminar situation where, tentatively at the beginning of the year, pugilistically by the end, they take me and "my" Shakespeare on, to make him their own.

Their irreverence can strip the gloss off my favorite ideas like Nitromors stripping paint off lacquered doors. This past year they were impatient with Rosalind "fannying about in Arden"; intolerant of (and certainly not entertained by) Falstaff's dangerous, wasteful self-indulgence ("not the man you'd want covering your back in Fallujah"); initially scathing of Anne's capitulation to Richard: "she's spineless!" But couldn't they see the "bunch-backed toad" as a mesmerizing cobra? Then, responding to my exasperation with their dismissiveness, they put the scene on its feet, directing it themselves – I kept my mouth shut – from behind desks shoved against the classroom walls; 30 minutes later, limp from the exertion of releasing the energies of this dialogue in performance, and genuinely stunned by what they'd discovered: "Oh my god, they're *making sex* in this scene"; "Ummm" – this from the student playing Anne – "I think I know now why she does it." (Score one for the teacher. And the playwright.)

Of course they frequently defer to me. It's not that I know "better"; just that I know "more." They're coming to a seminar after a first or second reading of *King Lear*; me, after 40 years of reading and reading again – and again. But what they lack in readerly and spectatorly experience, they more than make up for in direct reaction, delivering to me that most precious of things, the *first* experience, the shock of the new, taking me back, over and over, to first things: Othello's "I will chop her into messes! Cuckold me!" *for the first time*; Cordelia's "Nothing" *for the first time*; Hotspur's report, *for the first time*, of that maddening, spruce gadfly of a king's messenger (with his pouncet box) mincing his way across the battlefield, demanding Hotspur's prisoners even before his comrades' corpses have been cleared.

And they constantly stop me in my tracks when they pause to look at something I've been trotting by for years: the student who made me look, really *look*, at Antigonus, hunched over that baby bundle, alone on that vast desert shore (the empty stage), saying goodbye to Perdita; the student who asked me about where little Lucius had suddenly sprung from in the closing scene of *Titus Andronicus*; the student who wondered, incredulously, about Cassio's loose-mouthed sleep-talking, "Iago 'lay with Cassio lately' – Iago *in bed with* Cassio?" (Everything I've published in the last 20 years is, *inter alia*, an attempt to think through the conversations they've started. Teaching, for me, is research.) I'm fascinated, year by year, at the way the latest batch of finalists acts as a barometer of cultural and political shift as they reinvest in Shakespeare to help them articulate what *matters to them*. Impatient with "silly" *As You Like It* last year, they bit hard on *Troilus and Cressida* and *Measure for Measure* not because they're worldly and cynical but because these plays, they say, set up real debates: "What's aught but as 'tis valued?"; "But can you if you would?"

A third reason why I teach is because there's always more to say – and because the last time I tried to say it, I didn't get the words right, didn't get the words I spoke anywhere close to the emotions I felt, the ideas I thought, brought to them by my latest encounter with the playwright. I constantly face up to the ludicrous futility of my teacherly words. How can anything I say be adequate to *King Lear* or *Henry IV* or *The Winter's Tale* – to either the early modern *King Lear* or the *King Lear* we're remaking on our own stage? ("Just read the play!" I want to say to students.) "Trying to use words" on Shakespeare, I'm with Eliot on poetry: "every attempt," he writes in "East Coker,"

> Is a wholly new start, and a different kind of failure
> Because one has only learnt to get the better of words
> For the thing one no longer has to say, or the way in which
> One is no longer disposed to say it.
>
> (Eliot 1969: 182)

The right words for Shakespeare are always elusive, fugitive – like "The voice of . . . the children in the apple tree" in "Little Gidding" (1969: 197). So what hope of me ever catching them when, as Virginia Woolf writes in "On Not Knowing Greek," Shakespeare's playground territory of meaning is always just beyond our reach: "The meaning . . . just on the far side of language," "the meaning which in moments of astonishing excitement and stress we perceive in our minds without words," *that* is "the meaning that Shakespeare succeeds in snaring" (Woolf 1992: 99–100). Perhaps the best the constantly empty-handed, slack butterfly-netted teacher of Shakespeare can do is to take solace from Beckett: "No Matter. Try again. Fail again. Fail better."[2] Teaching Shakespeare keeps me humble. In my professional life I see myself playing out versions of the tutor (*pace* Antony's schoolmaster) that Shakespeare recognized, drafted for the stage four hundred years ago, installed in the cultural memory bank for all time. (Like Antony, Shakespeare was someone who kept thinking about the schoolboy and the "magister," and kept the tutor whom he'd outgrown somewhere in his writerly consciousness near.) So I'm Miranda, squawking at her truculent pupil (mine, typically the Philosophy and Literature student who doesn't see the point of performance), that I "Took pains to make thee speak"; "I endowed thy purposes / With words that made them known" (*The Tempest*, 1.2. 357, 360–1). To which the grateful reply is – the one we all know. I'm little Rutland's tutor, standing helplessly by as revenge-crazed Clifford savages the child, then cuts his throat. (Well, most of the problems my personal tutees bring me aren't fatal, though some are, but even so, when faced with their betrayals, broken hearts, parental deaths, mind-crushing depressions, body-wasting eating disorders, I sometimes wonder about the usefulness of teaching. Even teaching Shakespeare. "Poetry makes nothing happen."[3] Except that I know that it *does*: there's nothing like *Troilus and Cressida* to locate a shared vocabulary of betrayal; or *King Lear*, deaths in the family; or *Macbeth*, conscience and consequence. Teaching Shakespeare helps me fast-track adolescents into adulthood.) I've never been tempted to play Lucentio-as-Cambio, to use teaching to cover seduction, though I'm perpetually aware of the charged intellectual intimacy between teacher and taught, and glad that I teach in an environment where students and teachers can still lay hands on each other as we work on text. (A student this year wrote feedback on a workshop: "It did occur to me to ask myself why I was spending my Saturday morning lying on top of my tutor." I did something particularly daft one day; a student observed: "You silly tart." I did not for a moment consider litigation.) I know that as a teacher I never act Holofernes to Mote, but fear that I sometimes play Parson Evans to little William, Evans with his Welsh "prabbles" and his "preeches" requiring double translation of Latin into English, me with my Californian accent and locutions. Like his, my tutorial catechisms are regularly exercises in total bewilderment. (But after all, there may be something to be said for the Evans method. A student this year reported in the course evaluation that Professor Rutter "ends seminars in the most sensational [I think he meant "opaque"] way imaginable – asking something like 'What's in a name?', then leaving the room. We then spend the rest of the day thinking about it." So, perhaps, score a glancing point for the teacher? And a "palpable hit" for the playwright.)

While Shakespeare humbles me, the fact of the matter is that teaching Shakespeare massively empowers me. He gives me academic street cred and departmental weight to throw around. He even gives me national visibility: the BBC asks me to talk about Shakespeare on the radio; the *Times* asks me to write about Shakespeare in their glossy Saturday magazine. Shakespeare gets me invitations to sound off at the Royal Society of Arts and the Institute of Contemporary Arts, and a summons to serve as an expert witness in a Crown case. He even gets me through the private entrance into the Royal Palace of St James's. Voted Man of the Millennium in the UK, situated at the epicenter of British theatrical life, unchallenged Governor of the Cultural Bank of England, "Will the Huge" (as Welsh actors call him) sheds some of his prestige onto any actor who plays him, film-maker who films him, teacher who teaches him. Teaching Shakespeare, I never have to explain myself (like, say, my colleagues, having to make a case for teaching Goldsmith – or Charlotte Smith). In the next round of departmental appointments we may not replace our eighteenth-century specialist. But our Shakespeareans? Their appointments are secure. Because in my department, Shakespeare isn't optional. He's required.

And he's required right across the UK. A century ago if you wanted a job in the Indian Civil Service you had to sit colonial government examinations and answer questions on Shakespeare. Today, if you want a place to read English in a British university, you have to sit national public examinations – and answer questions on Shakespeare. Indeed, at school, you're going to have to answer questions on Shakespeare at Key Stage 3 (when you're 14 years old) and Key Stage 4 (when you're 16 years old). And you'll have to answer questions on Shakespeare when you sit the statutory reading test for all 13 year olds, set by the Qualifications and Curriculum Authority. Shakespeare is studied (more or less, as option, module component, or requirement) on *every* university English syllabus in the kingdom. So to get your honors degree in English literature, you're probably going to have to answer questions on Shakespeare. In 2007, when Oxford University mooted plans to downgrade its compulsory undergraduate Shakespeare paper, the debate made the national news (Shields and Akbar 2007).

Of course, making Shakespeare bear the brunt of so much pedagogic (and political) work, as a kind of Hercules holding up the nation's English curricular globe, means teaching him to large numbers of little Williams who really aren't bothered, and making perfectly competent schoolteachers transform themselves into versions of Holofernes. Under the sign of Shakespeare, an awful lot of deadly (and anxious) teaching and learning goes on in the UK.

But the opposite is likewise true. For Shakespeare's centrality to the national curriculum means that Shakespeare is one of the regular places where successive governments rethink education policy, conduct their big debates about teaching and learning, implement change and innovation, all of this aimed at enhancing the shared experience of little William and Parson Evans – while improving not so much the cultural life and social soul of the nation as its economic productivity. In Margaret Thatcher's day, the twin imperatives driving education reform were curriculum content and entitlement; in Blair's premiership, the imperative was pedagogy. And, ventriloquizing Blair himself (or perhaps vice versa), the buzz word on every minister's lips these days is "creativity": "in the 21st century," Blair argued in a speech supporting Labour's 2001 Culture and Recreation Bill, "we are going to see the world increasingly influenced by innovation and creative minds. Our future depends on our creativity" (quoted in Mitchell 2001). "Creativity is about adding the deepest value to human life," wrote his Culture Secretary, Chris Smith, in 1998, and continued: "creativity, culture, national identity and the nation's future wealth are all inextricably bound up together and it is skilled, creative people that make the difference" (Smith 1998: 147). In June 2005, the Minister for Culture, Media and Sport, in a speech to the Institute for Public Policy Research, commented that his department had "set an ambitious but achievable goal . . . : to make Britain the world's creative hub" (Purnell 2005), while the 2003 Roberts Review, commissioned by the UK's four higher education funding bodies to review how research in university departments is assessed (and, on the basis of the Research Assessment Exercise, how government money is subsequently disbursed), observed, *inter alia*, that "the developing education policy context" offered "positive opportunities for the embedding of creativity in education."[4] Is this lip service paid to creativity only so much spin? Or is it a genuine commitment? Most educationalists would argue that Blair, for all the change in discursive tactics, merely continued the Thatcherite revolution and that, in the UK, education policy in schools is still driven by targets, by an obsession with frequent tests of basic skills and with standards based on what is measurable – that is, functional literacy. Depressingly, this trend looks set to continue: Brown is even more of a target man than Blair. But pulling in the opposite direction, the Roberts Review has argued for scrapping certain national targets, freeing up the schools curriculum for more creative teaching. So: targets vs. creativity. In this contradictory policy world, not surprisingly, Shakespeare is right at the forefront of the drive toward testing – and toward creativity.

I, at least, am the delighted beneficiary of progressive government policy, endowed with space and funds to "get creative" – and to rethink Shakespeare teaching in my department. In 2005, the Higher Education Funding Council for England (HEFCE) launched 74 Centres for Excellence in Teaching and Learning across England. Each of these CETLs has a specific project and remit, and is funded for five years. The CETL I direct, called the CAPITAL Centre (an acronym: Creativity and Performance in Teaching and Learning), is, as the bid document puts it, a unique venture to forge a partnership between a university and a theatre company: as it happens, our local Shakespeare rep, the one situated just down the road in Stratford-upon-Avon. CAPITAL's mission is to bring "the expertise of the Royal Shakespeare Company" to "the higher education community," to offer an "interdisciplinary approach to teaching and learning by creating a shared space for academics and practitioners – teachers, students, writers, actors – to inform each other's work." "Good teaching," we propose, "is like good rehearsal": both rely on "the arts of imagining other minds, role-play and improvisation, trust and teamwork, discovery through the creative process."[5]

I think of CAPITAL as "a third room": not exactly a rehearsal room; certainly not a classroom; but a space where the practices of actors and students can meet, converse, and learn from each other. And it's a *real* space. At the Centre – which opened, auspiciously enough on Shakespeare's birthday, 2007 – we have academic offices for tutors, a playwright in residence, and our Fellows in Creativity; a Writers' Room (complete with sofas, a collapsible stage, library and video collection); a computer room; a large foyer for public gatherings; long stretches of white walls for exhibitions and displays. And most thrilling of all: a white box rehearsal room, a fully kitted out black box studio, and professional standard dressing rooms. In short: a playground where we can put Shakespeare (and not just Shakespeare) on his feet to explore theatre poetry in space and time, to give students access to his physical performance texts as well as his literary playtexts, the wrighting of the writing. Stuck in my mind is Simon Russell Beale's oft-repeated notion that acting is three-dimensional literary criticism. Putting students on their feet doing Shakespeare, I want them to get out from behind desks, away from screens and keyboards, away even from "the book," to experience the thrill of practicing literary criticism in three dimensions.

So from autumn 2007, this teacher of Shakespeare will be abandoning the traditional university classroom for a white box rehearsal room. I'm going to be teaching "Shakespeare Without Chairs." I'll be using rehearsal methods, drawing on the work not just of the RSC but of CAPITAL's other collaborators (Cheek by Jowl, Northern Broadsides, the Coventry Belgrade, Shakespeare's Globe) and practitioners from their voice, movement, and education departments; using actors where I can; doing what actors and directors do in rehearsals, looking closely at text; thinking about folios and quartos; thinking historically; thinking theatrically; thinking about original staging and subsequent performance: the Elizabethan or Jacobean script and its meaning(s); the script that belongs to us, that is being remade in productions now. (So I'll be taking students to the theatre to see the RSC's current work, and to the cinema to see Shakespeare on screen).

But I'll be using, too, the vast experience of my academic colleagues – Skip Shand, Ric Knowles, Tony Dawson, Barbara Hodgdon, Miriam Gilbert, Bill Worthen, Tony Howard, Paul Prescott – who have been advocating "actorly reading" in university classrooms for years. I'll be using simple exercises, *moments* of performance (where the language seems to offer no difficulties) that open up the process of reading imaginatively. From *Antony and Cleopatra*, for instance:

> *Caesar*:   Welcome to Rome.
> *Antony*:   Thank you.
> *Caesar*:   Sit.
> *Antony*:   Sit, sir.
> *Caesar*:   Nay, then.
>
> (2.2.28–32)

Or from later in the same play:

> *Thidias*:   Thus, then, thou most renowned: Caesar entreats
>   Not to consider in what case thou stand'st
>   Further than he is Caesar.
> *Cleopatra*: Go on; right royal.
> *Thidias*:   He knows that you embraced not Antony
>   As you did love, but as you fearèd him.
> *Cleopatra*: O.
>
> (3.13.52–7)

Working on extracts like these should explode any students' preconceptions that the Shakespeare text bears single and finished meanings – and prepare them for play reading as a labor-intensive activity where they're going to have to work hard on the words, on the poetry, on the rhetoric, on the choreography of the scene, on the material "stuff" the scene plays with, including, always, the actor's body. From simple beginnings, I'll be moving students on to heavyweight scenes and speeches that will invite them to engage with this playwright as a *maker*. Hector meeting the Greeks; Romeo trading wit with Mercutio; Hamlet on Hecuba, Brutus on assassination, Macbeth on "If"; Rosalind as Ganymede schooling Orlando; Iago seducing Othello; Othello remembering a handkerchief; Diomedes corrupting Cressida as Thersites watches Ulysses watch Troilus watching (then splitting "Cressida" from "Cressida" to disavow what he's seen): in Shakespeare, there are no "ideas" that float free from immediate context, from the urgent need to speak inside a situation, where speaking is both thought and character simultaneously.

When he hears what I'm up to, I think George Hunter will be pleased. An eminent Shakespearean, editor, and "new historicist" *avant la lettre* – in his day, academics like him were called "scholars" – Hunter was the man who devised the English Literature degree at my university. It was he who made Shakespeare compulsory for *every* English Literature student, who made Shakespeare a full-year, final year module: the culmination of the English degree when undergraduates were grown up and ready to take on the playwright. His inspiration was that Shakespeare should be taught (in what was then, 40 years ago, one of England's new universities) not only as a poet, a writer of what subsequent centuries would call "literature" whom students would encounter in the study, but as a jobbing playwright: a practical man of the theatre whose plays had to be understood in performance; a man to meet on stage. My teaching in the past 25 years has been an extension of Hunter's vision. The CAPITAL Centre is its logical outcome.

I'm one who thinks that theatres and universities need each other, that actors and students interpret each other to each other. Shakespeare, it appears, thought so too. In *Love's Labour's Lost*, it takes a pedant and his crew performing that play of the Nine Worthies to deliver the final *coup de grâce* that shows us, the audience, just how foolishly doomed is the antisocial project of those crass, would-be academic recluses who intend to dedicate themselves to books rather than life. And in *Hamlet*, the players, the *play*, need Horatio, the postgrad student from Wittenberg, to witness, to spectate, to make sense of what's being performed. As Tony Howard (my friend and colleague, and the greatest Shakespeare teacher my university has yet produced) reminds me of this symbiotic relationship between the theatre and the academy, these two organs of culture expose each other in revealing ways:

> *Love's Labour's Lost* is about would-be intellectuals who see the academy as about exclusion. They patronise and mock the players – brutally – and this forces the women to understand that if the men can't embrace the collectivity of theatre, then they're not ready for life or love either. Hamlet is the opposite. He's a university man collaborating with theatre people for a larger purpose – and he needs the academic, Horatio, to study not the play but the audience.[6]

Certainly, in Shakespeare, if playing mirrors nature, nature just as often mirrors playing, and actors and academics double each other. When the need arises, Horatio knows how to act the "antique Roman" no doubt just as Polonius does – because he "played" the part "once i' th' university" (5.2.293, 3.2.95).

Ending, I want to return to my beginning, and to Mote and Mark Antony, the dwarf and the giant. I teach Shakespeare because he's the biggest subject I know; because he makes us face up to beginnings and endings (and middles); civilization and the wilderness; ourselves as angels and brutes; horrible imaginings and the sweetness of life. He's mighty. But he's also somehow midget. His imagination – its reach and resources – is cathedral-sized. Yet its particularity, the metaphors it utters itself in, are as familiar, as human-sized as the parish church still standing in a Warwickshire that is still recognizable from the writing, where the lark still sings at "heaven gate"; where winter rain still runs down "eaves of reeds" and the daffodils "come before the swallow dares"; where latter-day greasy Joans still "keel the pot" and slug-a-bed schoolboys still "creep like snail" unwillingly to class, stepping over drunkards who've been thrown out of public houses and will wake up in the gutter. The mighty is contained in the midget. Lear, dying, wants a button undone. Prospero, renouncing his power, remembers "the sour ringlets . . . Whereof the ewe not bites." Desdemona, reeling from Othello's incomprehensible rage, simply remarks that they who "teach young babes / Do it with gentle means and easy tasks" and that "He might have chid me so; for . . . I am a child to chiding." Shakespeare makes me laugh. ("Agamemnon . . . has not so much brain as ear-wax."). And weep ("Oh my dear mother, do I see you living?"). He gives me such astonishing scenes: Lady Macbeth *sleepwalking*, Ophelia handing round her memory flowers, Hamlet talking to a skull, Richard Plantagenet counting time. And of course, Shakespeare gives me language. To know myself, and others; to conduct my business in worlds immediate, actual, eventual, and imaginary.

So here I go, at the beginning of another academic year, Mote and Mark Antony leading me on my teacherly way, remembering my schoolmasters, and, equipped with Shakespeare's books, "parted" to play Hercules.[7]

Notes

1   My text is Wells and Taylor (1986).
2   This line, which probably should be adopted as the university teacher's occupational logo, emblazoned on our sweatshirts (and tattooed on our chests), comes from his *Worstward Ho* (1983: 1).

3   I am, of course, quoting W. H. Auden's "In Memory of W. B. Yeats" – who himself had thoughts on the effectiveness of poetry.
4   The report can be accessed at <www.ra-review.ac.uk/reports/roberts.asp>. I owe this information to my colleague, Jonothan Neelands, one of the UK's leading experts in the field of drama and education.
5   See the CAPITAL website at <http://go.warwick.ac.uk/capital>.
6   From a public lecture May 12, 2007.
7   This essay is dedicated with gratitude to the memory of George Hunter, who died April 10, 2008, when this collection was in proofs. I am grateful to the students who have appeared in this essay: Becky Allen, Ben Fowler, Bronia Evers, Naomi Everall, Jonny Heron, Julia Ihnatowicz, and Oliver Turner. And to my big sister, Roberta Skelton, a star teacher whose excellence I aspire to.

References and Further Reading

Beckett, Samuel (1983). *Worstward Ho*. London: Calder.
Eliot, T. S. (1969). *The Complete Poems and Plays*. London: Faber and Faber.
Foakes, Reginald (2005). *Imagined Places: A Life in the Twentieth Century*. Philadelphia: Xlibris.
Mitchell, Paul (2001). "Britain: Labour Government Outlines the Next Stage in its Assault on the Arts." April 10. Available at <http://www.wsws.org/articles/2001/apr2001/arts-a10.shtml>.
Purnell, James (2005). "Making Britain the World's Creative Hub." June 16. Available at <www.culture.gov.uk/Reference_library/Minister_Speeches/Ministers_Speech_Archive/James_Purnell/James_Purnell_Speech01.htm>.
Shields, Rachel and Arifa Akbar (2007). "Shakespeare in Peril as Oxford Rethinks English Syllabus." *Independent*, June 30. Available at <www.independent.co.uk/news/education/education-news/shakespeare-in-peril-as-oxford-rethinks-english-syllabus-455354.html>.
Smith, Chris (1998). *Creative Britain*. London: Faber.
Spencer, T. J. B. (1964). "The Life of Marcus Antonius." In *Shakespeare's Plutarch: The Lives of Julius Caesar, Brutus, Marcus Antonius and Coriolanus in the Translation of Sir Thomas North* (pp. 174–295). Harmondsworth, UK: Penguin.
Wells, Stanley and Gary Taylor (Eds) (1986). *The Oxford Shakespeare: Complete Works*. Oxford: Clarendon Press.
Wertenbaker, Timberlake (1989). *The Love of the Nightingale, and The Grace of Mary Traverse*. London: Faber and Faber.
Woolf, Virginia (1992). *A Woman's Essays*. Rachel Bowlby (Ed.). London: Penguin.

Index